Beyond Coercion

Beyond Coercion offers a new perspective on mechanisms of social control that authoritarian regimes practice. Focusing on the Chinese state, Alexsia T. Chan presents an original theory and concept of political atomization, which explains how the state maintains social control and entrenches structural inequality. Chan investigates why migrant workers in China still lack access to urban public services despite national directives to incorporate them into cities, reported worker shortages, and ongoing labor unrest. Through a meticulous analysis of the implementation of policies said to expand workers' rights, she shows how these policies often end up undermining their claims to benefits. The book argues that local governments provide public services for migrants using a process of political individualization, which enables the state to exercise control beyond coercion by atomizing those who might otherwise mobilize against it. This title is part of the Flip it Open Programme and may also be available Open Access. Check our website Cambridge Core for details.

Alexsia T. Chan is Associate Professor of Government at Hamilton College.

STUDIES OF THE WEATHERHEAD EAST ASIAN INSTITUTE, COLUMBIA UNIVERSITY

The Studies of the Weatherhead East Asian Institute of Columbia University were inaugurated in 1962 to bring to a wider public the results of significant new research on modern and contemporary East Asia.

Beyond Coercion

The Politics of Inequality in China

ALEXSIA T. CHAN
Hamilton College

CAMBRIDGE
UNIVERSITY PRESS

CAMBRIDGE
UNIVERSITY PRESS

Shaftesbury Road, Cambridge CB2 8EA, United Kingdom

One Liberty Plaza, 20th Floor, New York, NY 10006, USA

477 Williamstown Road, Port Melbourne, VIC 3207, Australia

314–321, 3rd Floor, Plot 3, Splendor Forum, Jasola District Centre, New Delhi – 110025, India

103 Penang Road, #05–06/07, Visioncrest Commercial, Singapore 238467

Cambridge University Press is part of Cambridge University Press & Assessment, a department of the University of Cambridge.

We share the University's mission to contribute to society through the pursuit of education, learning and research at the highest international levels of excellence.

www.cambridge.org
Information on this title: www.cambridge.org/9781009355636

DOI: 10.1017/9781009355643

When citing this work, please include a reference to the DOI 10.1017/9781009355643

First published 2025

A catalogue record for this publication is available from the British Library

Library of Congress Cataloging-in-Publication Data
NAMES: Chan, Alexsia T., author.
TITLE: Beyond coercion : the politics of inequality in China / Alexsia T. Chan, Hamilton College, New York.
DESCRIPTION: Cambridge, United Kingdom ; New York, NY : Cambridge University Press, 2025. | Includes bibliographical references and index.
IDENTIFIERS: LCCN 2024020358 | ISBN 9781009355636 (hardback) | ISBN 9781009355643 (ebook)
SUBJECTS: LCSH: Internal migrants – Civil rights – China. | Migrant labor – Political aspects – China. | Citizenship – China. | Marginality, Social – Political aspects – China. | China – Politics and government – 1949–
CLASSIFICATION: LCC HB2114.A3 C4197 2025 | DDC 307.2/40951–dc23/eng/20240711
LC record available at https://lccn.loc.gov/2024020358

ISBN 978-1-009-35563-6 Hardback
ISBN 978-1-009-35567-4 Paperback

For Avery

Contents

1 Inequality and the Autocrat's Toolbox — *page* 1
2 A Theory of Political Atomization — 20

PART I PUBLIC SERVICES AS SOCIAL CONTROL

3 Deflecting Migrant Workers — 55
4 Demobilizing Migrant Workers — 73

PART II MIGRANT WORKERS BLUNTING CONTROL

5 Playing with Institutional Leeway — 101
6 Making Do and Muddling Through — 122
7 Conclusion — 146

Notes — 163
References — 177
Index — 195

1

Inequality and the Autocrat's Toolbox

Local governments in China face the daunting challenge of the world's most rapid urbanization. One of the latest endeavors in central planning aims to boost urbanization as an engine of the country's economic growth. By 2030, 70 percent of the population, or approximately one billion people, will be living in cities, 292.5 million of whom are currently migrants (The World Bank and Development Research Center of the State Council 2014, National Bureau of Statistics 2022). About one in five people in China is an internal migrant, and they have practical demands they need met after they find a job and settle down in urban areas. After four decades of moving from the countryside to metropolitan destinations to work in factories manufacturing goods for export, serving as nannies and security guards for their fellow citizens, and doing a number of other often low-paying and physically demanding jobs, most of these rural migrants do not yet hold the full set of social rights that their urban counterparts enjoy. At first glance, this seems to be changing as a few begin to gain access. Promises of reforms and renewed attention to remedying the inequality gap appeared to be a turning point in the early 2010s, but city officials' policy moves toward incorporation have counterintuitively generated new forms of exclusion through political atomization.

What is political atomization? This original concept explains the process by which the state creates policies that structurally treat marginalized people as individuals to enact selective inclusion over group-based exclusion. It effectively makes migrants responsible for their own public service access and shifts the focus from the state's obligation to provide basic benefits to citizens to those people's role in obtaining access.

By dampening expectations and diluting claims, it undermines group-based claims of discrimination. A system of political atomization is embodied in the policies, procedures, and practices that determine migrant entitlements and these migrants' interactions with various bureaucracies and government officials as they seek to access and use these privileges. Structural forms of control through these systems and the policies that make them up help give an illusion of agential power for migrants while keeping most of them out of urban welfare systems. Political atomization enables the authoritarian Chinese state to divide and conquer migrant workers and exercise control beyond coercion.

Political atomization entrenches migrant inequality in China. Reforms for incorporating outsiders into cities are not improving overall welfare for most migrant workers. But the process has not simply stagnated. Devolved policies at the municipal level are introducing new barriers for many to qualify for, access, and use urban social services. Atomization makes distribution and social citizenship for Chinese migrant workers a complicated city-by-city, case-by-case issue.[1] This book offers a novel conceptualization of the process by which a few migrants gain access to urban entitlements while others are excluded and most, more pointedly, are deflected and demobilized. Political atomization differs from existing understandings by unraveling the process of how people become individualized and explaining why mechanisms of social control extend beyond coercive repression and protest response in authoritarian regimes. Alternative explanations based on factors such as wealth, labor shortages, and generational differences do not account for the ways in which some cities are more inviting and others more exclusive. Nor do they show the logic behind the decentralized and frequently evolving patchwork of policies across the country that has emerged over recent decades.

Inequality and political atomization are understudied components of the autocrat's toolbox. Coercion and force are well-known parts of it, but there are softer forms of social control that shape the daily lives of people living under authoritarian regimes. One element of this is inequity. Inequality in society is universally criticized as government leaders and international organizations deride its harmful effects on the economy, innovation, people's general health and well-being, and more and thus seek to reduce disparity. Though there are many reasons why socioeconomic inequality persists, there is one under-explored source. States themselves may preserve or exacerbate some level of inequality while they pursue other government goals, such as social stability and productive labor flows. The government recognizes that inequality creates an opportunity for social control via access to social welfare programs.

Political atomization benefits the state even without perfect central coordination and capacity. In the case of China, decentralization facilitates political atomization; more specifically, variation in public service provision for migrants aids social control through individuation. While it is difficult to impute the central government's intention, it is also not necessary in order for individualization to work. Nor is extremely high state capacity required. A baseline level of state capacity is helpful because the central government can credibly signal its commitment to incorporation while local governments construct and implement migrant social policy. Evaluating the exact level of central planning and overall state capacity are not the focus of this project and are left for future research. The challenges for municipalities and outcomes for migrants on the ground remain the same. The effectiveness of incomplete coordination and capacity in facilitating atomization mirrors the state's desire for a zone of control in which it wants some level and kind of inequality but not too much.

This opening chapter maps out the challenge of urbanization as development and situates the concept of political atomization and the main findings of this book in the larger context of inequality and authoritarian distribution. The concept of political atomization helps us understand four phenomena better: how authoritarian regimes exercise social control beyond coercion, why the perceived exchange of promised services for loyalty bolsters authoritarian resilience, how public service provision works without elections, and why there have been new gradations of second-class citizenship and structural inequality in China. To show how political atomization works, this book tracks the dynamics and consequences of the process from the state's perspective through migrants' points of view. The path first traces central directives to provincial, municipal, and district policies and the officials tasked with formulating them. Then it follows migrant interactions with frontline service providers who deliver health care and education in hospitals and schools and migrant workers' experiences with trying to access social services and thereby undermine political atomization. This book uncovers emergent and evolving structural sources of inequality, social control, and everyday marginalization in China.

WRANGLING URBANIZATION

The central puzzle and research questions of this book arise out of several cross-cutting frictions produced by urbanization: Why do most migrant workers still lack access to urban public services despite national directives to incorporate them into cities, reported worker shortages, and ongoing labor unrest? How do policies said to expand workers' rights end up undermining their claims to benefits owed to them? This book argues that local governments use political atomization aided by variation in public services for migrant workers to maintain social control and structural inequality. Through this, the Chinese state is able to regulate a large, marginalized, and mobile group of people whom they need, and cities can keep a steady labor force without providing the full set of benefits owed to these workers. This section outlines the urbanization challenge for municipal authorities.

Urbanization presents a quandary for city governments. The difficulty for local authorities is to maintain a steady and replenishable labor force without having to provide and pay for migrant entitlements. Municipalities therefore must juggle priorities that can pull them in opposite directions. They need to attract migrant workers to provide labor, foremost to support local economic growth and the future of one of the world's largest economies. The central government hopes they will eventually become middle-class consumers whose spending boosts the economy. These people, however, are not only workers but also citizens whose quality of life and well-being are at stake. And there is a practical issue. City and district governments have to respond to newcomers trying to use their health insurance at an urban public hospital or enroll their children in school, but they are not always willing to shoulder the burden of paying for and expanding public services for people they distinguish as outsiders. Multiple interests across levels of government and different sources of pushback from native urban residents further hinder the full incorporation of people registered as rural residents. Bottom-up demands and pragmatic considerations are but two sources of pressure to include migrants more in urban welfare systems.

Pronouncements from the central government put the squeeze on cities from above. They call for the further integration of migrants, and in March 2014, the Party Central Committee and the State Council jointly issued a National New-Type Urbanization Plan (*guojia xinxing chengzhen hua guihua*, 国家新型城镇化规划) (2014–2020) that among other things called for increased funding for public services (State Council of the People's Republic of China 2014). In July 2014, the State Council announced a goal of eliminating the distinction between rural and urban household registrations (*hukou*, 户口) and converting 100 million rural residents' *hukou* into urban registrations by 2020. National officials, then and since, have recognized the need to improve services for migrants and have frequently emphasized the importance of a "people-centered" (*yiren weiben*, 以人为本) approach to urbanization. Rhetoric surrounding this set of proposals and goals is couched in broader aspirational goals: as a next step in China's path of modernization and in terms of its potential to boost domestic demand and drive future economic development. One piece of the plan includes reforming the residency system and improving access to benefits in the city for outsiders and long-term residents. At a press conference on the plan, Xu Xianping, Vice Minister of the National Development and Reform Commission, said, "[T]he plan requires us to promote the reform of the household registration system and the equalization of basic public services."[2] Yang Zhiming, Vice Minister of Human Resources and Social Security added, "We'll help more migrant workers ... enjoy fundamental public services through settling down in cities and towns. Even for those who do not settle in urban areas, we'll allow them to gradually benefit from fundamental public services. We'll make relentless efforts."[3] These statements signal attention from multiple senior officials at the national level to migrants' lives as part of their strategies for making China more urban.

Cities therefore have an unfunded mandate to provide public services for newcomers in a system where there has been devolution of responsibility to city authorities. In the Xi Jinping era of authoritarian consolidation and recentralization of power, this remains one area where policy formulation and implementation have remained relatively decentralized and have been left in the hands of provincial, municipal, and district officials (Chan and Buckingham 2008, Guo and Liang 2017, Chan 2024). The Chinese Academy of Social Sciences estimated it would cost approximately 650 billion RMB (or US$106 billion) a year to ensure that rural migrants have the same health care, education, and housing benefits that their urban resident counterparts have (Reuters 2013). Without fiscal restructuring and larger transfers from the central government to pay for these extensions, municipalities are hamstrung.

A mismatch between state priorities and migrant preferences further strains the unfunded mandate. To reap the benefits of urbanization without congesting already crowded mega-cities, the central government often encourages people to move to small and medium-sized cities.[4] These less developed cities are not as attractive to many internal migrants. Like most others in their position elsewhere and contrary to national authorities' main concern, migrant workers tend to favor large metropolises that offer more and better paid work opportunities, contain established networks of co-migrants from home, and allow more flexibility to switch jobs or industries when one does not pan out as expected. Restrictions on acquiring local *hukou* do not deter migrants from moving to those cities, but welfare benefits associated with local registrations are appealing (Pizzi and Hu 2022). An ongoing tension lies in the incongruence between where migrants want to live and work and where Beijing would prefer they go.

The limited integration efforts so far have been decentralized and disjointed. Changes to migrants' participation in urban welfare schemes have been made incrementally in the name of gradual reform to a big, unwieldy system. Counterintuitively, piecemeal improvements have made things the same or worse for most migrants. Differences, particularly in rights, can help keep marginalized populations divided and potentially undermine their collective consciousness. Group-based demands lose their bite, and individuals learn it is pragmatic to negotiate one-on-one with local government bureaucrats to get their needs met. By making access to social rights an individual process, the state can provide fewer services while maintaining a pool of labor to support economic growth in the city or province. Adding to the effectiveness of these informal and formal institutions, many migrants end up blaming themselves when they are excluded from urban public services.

Breakneck urbanization supported by the state raises questions about intentionality behind political atomization. Regardless of whether a coordinated top-down plan existed from the outset, migrant social policy has evolved into a useful tool of control for the government. It is difficult to definitively determine if it was a wholly formed, premeditated master plan from the start, but it need not be to work. Differences among municipalities designing residency points systems and regulating public school and hospital access are more easily discernable as reflecting official orientation toward policy than a centrally led and synchronized plan with and among all of them together. Intentionally or not, the degree of variation between localities, over time combined with the persistent gap between central directives and sub-national administration of public goods, shows the underlying political logic of sustaining this system. Migrants can experience individualization through a system cobbled together from local subsystems without a puppet master in control of everything.

INEQUALITY AND AUTHORITARIAN DISTRIBUTION

Authoritarian Control beyond Coercion

The world is moving into a new era of democratic recession and authoritarian upsurge (Diamond 2015, Freedom House 2017). Old paradigms focused on democratic transition are becoming obsolete as we move into a period of global authoritarianism, and China is the ideal case for studying this. The country's tremendously successful economic transition and stable regime illuminate the role of states in development under consolidated nondemocratic rule. And while there are many studies on democracy and inequality, there is a dearth of research on the dynamic in autocratic countries. This book stands on the cusp of a new wave of research on autocracy. It challenges existing scholarship on authoritarian durability, public service provision, and citizenship in China.

Regulation of migrants provides a window into state control and day-to-day authoritarian governance. The literature on authoritarian durability focuses on the institutionalization of elite power transitions and harbingers of regime change (e.g., Nathan 2003, Svolik 2012) but sometimes forgets that stability maintenance is a pressing daily task never far from rulers' minds. This book shows a slice of nondemocratic rule in the days and years between elite transitions that come every half decade in China: mundane forms of social control built into institutions and structures that encourage citizens to make decisions that are consistent with the state's goals. They are ordinary features of daily state–society interactions that systematically shape inequality. Taken together, they are powerful ways the state manages citizens' expectations, maintains social stability, and sustains a labor force for economic growth.

The provision of public goods to migrants in China is not designed to primarily improve their welfare. A hitherto less exposed part is its role in supporting state-led urbanization, social stability, inequality, and other aims of the government. How they pursue these goals through this mechanism helps explain the political atomization that many migrants experience when they attempt to make claims and demands that are within the bounds of policies but still cannot prove eligibility, acquire access, or use services. Authorities use the social assistance program colloquially known as *dibao* (低保) for surveillance and repression (Pan 2020), and the stratified expansion of social health insurance privileges elites over masses (Huang 2020). Furthermore, political atomization and decentralized provision of social services are not particularly efficient. Migrant workers move around by definition, so a national system with transferrable benefits would be a more straightforward choice. But when other state goals in addition to providing benefits enter the picture, it becomes clearer why devolved policies persist despite being less effective for the population they are supposed to help as a whole.

While there has been extensive research on the use of force in authoritarian regimes, tools of social control beyond coercion are underexplored. Scholars understand less about authoritarian consolidation (Göbel 2011), especially outside crises of power transitions. The military and police are important and necessary when, for instance, imminent regime collapse is pronounced and obvious. The goals that can be achieved through physical suppression and violence are limited. And focusing on force in authoritarian regimes occludes the multitudes of ways in which marginalized people experience and become familiar with state power in practice and therefore inform how they come to challenge it, bow to it, or simply live with it. In the same way that Lisa Wedeen (1999) discussed the centrality of rhetoric and symbols in Syria to expand the narrow focus of the study of politics on material interests, this book problematizes previous studies' overwhelming convergence on police coercion as the main means of state control over society.

Examining nonviolent forms of control uncovers some hidden dimensions of state–society relations. Many studies focus on protest as a channel for contention in such relations in China and other authoritarian regimes. This book unpacks a form of state–society relations that is less about direct mass contention and more about access and negotiation. The spaces are liminal but also showcase a deliberate part of local governments' design of urban public welfare. The book better reflects the common lived experience for most people living in China. This book echoes Piven and Cloward's (1971) finding on the relationship between the welfare system and civil order in the United States and builds on it by showing how the dynamics and outcomes differ in a developing country with an authoritarian regime.

Political atomization sits between two of James Scott's concepts: "seeing like a state" in grand projects of authoritarian vision (1998) and "everyday forms of resistance" (1985). The process requires municipal authorities to have some sense of societal legibility to know who does and does not count as interlopers and whether they deem them deserving of benefits. At the same time, these outsiders are not uniformly or completely powerless. Their everyday experiences of power typically reflect how the state perceives them in terms of overall desirability as a permanent resident, potential threat to social stability, and economic value. Some are more appealing than others and therefore receive more benefits. These workers are also subject to authoritarian legality, which further emboldens some to claim rights as legislation grants more to them and then eventually falls short of expectations in practice (Gallagher 2017). Political atomization follows a similar course of initial, cautious hope followed by disenchantment, but with even less high-level political willpower and fewer resources behind it than many labor law reforms. This book identifies this process as a feature and not a bug of the systems which distribute urban entitlements to rural migrant workers. Disillusionment from experience and being told to wait for coming substantial reforms that never materialize make it harder for people to pursue claims and help to disempower the rest.

Authoritarian Distribution

Modern autocrats can draw on a diverse toolbox, as evident from examples from around the world. Major dimensions of authoritarian control are often categorized into tools of repression or cooptation, the latter of which includes variations of making concessions and buying loyalty. Leaders must weigh whether to use repression to, for example, counter challenges to the status quo (Davenport 2007) or deal with threats to the regime from a mass, organized, and potentially violent opposition (Svolik 2012). Numerous studies have considered the trade-offs between repression and cooptation from different approaches and across various governments (e.g., Wintrobe 1998, Gershenson and Grossman 2001, Gandhi and Przeworski 2006, Davenport 2007, Gandhi 2008, Frantz and Kendall-Taylor 2014, Xu 2021). Repression in authoritarian regimes is costly, can be ineffective, and may generate backlash though. Political atomization serves as an alternative mode of social control that may risk less overt and violent repercussions than coercive repression.

Coopting potential threats or giving policy concessions is another tool of authoritarian regimes. Autocratic leaders may induce loyalty or coopt segments of society through different power-sharing institutions, such as political parties, elections, and legislatures (e.g., O'Donnell 1979, Gandhi and Przeworski 2006, 2007, Brownlee 2007, Gandhi 2008,

Magaloni 2008, Svolik 2012). Dictators, for instance, make more extensive policy concessions and share fewer rents when they need more cooperation, and they make larger concessions and distribute more spoils when there is a higher threat of rebellion (Gandhi and Przeworski 2006). A combination of performance-based loyalty and repression explain a number of East Asian cases, and the regime in China adopted policies of both carrots and sticks to gain support or acquiescence from coalitions (Gallagher and Hanson 2009). Gallagher and Hanson's (2015) challenges to applying selectorate theory to authoritarian regimes based on Bueno de Mesquita et al.'s (2003) assumptions on the unrealistic linking of public goods and political rights and the exclusion and underestimation of the unenfranchized are relevant. This book builds on this further by examining a large subset of the masses, migrants, and the concrete process of providing, in addition to granting or withholding, public goods in the case of China.

Autocrats have long structured distribution through clientelism and patronage for political ends, and the literature often focuses on whether to provide or restrict public goods.[5] Scholars have studied clientelism across different regions, ranging from the roles and limits of patronage in Southeast Asia (Pepinsky 2007, Slater 2010) to neopatrimonialism in Sub-Saharan Africa (Bratton and van de Walle 1997) to the involvement of Bolivarian circles in receiving services in Venezuela (Hawkins and Hansen 2006). The study of social protection policies in developing countries is growing (e.g., Mares and Carnes 2009, Wibbels and Ahlquist 2011), but insufficient attention has been paid to the authoritarian roots of developing countries' social policy (Mares and Carnes 2009). The case of China is ideal for studying the provision of these benefits without electoral incentives in authoritarian regimes and underlines how the political logic of social policy may differ in nondemocratic regimes.

Political atomization differs from existing literature on patronage and clientelism in several ways and opens new paths for research on authoritarian welfare states. One key distinction is that perceived exchange of promised services for loyalty works for now in China, even in the absence of fully actualized incorporation. The allure of diffuse promised benefits, moreover, for Chinese migrants stands in contrast to targeted actual entitlements common in the literature. And how, not only if, public services are provided is an arena of concession and cooptation that merits more scholarly attention. The level of more targeted provision of public goods for groups within society, the interaction between economic growth and the development of the welfare state, and the ways in which entitlements are available for a few but held seemingly just out of reach for many afford the state novel ways to use inequality as a tool of social control.

Public Service Provision without Elections

China is a useful comparative case for understanding public service provision in a developing, nondemocratic country. Studying distribution in an authoritarian context helps with identifying incentives and disincentives for providing public goods in the absence of electoral pressures. This also enables this book to disentangle the other functions of welfare aside from the services themselves. The ways in which Chinese officials sometimes restrict benefits or construct phantom services contradict existing explanations and introduce new approaches to evaluating public service provision for marginalized groups. Within case, it features decentralization and regional variation that provide fertile grounds for identifying the gaps (and spaces for opportunities) between broad central directives, local policy formulation, and ground-level implementation.

Local authorities in China provide entitlements despite not having to stand for public election or fear being voted out of office. The study of public goods is wide-ranging, and extensive work addresses clientelism and electoral pressures that officials face in deciding whether and when to incorporate outsiders into their public welfare systems. Political parties and incumbents compete for voters who may cast ballots as levers to increase the provision (or lack thereof) of benefits (Garay 2016) or to allow forebearance to continue (Holland 2017) in Latin American contexts. Studies like these explain development of social welfare policies in newly consolidated democracies (Jamil 2021) but tell us little about the pressures municipal Chinese officials face to expand or contract privileges such as pensions and low-income housing. Nor does it account for the pattern of selective inclusion of migrant workers in Chinese metropolises.

Political atomization exposes functions of welfare for the state beyond the social services themselves. Selective provision can forestall unrest at politically sensitive times and enable officials to contain and channel migrant demands. The state can divide and conquer a large, marginalized social group by appeasing a few and making it harder for the rest to organize collective action against it. Likewise, sudden restrictions on access and the complete shutdown of public goods like electricity, water, and schools can drive undesired social groups out of a neighborhood or the entire city. Moreover, people become atomized through modes aside from repression of protests, namely social control via public service provision. Unpacking the process of individualization shows how society becomes fragmented in an authoritarian regime that divides and rules those who are historically marginalized. Atomization is often thought of as the byproduct of crackdowns on group contention, making it more difficult for organizers of collective action and perhaps dissuading joiners. Here it functions closer to prevention and preemption. Although I first observed this phenomenon in China, there is nothing inherent to the concept itself that isolates its applicability to an authoritarian or middle-income country. Its utility, flexibility, and efficacy are far-reaching and can be used by almost any state with the appropriate capacity and need.

And the mere expansion of services is not always better. Bureaucrats at first appeared to be dismantling old national systems of discrimination such as the *hukou* system. Year after year of supposed incremental reform has shown that municipal and district authorities are constructing new, smaller systems of partial inclusion devolved at the municipal level. When announcements about migrant students in Shanghai gaining the right to compulsory education in the city were made, international and domestic news outlets seized on it as evidence that meaningful reform and incorporation were underway. By the time stories of segregation, blocked enrollments, required "voluntary" donations, and other developments trickled out, public attention had turned elsewhere. These outcomes are products of a patchwork system designed to individualize distribution rather than expand it. They are far from short-term hiccups of new policy rollouts and have not led to heftier national reforms.

In some cases, the opposite has been true. Retrenchment has occurred as some of the most overcrowded mega-cities seek to contract their populations or stop any further growth in the coming years. Beijing and Shanghai, for example, are aiming to cap their populations, so urbanization is not a uniform process across localities. Different cities receive migrants looking for work in varying industries and from places ranging from villages that surround the city to ones in provinces on the opposite side of the country. Small cities may experience a boom and bust, while large cities see a steady inflow of people because they are consistently appealing locations. Migrant workers' demands and needs, therefore, are not identical across cities, prompting additional fluctuations in policies and practices.

Chinese officials sometimes restrict benefits instead of giving concessions to groups they view as a potential threat to social stability. Contrary to some scholars of authoritarian durability who find governments give concessions to target groups who might challenge the regime (Knutsen and Rasmussen 2017), Chinese officials sometimes do the opposite. Other research finds that increasing distribution in authoritarian regimes may undercut opposing elites and enmesh people in a relationship of coercive dependence (Albertus et al. 2018). The Chinese Communist Party (CCP) is not particularly focused on giving benefits to migrant workers as a way to fend off rival elites, and in many cases, outsiders are excluded or deflected rather than becoming enmeshed. Neither accounts for the periodic and place-dependent expansion and cutback of social rights given to migrants as they move around China. Moreover, wholesale inclusion or exclusion is not the only decision that officials have to make regarding migrant social policy. Through seepage, one policy can change the allocation of resources and goals of unrelated areas of government (Pan 2020).

Unlike other studies that focus only on whether services are provided (often to maximize efficiency or buy loyalty) (Bueno de Mesquita and Smith 2010), I find that *how* public services are provided is itself a tool of social control. Moving from a primarily binary understanding to a qualitative one broadens our categorization and more accurately reflects the grounded experience of marginalized people. This deeper conceptualization considers the ways in which eligibility, access, and use can be manipulated, thereby questioning and recognizing under what conditions the expansion of public goods (formally and in implementation) is not always uniformly positive. Ethnographic observations and in-depth interviews capture power relations and mechanisms in the delivery of social rights. How, not only if, the government provides services is important. The approach to understanding public service provision in this book adds a new dimension to be assessed.

New Gradations of Citizenship and Structural Inequality

Achieving Xi Jinping's "Chinese Dream" and "common prosperity" will require addressing inequity, and reducing inequality is a stated priority for the central government. Building on the notion of national rejuvenation on the world stage, the party-state responded to increasing grievances and unrest about social inequity by connecting the Chinese Dream with the domestic public and their concerns about housing, employment, public health, education, and the environment (Wang 2014). In a 2017 speech after the conclusion of the 19th National Congress of the Communist Party of China, Xi Jinping said, "On the march towards common prosperity, no one must be left behind. We will mobilize the whole Party and the whole country in a resolute push to deliver on our pledge and eradicate poverty in China."[6] In the same speech, he emphasized a "people-centered philosophy of development." The 2014–2020 national urbanization plan set milestones that matched the lofty and alluring aims. Besides numbers on who would receive city *hukou*, railways would connect all cities with more than 200,000 residents, and high-speed rail would link cities with more than half a million residents (State Council of the People's Republic of China 2014). Discussions of inequality in China often converge on two points: remarkable progress in poverty alleviation and the ever stubborn rural-urban divide (e.g., Whyte 2010b, Ang 2016).[7] Migrants and policies toward them bridge this divide literally and figuratively, and much has changed since previous studies found that rural migrants in urban China are second-class citizens.

A number of demographic, economic, and social changes have occurred since the initial wave of migration in the early 1980s after Reform and Opening began. Some migrants were born in the city and have never lived in, much less visited, the villages where their household registration is located based on their parents' status. The second generation is enjoying higher minimum wages and seeking a better quality of life than many of their parents who first ventured out of their villages to work in factories. Most are less willing to "eat bitterness" (*chiku*, 吃苦) and want safer, more lucrative, and more stable employment and residence. Migrants on the whole are older,[8] which follows the wider societal pattern of an aging working population. The larger economic landscape in which they work is changing. Industrial upgrading is part of a plan to reshape the foundations of the Chinese economy, which has relied on exports over the last four decades. While these factors have shaped the lives of migrants, none explain political atomization, or the array of differential citizenship that migrant workers have across cities in China.

This book builds on the foundational scholarship of my forebears, including Dorothy Solinger's seminal work among many others. By the mid-1990s, two simultaneous processes were happening: Chinese migrants submitted to the state as they were being incorporated into official systems, and transients' presence was unintentionally undermining the "urban public goods regime" (Solinger 1995). Solinger has argued that the outcomes of marketization must be understood alongside institutional legacies from the former socialist system and that, as of the late 1990s, the state and markets were blocking the realization of what she calls normal urban citizenship (Solinger 1999). Since then, systems and practices of urban public goods provision have continued to evolve.

Among the new contributions of my book is the focus on how political atomization enables the Chinese state to divide and rule migrants.

In contrast to the bright line distinction between rural migrants and urban residents that once existed (Chan 1994, 2009, Solinger 1999, Chan and Zhang 1999, Fan 2002, Chan and Buckingham 2008) due to the *hukou* system (Cheng and Selden 1994, Solinger 1999, Chan and Zhang 1999, Fan 2002, Wang 2005, Chan and Buckingham 2008, Chan 2009, Whyte 2010b, Wu 2010, Chan et al. 2018), gradations in second-class citizenship among migrant workers have emerged. While the rural–urban dichotomy has not vanished, differences among migrants, such as informal workers in China's construction industry (Swider 2015), have come to the fore. More highly educated and wealthier migrants from other cities tend to fare better than those with less formal schooling and with lower socioeconomic status who hail from the countryside. Disparities in the attainment of social rights also exist among people in the latter group, so a migrant from within Sichuan Province, for example, has more access to public schooling and can more easily use their social insurance in the provincial capital Chengdu than a similarly positioned person who has traveled from Anhui Province. Whether each of them is employed in a company with a signed labor contract or working in the informal economy without this paperwork further divides them in some cities. These within-group differences transcend an us-versus-them mentality and manufacture a them-versus-them cleavage because of the variation within rural migrants as a group.

In order to show how systemic political atomization is, this book distinguishes structural sources of inequality from individual acts of discrimination. Regardless of whether a single official or bureaucrat is prejudiced against migrants or supportive of incorporating them, policies and practices behind political individualization dictate that they do their small, local part to construct the patchwork of policies that leaves migrants between having social rights and being able to access urban public schools or secure low-income housing in the city. Authorities who carry out policies and deliver services need not be anti-migrant in order for political atomization to emerge, function, or persist.

Structural sources of inequality have political and practical advantages over discrimination. They enable bureaucrats and service providers to feel some distancing. It is not only migrants who are unsure whom to blame but also officials themselves who frequently cite policies and directives coming down from higher level authorities as being the sources of their decision-making. They are carrying out policies and doing the best they can within the confines of an unfunded mandate and multiple incentives, such as promoting economic development while preserving social stability and incorporating migrants. Ironically, the transparency of some of these policies at the most local levels on paper allows street-level bureaucrats (Lipsky 1980) and service providers to evade direct blame and claims of exclusion. Though they may be clearly written somewhere, their accessibility and navigability are another matter to be dealt with by people encountering the system in a government office.

Nearly every government, international organization, and nongovernmental organization agrees that inequality is a problem and every effort should be made to reduce it. However, inequality can sometimes benefit the state, either by original design or by way of incremental structural changes that end up having the same effect. Political atomization is another tool in the autocrat's toolbox for regulating marginalized social groups. Because a few are able to gain access to services and there is often technically a path to full citizenship, it makes it more difficult for them to build a collective consciousness, much less engage in collective action. A national overhaul of social service provision that would, for instance, make pensions transferable between provinces would make migrants better off overall. A hodgepodge system with power devolved to local governments enables localities to keep a renewable supply of migrant workers without having to pay for the full costs of integrating them as equal urban citizens. Sources of intergroup inequality, methods of less coercive and noncoercive control, and maintenance of a labor force to support local economic development are deeply intertwined in China. This expands our understanding of how nondemocratic states hone their methods of social control through bureaucratic demobilization and individualization.

This book advances an explanation for the political logic of inequality in China. The central government has made extraordinary strides in reducing poverty, and that accomplishment shows China's state capacity (even if it can be uneven or fragmented at times)[9] when a policy goal is a priority. But migrant inequality remains an unsolved problem. While outright discrimination against migrants can and does occur, the bases for discretionary provision and selective inclusion are built into the institutions themselves and are a consequence of the nature of decentralization in this policy area. Inequality can benefit the state, even as institutions of social control are updated and repurposed at the same time that national pronouncements about the undeniable need to address inequity are disseminated. By identifying this specific form of structural inequality that is between wholesale exclusion and complete inclusion, political atomization pinpoints a different form of selective incorporation that allows the state to appear to be dedicated to improving migrant welfare without having to actually do so in full (at least yet). Furthermore, in the Xi Jinping era of increasing centralization and consolidation of power at the top, there has been more continuity than change between Xi's and his predecessor's administration in this particular policy area, and migrant welfare provision in cities remains relatively decentralized because such pliable citizenship serves the state (Chan 2024). Overall, political atomization augments structural sources of inequality.

ROADMAP

This section explains the division of chapters in the book. Chapter 2 presents a theory of political atomization, how it works, and why it persists. The remaining arguments and evidence of this book are organized into two main parts. Part I (Chapters 3 and 4) lays out how the provision of public services is a tool of social control for the state in urban China. Part II (Chapters 5 and 6) shows how migrants can blunt elements of control and gain some access to services. Chapter 7 zooms out to examine the broader implications for China and provide a comparative perspective.

Chapter 2 identifies and conceptualizes political atomization. This process explains two phenomena better than existing literature: why incremental expansions in social policy can entrench inequality and how authoritarian states sometimes use public service provision as a tool of social control. It also accounts for how policies said to expand workers' rights end up undermining their claims to benefits owed to them in China. The chapter considers why alternative explanations are inadequate and then describes the research design, methods, and sources of the book. The main section begins by situating the theory of political atomization within the literatures on authoritarianism, immigration, and welfare states. The rest of the section elucidates in detail how political atomization works and why it persists. There are trade-offs and risks to this approach, but embedded inequality ultimately serves the state. Unpacking political atomization illuminates how everyday marginalization of people works on the ground in their lived experiences.

Chapter 3 focuses on how municipalities deflect demands for benefits instead of meeting them or denying them outright to resist and undermine elements of the central government's urbanization strategy. This diffuse promise of phantom services operates at what is experienced by local officials and migrants as the person-by-person micro-level of provision. Urban authorities sometimes do so by establishing nearly impossible eligibility requirements or requiring paperwork that outsiders struggle to obtain. At times they also nudge migrants to seek health care or education elsewhere by enforcing dormant rules or by shutting down a locally available service provider. Local officials use these ploys for both political and practical reasons. Limiting access isolates and disempowers migrants and is cheaper than offering benefits. Phantom services are a consequence of the localization of the household registration system and a sign that new axes of inequality and gradations of second-class citizenship have emerged.

Chapter 4 shows how cities demobilize migrant workers through partial and incomplete inclusion at what is perceived by local authorities and migrants as the higher meso-level of regulation of institutions. The local state plays two main roles in migrant education services. As regulators, municipal authorities shut down, take over, or certify private, "people-run" migrant schools that serve as informal substitutes when rural students cannot enroll in urban public schools. At the same time, they exclude, segregate and separate, or include those students in public schools as providers. Three main approaches to regulation and integration are: (1) suppression and exclusion, (2) selective absorption and segregated inclusion, and (3) certification and full inclusion, as exemplified by Beijing, Shanghai, and Chengdu, respectively. Municipal and district officials use migrant social policy in this area to push visible results, avoid blame and criticism, and employ complementary approaches between private regulation and public integration.

Although rural migrants are frequently deflected and only selectively incorporated into urban public benefits, Chapter 5 shows that they have ways to undercut elements of social control and attain some education and health care. Resourcefulness and practical priorities help them find bureaucrats who practice co-migrant empathy and work within existing formal institutions to pry open what institutional leeway they can. When those are insufficient or inaccessible, rural migrants create and turn to private alternatives to get health care and education in the city. "People-run" schools are informal institutions that fill the gaps of public service provision, enabling migrants to keep their jobs when they get sick or have families in their destinations. However, because they are makeshift and typically operate on the outskirts of cities and in the shadows of legality, they can become subject to sudden intervention or regulation by the state. At other times, the government allows them to operate. The subversion of control is possible but not without the risk of being reverted into a target of the state.

Chapter 6 looks at how individuals improvise around authoritarian control and government restrictions in everyday circumstances. By shifting the focus from gaining institutional access to meeting their needs, migrant workers make do and muddle through despite being relatively powerless vis-à-vis the Chinese state. Newcomers have devised strategies of survival to scrape together needs so that they can keep their jobs, save their disposable income, and attain medical treatment when necessary. At the individual level, they frequently rely on visiting illegal private health clinics or try to straddle the rural–urban divide. In community-based innovations, they negotiate with their employers to opt out of paying into social insurance schemes (and thereby run against the common notion that all outsiders want to be included) or craft small-scale, self-run insurance arrangements. These practices suggest that migrants have found ways to curtail some of the effects of social control, but notably it is mostly at the margins. The effects of political atomization are therefore muddled, and the state's use of public service provision as a tool of social control largely remains intact.

Chapter 7 concludes with broader implications. After recapping how the previous chapters fit together to form a larger window on social control beyond coercion, it scrutinizes the limits of political atomization with a focus on perverse outcomes that result from the accumulated effects of individualization. Next are implications for China for inequality, the economy, migrant welfare and citizenship, and the authoritarian state's social control toolbox. China is not alone in using political atomization, and a comparative perspective can spur future research on how the phenomenon already exists, not only in other developing and authoritarian countries but also in democracies and developed countries. It ends with an examination of inequality and the state, noting that individual-level schemes are no match for systemic deflection and demobilization to address the entrenchment of inequality in social policy.

This book brings together seemingly disparate studies of inequality, social control, and public service provision. The lens used here clarifies why policies about "people-centered" urbanization serve state ends other than improving migrant welfare. A convoluted patchwork of local policies does little for people who move around frequently for work opportunities and sometimes across thousands of miles. The persistence of this hodgepodge of policies shows other interests at stake that are familiar in other contexts but rarely highlighted in the question of inclusion and distribution. Inequality is in service to the state rather than being a threat to it.

2

A Theory of Political Atomization

IDENTIFYING POLITICAL ATOMIZATION

Mr. Wang grabbed an extra yellow hard hat from his friend's dorm bed and handed it to me before we headed out to meet his co-workers. It had taken me several subway line changes, a *heiche* ("black cab," 黑车) ride, and a few text messages indicating I was lost to reach them. We stood in the characteristic white dorm trailers with blue trim within walking distance of the construction site where most of the others had already started their workday. There were about ten bunks in the room, and individual beds were stacked with worn blankets, sundries such as small plastic cups with toothbrushes, and other personal belongings. Everyone had a pep in their step because it was Mid-Autumn Festival, and the company was giving each worker one large bottle of Tsingdao beer and the *bao gongtou* (chief labor contractor, 包工头) had promised a 50 RMB (approximately US$7) bonus to everyone for the holiday.[1]

Instead of sitting down for our interview, he insisted I go into (or, more accurately, onto) the structure being erected. As I climbed to the second and third floors that were under construction, he and his colleagues told me about their lived experience not only as workers but as rural migrants eking out lives with little social protection in the city. The workers were able to nimbly balance on the wooden planks and move more quickly through the scaffolding than me. I tentatively grabbed rebar that was sticking out, trying not to fall or accidentally shift something mid-build. I was grateful for the borrowed hard hat, but it was too big and kept slipping off my head as I chatted with the workers while they slogged through their tasks. We eventually wound our way to talking about concrete issues such as what they did when they got sick and where their children lived and were going to school. It was early in this particular fieldwork trip, and I was curious about whether they were receiving more or better benefits given what I had read about in the Chinese language news about improvements in social policy toward migrant workers. Their experiences not only clashed with formal policy but, more surprisingly, with each other's. As I interviewed more people and observed services being accessed (or not) at the point of delivery, it would become apparent that this was actually a larger pattern of political atomization.

Later that afternoon, news spread quickly that they were getting the last hour of the scheduled day off. Around 4 p.m., workers rushed to drop off their tools and clean up to prepare for a celebration. One person whom I had not yet met warmly proclaimed there was a guest (me) in the dorm and that he would go wash his face in honor of that. He later bought extra drinks for the group and explained how he had moved between the cities of Beijing and Shenzhen, depending on where there was work available. A small group, including the girlfriend of one of the workers, grabbed pastel-colored, wide, shallow plastic bins and headed to the company cafeteria to order food for the occasion. One of the interviewees was unsure of my age as I was a graduate student at the time and bought me a bottle of a sweet milk-flavored drink typically given to children. We passed around bowls of rice and a green plastic tub (sometimes repurposed for laundry) of pork, and they explained that meat dishes were expensive but today was a treat for everyone. Another person walked in carrying a container of cooked green vegetables to share and said that the company paid for housing and electricity while they lived in the dorms but not for food or drink. An elderly man who spoke only his local dialect smiled as his colleagues told me that he was working to support his children's family back home in Shaanxi. They concluded the main meal with the fruit and cigarettes I had brought as a token of gratitude for allowing me to interrupt their day of work and night off. As they became more comfortable, they more openly expressed their frustrations with how their social protections, timing of wage payments, and other issues were much worse than for others on the site. They compared their benefits to those of the people who made up the layers of subcontractors between them and the company and to those of the supervisors who worked directly for the firm paying for the building.[2]

The workers' experiences of accessing and using urban public services stood in stark contrast to their mid-level boss'. The supervisor had two children, a fourteen-year-old daughter who wanted to pursue a career in medicine and a ten-year-old son. Both were in Shaanxi Province with his wife while he stayed in Beijing for the year. He paid his workers once a year and was clearly higher in the company hierarchy than those whom I met in the dorm. When I asked him questions about social insurance, health care, education, pensions, and other benefits, his answers were straightforward and simple. He said, for example, "If I am seriously sick, the company pays."

Those whom he employed had a significantly wider range of experiences. Some had left their children in the care of grandparents in their home villages so their children could attend school there, while others had heard stories of migrant children being allowed to enroll in public schools in certain cities and were considering bringing their children and wives to the city to try their luck with the new regulations. Depending on the severity of their injury or illness when they did need medical care, some attempted to use their rural insurance at urban public hospitals while others toughed it out until they went home for Spring Festival or another occasion when they would not have to miss work. As they regaled me with stories, they began to compare nitty gritty details with each other. Some workers followed a particular subcontractor from their hometown to whatever construction sites they found, whereas others drifted between industries. Sometimes they would have health insurance that could be used at the nearest public hospital in the city if they had a work unit (*danwei*, 单位), and other times their access was more uncertain. Often, they did not know if they could use any of their supposed entitlements until an emergency arose. For these particular employees, housing was not a concern because most lived in the company dorms on site. But construction workers' access, eligibility, and use differ from people who work in factories assembling goods for export or in restaurants as waiters and dishwashers. For all of these people, their benefits depended on what city they were working in that year. This was only a brief preview of the ways that the state does not treat migrant workers as a monolithic group.

These construction workers' experiences embody the puzzle motivating this book. First, policies that appeared to support their incorporation into cities were not improving their social protection in practicable ways. Second, the variety of experiences with accessing and using services depended on a wide set of factors, ranging from their specific hometown to which city they happened to be working in at the time to the industry in which they were employed. It was difficult for any one individual or household to identify a systematic pattern of discrimination and exclusion being used against them because local governments seemed to handle and channel their demands on a case-by-case basis. Many were deflected with what seemed to be person by person phantom services and blamed themselves for their lack of services (Chapter 3). They navigated complicated, seemingly ever-changing regulations of institutions in each city as a few gained access while others were demobilized (Chapter 4). Some opted to send their children to makeshift alternatives such as private migrant schools (Chapter 5) or developed informal substitutes for health insurance (Chapter 6). Nearly all faced political atomization.

This chapter proceeds as follows. The next subsections offer a preview of the concept of political atomization and discuss why alternative explanations for the uneven provision of services for migrants are lacking. The section after that describes the research methods of the book. The chapter then proceeds to unpack the conceptualization of political atomization, explaining how it works, why this form of everyday marginalization persists (including potential downsides of this approach), and why it structurally entrenches inequality. Unpacking political atomization illuminates how marginalization of people works on the ground and in their lived experiences.

A Preview of the Concept

Political atomization is a process by which the state creates policies that structurally treat marginalized people as individuals to enact selective inclusion over group-based exclusion.[3] It makes migrants responsible for their own public service access and shifts the focus from the state's obligation in providing basic benefits to citizens to those people's role in obtaining access. By dampening expectations and diluting claims, it undermines group-based claims of discrimination. A system of political atomization is embodied in the procedures and policies that determine migrant entitlements and their interactions with various bureaucrats as they seek to access and use these privileges. Structural forms of control through these systems and the policies that make them up help give an illusion of agential power for the migrant while effectively keeping most of them out of urban welfare systems. Political atomization enables the Chinese state to exercise control beyond coercion.

How do policies said to expand workers' rights end up weakening their demands? I contend that a process of political atomization undermines most migrants' claims on the benefits owed to them. When people were excluded nearly wholesale based on their household registration statuses, registered rural residents who live and work in cities could allege group-based discrimination. They at least had a clear basis for collectively organizing, although many felt it would be largely ineffective because of their limited political power and marginalized status as second-class citizens. For many years, the household registration (*hukou*, 户口) system prevented most from accessing public services in their urban destinations.

The central government has distributed directives for cities to incorporate migrants. Through initiatives such as the National New-Type Urbanization Plan (2014–2020),[4] Li Keqiang drove state support for deepening China's urbanization process as a tool for economic development. Some policy changes appeared to follow suit and began to integrate outsiders into urban centers. More avenues for migrants to change their registrations from rural to urban emerged, especially in small- and medium-sized cities. Scattered increases in their access to education, health care, housing, pensions, and other benefits in cities seemed to follow. *Hukou* reform, however, has taken a particular form and led to localization of policies instead of a deep and systemwide overhaul. These seeds of change have not only come from central leaders in Beijing. In the Xi Jinping era of centralization and consolidation, public service provision for migrants has remained surprisingly devolved (Chan 2024).

Many city governments have issued their own policies. Changes have occurred in areas such as social insurance (Zhang 2012, Huang 2014), education (Chan and Wang 2009, Lan 2014), and housing (Huang 2012). Reforms to the *hukou* system (Chan and Buckingham 2008, Hong et al. 2022) and complicated points-based residency systems have also been introduced. While there have been some meaningful improvements in migrants' lives more broadly, local policy modifications and adaptations have not been uniform across provinces and cities within the country. Most mega-cities, for example, tend to be more restrictive toward outsiders while some lower tier cities have begun to incorporate migrants more. This piecemeal reform has led to limited headway on resolving the core issue.

Overall progress has been slow and uneven. Despite both central endorsements and local reforms, migrant workers' access to urban social services remains patchy. Instead of being provided or denied benefits outright, many migrants are being deflected (Chan and O'Brien 2019). Under novel points systems, few can accumulate enough points to qualify to change their official residence change. Housing ownership, for example, counts toward their totals. But when migrants are 92 percent less likely to own homes than locals in Shanghai (Qian et al. 2019), they tend to encounter new obstacles to changing their residency status instead of fresh opportunities. Guangzhou granted 5,000 *hukou* in 2015, and, according to Mayor Yang Xiong, Shanghai granted *hukou* to 26,000 migrants total by the end of that same year (Zuo 2016). Beijing extended *hukou* to 6,019 people who had the most points out of 124,000 applicants in 2018 (Xinhua 2019). The same policies said to expand migrant social rights have in effect thwarted more substantial, institutional, and group-wide integration that would significantly protect their benefits across the country. Developments in urban integration sometimes stall altogether when other policy priorities take precedence. Because public service provision for non-locally registered residents is decentralized, policies that vary city by city constitute the complicated patchwork that people who move around need to navigate.

Alternative Explanations

It is helpful to consider a number of alternative explanations before showing how political atomization works and why it persists. The simplest reason for why various local governments treat migrant workers differently could be wealth: richer cities can afford to spend more on public services for outsiders. But wealth does not explain why, for example, Beijing is generally exclusionary, Shanghai has had limited success, and Chengdu is doing especially well in making education accessible to migrant students. Nor does it explain variation over time within these cities or differences between regional cities such as Dongguan and Hangzhou. Wealthier cities should be better equipped to manage an unfunded mandate, but they have other competing policy priorities. In addition, local officials and urban residents are sometimes reluctant to share resources with rural migrants, whom some see as undeserving outsiders and troublemakers.

Furthermore, the wealthiest cities are typically overcrowded megacities. A few of the largest cities are attempting to cap the number of people living in those metros and are seeking to disincentivize further population growth. The Beijing Municipal Master Plan (2016–2035), officially approved by the Party Central Committee and the State Council (People's Government of Beijing 2018), set a goal of capping the city's population at 23 million by 2020 (People's Republic of China Central People's Government 2017). Shanghai followed in the capital's footsteps with a 25 million goal cap by 2035. Cities in these circumstances are unlikely to do anything that would lure more people, such as dramatically expanding their public goods provision. Nor do their public service policies toward migrants take on the same levels or forms of opening and restriction as each other.

Labor shortages are another potential alternative explanation for why certain cities treat migrants better and others worse. Cities in the Pearl River Delta in Guangdong Province have experienced labor shortages since about 2004 (Yang 2005), but improvement in services has been more recent and dependent on limited local *hukou* reform. The mechanism seems plausible, but municipalities and companies often turn to other levers to draw in workers when they are needed. Low-skilled labor shortages do not usually lead to changes in social service provision. Moreover, the relationship may run in the opposite direction: the *hukou* system (and associated restrictions on benefits for those who have relocated) may be part of the cause of labor shortages (Cui et al. 2018). According to small- and medium-sized factory owners in Guangdong and Sichuan Provinces that I interviewed, only the largest factories with tens or hundreds of thousands of workers have enough economic and political sway to try to influence local, never mind national, policy. They explained that only when a company offering as many new jobs as a large multinational company could deliver would the local government respond directly to a particular labor shortage.[5] In those cases, the local government may offer to bus in laborers from nearby villages or provide support, such as worker training.[6] Furthermore, the 2008 global economic downturn affected firms across the country, but not all cities have improved services in response. Meanwhile, workers are flocking inland, where services had already been improving. And it takes time to build capacity in public service provision and effectively incorporate new recipients, which would result in a possible lag until an expansion in benefits would attract new workers. Social policy is not a quick fix for metropolitan areas trying to resolve immediate labor shortages.

The education of migrant children is steeped in discourse around the term *suzhi* (素质, quality), which some urban parents raise concerns about and use as a reason to disallow those students. *Suzhi jiaoyu* (素质教育, education for quality) was part of the reform of education policy during the late 1980s, and *suzhi* has come to signify hierarchy in society as inequality becomes more visible and Chinese society is increasingly competitive (Kipnis 2006). Differences in class formation between urbanites, rural residents, and migrants occurred in the context of a related program in Xiamen (Lin 2011). Parents who are registered urban residents have used the term in practice to denote superiority and serve as a reason to justify bias against migrant students who do not have local household registrations. Popular discourse insinuates that students with higher *suzhi* get spots in universities while those with low *suzhi* are disadvantaged (Murphy 2004). Discourse, while important, does not necessarily translate directly into matching social policy toward migrants. Urban parent discrimination against migrant students does exist and is likely present in most cities, but their occasional complaints to school-level administrators are insufficient to explain systemic differences in migrant education policy. (See Chapter 4 on bias on the part of parents and bureaucrats and Chapter 5 on the consequences of discrimination by doctors and teachers.) Fieldwork for this book suggests that the mechanisms by which they can systematically shape overall policy toward those whom they perceive city as outsiders are limited.

Recent developments indicate that migrant workers may be gaining more leverage and therefore should be in a better position to demand more social protection. To be sure, some aspects of migrants' quality of life are improving, such as earning higher wages (Li et al. 2012). Labor shortages also tip the power imbalance more toward workers, but they continue to face high institutional barriers. Meanwhile, labor unrest is on the rise. China Labour Bulletin's online data show that reported strikes (which likely represent a small fraction of total strikes for the year) increased from 184 in 2011 to 1,257 in 2017.[7] In the first eight months of 2018 alone, 1,134 strikes had been logged into the strike map.[8] In 2014, as many as 40,000 workers at the Yue Yuen shoe factory complex in Dongguan, Guangdong Province, in "the world's factory" in southeastern China went on strike for two weeks. They protested what they claim had been years of inadequate social insurance and housing fund contributions that the company should have paid. Yue Yuen facilities produced shoes for global brands including Adidas, Nike, and Saucony. Though social benefits are not the most common reason that workers participate in strikes, this was one of the largest in recent memory according to labor activists. A Guangzhou Labor Dispute Litigation White Paper stated that unpaid social insurance accounted for more than 40 percent of arbitration cases from 2014 to 2016.[9] Some workers are beginning to seek redress for benefits they are owed, but the scope of their requests are often limited to companies not paying their part instead of putting the onus on the state. Labor unrest has also become more offensive (Elfstrom and Kuruvilla 2014), suggesting there are at least perceived openings in political opportunity. Workers have demanded repayment of wage arears, better working conditions, and more. Systematic reform of urban social services for migrants has not yet followed increasing migrant worker assertiveness or rising wages.

Demographic changes do not account for changes in public service provision for migrants either. Many observers have assumed that the second generation of migrant workers could and would push for a stronger social safety net. Second-generation migrants are the children of the migrant workers who were part of the initial massive rural-to-urban migration in the 1980s. Many are born and raised in the city, but their household registration status is still tied to that of their parents who retain their rural registration. Some experience more anger and dissatisfaction than the first generation (Pun and Lu 2010b), and most are more highly educated than their parents. While the identity of second-generation migrants is different from that of first-generation migrants, the fact that second-generation migrants are younger also means that they are healthier and less likely to have children.[10] From construction workers to those working on a factory line, they are more concerned about quality of life (e.g., working fewer hours or in less potentially toxic job environments) than about public education or health care.[11] Though individual companies may face different demands from first- and second-generation migrants depending on the type of worker most suitable for their business, the overall cohort breakdown in a city does not map onto broader government policies. When migrants do band together to access social services in the city, it is often to circumvent rules of exclusion from government-sponsored schemes or form informal institutions to serve as private alternatives. Differences between cities in the proportion of first- and second-generation migrants do not explain how the state treats migrants overall. City wealth, labor shortages, labor unrest, or the second generation of migrants alone does not account for patchy integration of city newcomers. Political atomization and other overriding state goals better explain public service provision for migrant workers.

METHODS

This book examines the political atomization of migrants based on fieldwork across six cities in four regions, three sectors, and two types of services. The findings are drawn from multiple trips to Beijing, Chengdu, Shanghai, Guangzhou, Hangzhou, and Dongguan between 2010 and 2019. I focus on large, top-tier municipalities rather than smaller cities,[12] because many workers prefer more developed cities, where there are more job opportunities and higher wages, and it is usually in these desirable destinations that social services are most contested. A fruit and vegetable seller from Shandong Province working and living in Beijing put it succinctly, "I have no interest in going to small cities because there aren't opportunities there."[13] These cities are located in four different regions of the country, including three areas along the coast that have been migrant worker destinations for four decades and an inland city that has more recently seen an influx of outsiders.[14] Of the many public services, I focus primarily on health care and education. Both are crucial to human development and China's long-term growth prospects and are of key importance to migrant worker families. Two of the three dimensions of the Human Development Index (HDI) are health and education.[15] I also bring in additional evidence on other benefits such as housing and pensions.

I conducted 150 semi-structured, in-depth interviews with migrant workers, officials, doctors, teachers, and other knowledgeable professionals.[16] Semi-structured interviews with open-ended questions give respondents an opportunity to be experts (Leech 2002: 668). Because responsibility for migrants is spread across many bureaucracies and includes several levels of government, this involved speaking with provincial, municipal, and district officials in health and family planning, education, human resources and social security, development, and public security. Conversations with doctors, hospital administrators, teachers, and school principals clarified how policies are implemented on the frontlines of health care and education. Migrant worker interviewees were drawn mainly from the construction, manufacturing, and informal sectors. Those in the gray economy include people who work as fruit and vegetable sellers, roadside food vendors, nannies, house cleaners, street sweepers, and building security guards. The structure of each of these sectors affects how long workers stay in a single given city (and therefore how likely they are to bring their families or demand urban services) and their social services eligibility.

I triangulated what I learned from interviews with other sources of information. In addition to in-depth interviews, ethnographic information was collected from migrant villages, construction sites, factories, dormitories, schools, and hospitals. I spent up to a full day or more on site to observe interactions between relevant stakeholders and decision-makers and power relations among government officials, frontline service providers, and migrant workers. The importance of immersion and an "ethnographic sensibility" inform my approach to understanding migrant workers' lived experience and how they make meaning of and understand their political reality (Schatz 2009). Local officials must interpret broad directives and translate them into policies, and the policies on paper may not be implemented as planned or uniformly enforced. I also analyzed government documents, official policies, and other archival materials such as reports and informational pamphlets handed to me by local governments, companies, and migrant NGOs. The general process of political atomization holds across all six cities and is the focus of this book, while the roots of variation in specific modes and patterns of defining and implementing urban welfare that diverge across cities and regions are left to future research.

UNPACKING POLITICAL ATOMIZATION

Situating the Concept of Political Atomization

Political atomization is an original concept and the main theoretical contribution of this book. This process explains two phenomena better than extant literature: why incremental expansions in social policy can entrench inequality and how authoritarian states sometimes use public service provision as a tool of social control. Inequality can serve the state rather than be a threat to it. The path to more equity may involve higher inequality as piecemeal reforms in integrating outsiders become stalled way-stops in themselves. This is consistent with evidence that shows Chinese migrant workers are still unhappy despite higher wages and greater mobility compared to the 1980s. One report found that, seven and a half years after migrating to urban areas, rural Chinese migrants are on average less happy than they might have been had they not moved (Knight and Gunatilaka 2018). Furthermore, the ways in which political individualization disempower them could help account for why overall protest rates remain surprisingly low among migrant workers, despite their strength in sheer numbers and economic importance. It also offers a fresh explanation for how authoritarian regimes use distribution for political ends. Cities maintain a sustainable labor force for economic growth while preserving social stability without having to pay for or maintain hospitals, schools, and other institutions for migrant workers and their families.[17]

Political atomization is distinctive from (but related to) existing terms in the study of authoritarianism, immigration, and welfare states. Previous accounts of authoritarian distribution mostly cover ways of fending off threats to the regime. Rulers can mitigate regime threats by buying support with public goods (Bueno de Mesquita et al. 2003) or coopting and compensating those who might revolt (Gandhi and Przeworski 2006, 2007; Gallagher and Hanson 2009).[18] More recent work posits that rulers can use entitlements to make the masses dependent on them through enmeshment and undercut elite rivals (Albertus et al. 2018). Other scholars emphasize the role of actors and ideas in policymaking in rural China (Duckett and Wang 2017). I find that China uses both the expansion and restriction of public services at the same time to exercise social control. Preceding studies focus overwhelmingly on whether social services are provided, but how officials extend them is equally important. Moreover, the methods they use help them pursue state goals other than neutralizing rebellions. Political individualization deepens social control and inequality, but selective inclusion is not necessarily extended to those migrant workers who directly threaten social stability or portend rebellion. If it did, one might expect broad (if shallow) integration of migrant workers into urban public services given their collective importance to sustaining economic development and growth. Rural fallback options are of little practical use to people who live a two-day train or overnight bus ride away from their home village, and political individualization over time reduces citizens' expectations and therefore their vocalized demands of the state. De facto exclusion through practices such as deflecting does not enmesh migrant workers and often drives them to create alternatives outside the state, which decreases their reliance on them.

Authoritarian states need a grasp of who their citizens are in order to govern them. They engage in projects of legibility which seek to simplify the population and group together individuals (Scott 1998). However, political atomization does the opposite: it makes policies and practices more complex. This involves including some and excluding most in a way that is pragmatic and cost-effective compared to the alternatives. More bureaucracy is needed to create, implement, and support these evolving procedures and regulations, and it is about dividing the population into smaller subgroups and treating them differentially. Individuation enables the state to divide and conquer this large marginalized social group in China, a different dimension of governance than the one Scott emphasizes. Keeping a labor force and maintaining overall social stability in China entail a delicate trade-off between increasing legibility and avoiding the burden of responsibility for citizen benefits.

Most reports on and studies of migration focus overwhelmingly on international migration.[19] But parallels do exist between internal migration within China and international migration between other countries. The chilly receptions that many rural migrants receive in their urban destinations from local officials and native residents are similar to those that immigrants may experience when they first settle in a new country. Comparing the status of undocumented immigrants in the United States and internal migrants in China show that some people are suspicious of their motives for moving in similar ways. The misgiving is that access to the welfare system in the destination city is a "pull" factor, as opposed to, for example, the "push" of lack of economic opportunity in their sending village or the "pull" of higher wages in more developed regions. And while the pace and scale of urbanization in China are on the high end globally, it is hardly the only government facing these pressures. Other developing countries such as India and Brazil are dealing with comparable issues.

Much of the literature on labor migration and migrant workers' rights likewise specifically aims its attention on international movement and mobility. In high-income countries, for example, increasing migrant workers' rights can come at the cost of more restrictive admission policies, especially for low-skilled workers (Ruhs 2013). The study of international labor migration may have implications for that of internal migration, but the transferability of insights is not automatic. The dynamics of international migration often involve people moving from lower-income countries to higher-income ones. Because people cross national borders for international migration, immigration policies involve admission decisions and programs at the border in a way that internal movement of people does not. The obligation of the state to their own constituents is likewise a different dynamic, making the function of social control through public service provision and political individualization distinct. They are, by definition, citizens of the country and therefore within the purview of the national government. In addition, local politics may play out differently when municipal officials share a home province with migrants living and working in their jurisdiction. Despite similarities between the lived experiences of China's internal migrants and immigrants elsewhere, applications of theories about migrant worker rights from the latter are limited.

Political atomization overlaps not only with the study of immigration but also that of welfare states. Research has been predominantly about welfare states in liberal democracies and advanced, industrialized countries. Piven and Cloward's (1971) classic book posits that relief-giving in the United States expanded during periods of higher unemployment to dampen civil disorder and contracted once political stability returned. In Western Europe, the welfare state compensated for the ills that industrial growth created (Offe 1972). Both shun the oversimplified view that welfare systems reflect state benevolence and acknowledge that they play a role in the national economy, but they cannot explain the dynamics of public service provision for migrant workers in China. There it is neither predictably "cyclical" as it was in the United States nor does it serve as a "safety valve" as it did in Europe (Piven and Cloward 1971, Offe 1972). Rather than being handed down from the national level, it is highly localized in China. Municipalities determine their own levels and timing of expansion and contraction, and many offer more to certain migrants and less to others. And they do so through services beyond low-income assistance. The case of China demonstrates how social control is exercised through a variety of entitlements in an entirely different context, that of an authoritarian regime and developing country.

Other work has surveyed welfare systems in developing democracies. They seek to explain the unlikely extension of social rights to underserved citizens. Certain marginalized groups have been able to get concessions of formal and informal welfare from the state in Latin America through voting pressures (Diaz-Cayeros et al. 2016, Garay 2016, Holland 2017). That electoral mechanism does not apply in China and thus does not explain the pattern of political individualization evident in the provision of welfare there. Keeping most migrant workers out of the public services in the city while allowing a few in disperses potential pressures from collective action that could demand more systematic changes. The nuanced ways in which access to and use of social services are regulated become channels through which the state is able to frustrate and dampen migrant expectations over time.

Public services as social control is part of a broader trend of what I characterize as the individualization of Chinese politics and state–society relations.[20] Versions of this tool in the state toolbox have been observed in other contexts, including judicial matters, rural land politics, protest prevention, worker activism, and more (e.g., Chen and Xu 2012, Lee and Zhang 2013, Chuang 2014, O'Brien and Deng 2017, Fu 2017,

Gallagher 2017, Chen 2019). What they have in common is the focus on managing individuals rather than dealing with an entire group (defined by their socioeconomic status or another politically salient characteristic) as a whole. It is a time- and resource-consuming process but has also been effective enough for the overarching goals of maintaining social stability and promoting economic growth.

How Political Atomization Works

Political atomization is a process to divide and conquer migrants. The major components of the process include differentiating migrants and distributing services selectively, which in turn dampen expectations and dilute claims. This subsection unpacks how the state creates policies that structurally treat marginalized people as individuals to effectively enact selective inclusion over group-based exclusion.

Differentiating among migrants is the first step, and the delineation of subdivisions of groups within migrants extends past the familiar divide between a registered rural citizen and an urban one. More highly educated and "high-skilled" migrant workers typically receive preferential treatment over those with less formal schooling or who are "lower-skilled."[21] Their hometown and place of origin (at least on paper) may also matter. Those moving to a city from another city often have better access than those originating from rural villages. People transiting within some provinces have more benefits in the provincial capital than interprovincial migrants working in the same destination city.[22] After they arrive, members of the "floating population" are further separated into categories depending on their residency and employment standings. Non-residents are split off from registered permanent residents and local household registration holders. Employees with formal employment and the proof to show it are usually entitled to more than those who work in the informal or gray economy, who will often lack a labor contract.[23] A migrant worker who is fortunate enough to have a job at a state-owned enterprise generally has more stable, formally recognized employment than someone who makes and sells homemade dumplings out of the back of a tricycle near a construction site on the outskirts of the city. These are a sampling, but not necessarily an exhaustive list, of the ways to divide migrants into numerous subgroups.

Policies that dictate differential treatment of subgroups of migrants pave the way for disparities in the treatment of individuals. The connection between the two operates sequentially between local policy formulation and implementation on the ground. Both contribute to hyper-differentiation among migrants that undermine the effectiveness of broader group-based claims around exclusion or demand-making for more incorporation. Providing different levels of health insurance reimbursement due to a client's place of origin, making it harder or easier to clear the paperwork for enrolling a child in school depending on whether they can prove residence in the city, or tying housing spaces to high-skilled versus low-skilled jobs opens room in each of those criteria and others for judgment calls. Bureaucrats make granular decisions around eligibility and access that involve interpreting these rules and procedures to determine individual-level integration in benefits systems. case-by-case provision thus becomes hyper-differentiated and individualized.

The hyper-differentiation within migrants serves several purposes. Rather than being treated uniformly as one group in terms of being provided or denied assistance, each subdivision offers the option to make distinctive openings and obstacles for obtaining their share of the welfare state. A local government could opt to give more education, health care, or housing to certain migrants they prefer. Or they can make it easier for some to stay long-term (i.e., decades) in the city. They may prefer for others, on whose labor the local economy depends and therefore from whom the municipal government benefits, to work for a few years while in their physical prime and then move back to the countryside or smaller city from where they came. These policies shape migrant workers' work and life decisions, such as whether to bring their children to the city with them and how much effort to expend while seeking social services. If someone's children cannot go to primary school or, more importantly for those who are seeking socioeconomic mobility, attend high school and take the college entrance exam in the urban destination, then migrant parents are likely to continue to make alternative arrangements. They may send their children to private migrant schools, enroll them in boarding schools, or have them live separately with their grandparents in the countryside where they can attend rural schools.[24]

Multiple divisions, moreover, make the mobile population more "legible" (Scott 1998) to the state. Migrants are notoriously difficult to track, and the national census did not begin recording where people actually lived instead of where they were officially registered until 2010. Officials in the planning department of the National Development and Reform Commission even turned to the "pickle index." They looked to see where sales of a staple dish (pickled mustard plant stem, *zhacai* 榨菜)

for migrants were up or down each year. The country's largest producer of this preserved vegetable saw its sales in southern China decrease drastically as sales went up in central China (Boehler 2013). On its face, differentiating migrants into more categories could increase the Chinese government's ability to incorporate them into urban welfare systems. If policies are intended to integrate them more fully, then knowing how many of them there are and who they are would enable municipalities to effectively reach them. Deciding where to build a school, how many teachers to hire, and what equipment to buy for classrooms requires being aware of how many students there are, who they are, and from where they will have to travel each day to attend class.[25] The same applies for health care. Whether a district or neighborhood needs a hospital or clinic, how to staff it, the level of advanced care that is essential, and what treatments will most often be provided entails knowing about their patients' medical needs and the ways in which they will pay for that care. Doctors and other medical professionals in hospitals close to migrant-heavy districts or more potentially dangerous worksites such as construction zones typically treat more migrant workers, and doctors in certain specialties such as eye care are likely to treat more older migrants than younger patients.[26] If they are more legible, the state should be able to allocate resources to serve them more efficiently.

However, improving legibility does not always serve the citizen. As would be the case in almost any setting, it simultaneously enables the government to exercise more fine-grained control over a large, marginalized group of people. Tracking them, regardless of whether the original intention could have been to improve their welfare by catering to their more specialized needs, gives the information necessary to treat them differentially. More highly educated migrants, such as lawyers or investment bankers, from another city usually have a fuller set of social rights than a so-called "lower-skilled" registered rural resident, such as a peasant who farms for subsistence. Those who benefit more can often choose from a wider array of options, ranging from buying into a system or changing their household registration altogether through their university or workplace. Paradoxically, migrants who are hardest to follow year to year as they move around are the ones whose access and long-term needs local governments are most interested in limiting. These rural migrants are more difficult to keep track of and most vulnerable to government intervention. The categorization of migrants becomes the basis of preferentially giving services to a few while providing phantom services to others (Chan and O'Brien 2019).

Selective distribution facilitates a divide and conquer approach to dealing with migrants. When migrants are cast together in one group by the state, their political identity becomes fused with the group status. They often self-identify as a rural migrant worker and say from where they originally hail when they introduce themselves. Separating them into further sociopolitical categories, at least in terms of rights associated with local citizenship, permits officials to manage them in smaller groups instead of as a monolith. Without having to tackle the financially and politically costly question of extending or withholding rights wholesale to millions of people at once, the policy decisions are more manageable. Putting procedures and regulations into place that favor some migrant groups over others makes it seem that everyone could potentially get benefits, even if many still do not in the end. When asked about what they do when they get sick or their children are old enough to start attending school, migrants explain, for instance, that they are "outsiders" working as street sweepers with little formal education themselves who are not as desirable (and therefore not as deserving of full benefits) as a doctor with an advanced medical degree in the view of the government.[27] The deeper subdivisions in migrant identity transfer to how the people see themselves vis-à-vis the state.

Divisions of migrant subgroups set the foundation for diluting their claims. Outsiders' stakes in their portion of the Chinese welfare state are contingent on who they are and what rights each city grants to different constellations of economic, political, and social indicators of their "worthiness" and interpretations of their "deservingness." If there is technically a path to full citizenship, it is substantially harder for migrants to assert discrimination or exclusion and full-fledged second-class citizenship. It is also qualitatively different. Many respondents described the reasons for why they personally failed to successfully enroll their child in an urban public school or have the proper social insurance card to be used in an urban hospital. The perceived problem was not being barred from entry, but rather that they did not complete the steps properly to register.[28] Some of them would emphasize, furthermore, that ticking every box was possible. When pressed for specific examples of success stories from their own lives or people they knew, it quickly became apparent that much of it was rumors rooted in a combination of broad hope and narrowly targeted self-blame. Individuals have to assess how well they measure up their prospects depending on what kind of migrant they are and other personal characteristics. Their claims of being excluded therefore are watered down.

Repeated experiences with diluted claims add up over time to dampen migrant expectations. Each school year that passes without a parent being able to successfully enroll their children in a public school in the city where they live wears down that person's resolve the next visit. Every time someone goes to the public hospital for a medical issue and figures out that their rural insurance will only cover as little as 10 percent of their procedure before bundling in the cost of an overnight hospital stay and other add-ons, they learn that they should expect less than what national pronouncements appear to be promising them.[29] Others receive outright denial because of their inability to pay in advance. Applications for housing that feel like mazes with no end likewise diminish expectations with each passing try. Conversations about individual experiences between migrants during a work break or three-day train ride home during Lunar New Year are shared stories (that sometimes serve as warnings) of initial optimism, eventual disappointment, and wasted time.

The process of political atomization shows how marginalization systemically unfolds in the daily lived experience of migrants. To a newcomer trying to secure housing in an unfamiliar city where they have moved for a job, a national patchwork system appears to be made up of as many smaller systems as cities that dictate who gets what from urban public welfare. Within each of these subnational frameworks, a migrant and their family must navigate a different tangle of rules and requirements. Under more ideal circumstances when the individual is the focal point, the personalization of service configurations could better meet their needs. In practice, these policies make the person responsible for negotiating their way through the system. Therefore, they also blame themselves when they are unsuccessful in getting through the morass of eligibility requirements, paperwork, and bureaucratic hoops.[30] The perception is that there is room for agency and it is the individual who botches the process, when in actuality the system is not set up for everyone across the board to be incorporated. Many experience diluted claims and dampened expectations as a function of individual inadequacy because they are told there is technically a path to full citizenship according to policy.

Structural sources of political atomization furnish an illusion of room for migrant agency. The reasonable thinking is as follows. If someone can become a full urban citizen, then it is conceivable for anyone to do the same. A slim, but real, possibility that a registered rural migrant from a county in Anhui Province is able to enroll their child in a Shanghai public school equipped with better facilities and filled with credentialed and experienced teachers exists. It is a matter of that individual's ability to jump over all of the bureaucratic hurdles to get there. This story of success spreads by word of mouth through that person's neighborhood or workplace and further out from there. Parents desperate for a reputable place to send their children to school and hopeful for one that could become the first step in socioeconomic mobility for the next generation of the family cling to these rumors of hope. Their own employers, including foreigners living in Beijing who employ migrant nannies and housekeepers, sometimes repeat the hearsay success stories themselves. What is less clear than the possibility is the probability that any given migrant is able to meet every requirement and surmount every structural obstacle to get these benefits. In addition to this plausible but all too often unlikely scenario, the state's supposed commitment to integrating migrant workers is not imagined.

While this process unfolds on the ground, the central government promulgates a steady stream of rhetoric about modernization. The state has supported the drive to urbanize people (and land) in order to boost domestic consumer demand and stimulate economic development. National targets support the move toward having more and more urbanites: hitting a 70 percent urbanization rate by 2030 and higher by 2050. According to logic based on other countries' historical experiences, developing countries must and do urbanize to become advanced, developed ones. The pace in China, however, is hastened. The movement of people into cities is part of a larger national economic vision for making China a fully modern and developed country, and the desired rate of this kind of modernization involves state-led urbanization.

Pronouncements about the latest urbanization ambitions also support political atomization. Terms such as "people-centered" and "new-type" urbanization suggest that circumstances will be different from the past and marginalized people will finally receive what they deserve as long-time contributors to local urban economies. They sew clothing in foreign companies' textile factories, check visitors' identification at the gates of luxury apartments, and toil in other parts of the city for decades. Having done their part and sacrificed not only for their families but also for the greater good of a country in economic transition amid marketizing reform, more and more feel they have earned their place in the urban social services scheme. This suggests that their incorporation, even if gradual and slow-going, into cities' social policy is underway.

Narratives behind the push for urbanization and modernization often have broad appeal. Rhetoric and plans around achieving "common prosperity," the Chinese Dream, the 2014–2020 urbanization plan, and other programs like these are frequently short on specific policy changes that expound how the goals will feasibly be met on the ground. Attractive visions encourage people to cooperate with the grand national aspiration to be realized while they wait for it to come to fruition in a meaningful way in their everyday lives. An easier way to secure a spot in public rental housing close to their workplace in Chongqing, for instance, is a concrete consequence for a construction worker who moved to the city with their spouse and children and therefore cannot live on site in the company dormitory. Urbanization and subsequent economic growth seem inexorable, but substantial structural changes that would support enhanced welfare for many migrant workers have not caught up yet.

In sum, political atomization works by effectively making migrant workers responsible for benefits owed to them by the state. Hyper-differentiation between groups of migrants first creates new subdivisions of beneficiaries based on characteristics such as their place of origin, level of education, or type of employment. Local governments then are able to divide and conquer using policies and procedures that in effect split people into different categories in order to provide more or higher quality services to some recipients over others. Because not everyone is excluded wholesale based on their status as a non-native resident of the city and a few are able to gain benefits, selective inclusion dilutes individual migrants' claims about discrimination. Over time, the experience of frequent deflection and denial of assistance dampens people's expectations of what the local government will actually provide to them. Without having to completely shut them out, the point of interaction and potential contention come over issues such as procedural correctness and paperwork. A patchwork of localized systems adds to the combination of largely structural constraints with the impression of room for migrant agency to contribute to the process of accessing their own rights. Primary responsibility, and therefore blame, falls to the individual migrant when they fail in navigating these numerous provincial, municipal, and district schemes. Rhetoric surrounding visions for Chinese urbanization and modernization prolong the patience of migrants as they wait their turn in what has been touted to be gradual reform that will eventually lead to the betterment of their well-being. Regardless of whether a coordinated top-down plan exists, migrant social policy has evolved into a useful tool of social control.

Why Political Atomization Persists

Now that the process of how this works has been unpacked, this section explains why political atomization endures. Individualization is an effective way to deal with migrant demands for their share of urban public services. Procedures and practices in the provision of services can relegate individual outsiders to having different social rights within the same city. Over time, individuation creates gradations of second-class citizenship, allows the state to fracture and regulate migrants, and moves the locus of contention from group-based to individual exclusion.[31] This section shows why it persists first from individuals' point of view and then from the state's perspective.

A policy approach that converges on individual responsibility undermines collective consciousness through several mechanisms. The categorization of migrants into subgroups based on their place of origin, labor status, education level, period of residency, and other factors separates people who previously were lumped together as migrant workers (*nongmin gong*, 农民工) in terms of their relationship to the state. Urban workers employed in the same position in Dongguan as their co-workers from outside the city might distinguish themselves as being locals (*bendi*, 本地) instead of outsiders (*waidi*, 外地).[32] This regional distinction has always existed, but its political salience is heightened because of the different benefits each receives according to their regional status within Guangdong Province. Instead of being fellow restaurant workers and migrants, the first person may have an easier time enrolling their children in school and may receive a higher percentage of reimbursement for medical care in an urban public hospital. Instead of an us versus them relationship between these individuals in society and the state, there is an us versus us demarcation among migrants that becomes relevant. The state treats them differently, so these two and others like them identify less as a cohesive group, thereby undermining their collective consciousness. Groups with collective consciousness believe the unfair treatment they receive is a societal problem rather than an individual one (Klein 1987). It forms the basis for contentious politics and social movements (Barnartt 1996). In effect, without this foundational element as a precursor, collective action is hindered and less likely. In cases where migrant workers are able to muster a collective consciousness, it still may not be clear whom to target.

The structure behind political atomization obscures who is to blame. The de facto emphasis on individual responsibility and eligibility in following procedures puts the person, not the system, at fault when the outcome is less than the broad policy ideal. While migrant children in China are aware of class differences, they attribute inequities to individualism and meritocracy (Chen and Wang 2021). Taking a single migrant's point of view on collating their documents shows how this looks in practice. A person who cooks and cleans for a family and cares for their children after school as a housekeeper may be contracted out from an agency or may be independently employed. If the first, she (because women typically take these jobs) may have a formal labor contract for her position that she can present as proof of employment and duration of how long she has been working in the city. The company can make social insurance payments on their behalf or find ways to avoid them.[33] The independently employed woman is likely doing the same work day to day and may have a longstanding relationship with the family for whom she nannies, shops for groceries, and cooks meals, but she may be paid under the table. Cash payments could be convenient and preferable for some, but without a formal contract, she does not have appropriate paperwork to show as formal proof of employment. Documents like these are frequently required to show eligibility for a municipality's entitlements. It is unclear if the policy, an official (a representative from the labor bureau or health or another division), the employer (the company or a family), or the migrant failed. The design of the system differentiates migrants into groups, some of whom are significantly more likely to be successful under it, but treats everyone as if they are equally eligible and able to attain benefits.

Variation in public service provision for migrants aids social control through atomization. The primary mechanism is one of divide and conquer in which the process of migrants trying to access or use benefits fragments them in two ways. First, differences in bureaucratic experiences limit the transferability between migrant case experiences. In the absence of uniform treatment, information sharing within communities is less useful because those who seem similarly situated may not receive the same treatment. Varying constellations of conditions such as eligibility criteria make people's cases seem incomparable to each other's and therefore reduces learning and adapting over time. A neighbor or friend's experience with an education authority or hospital doctor provides little experience building to help the next person gain access to or use their state-provided entitlements. Reduced utility of information sharing causes confusion, wastes time, and imbues a sense of powerlessness and vulnerability. This hampers collective organizing and information sharing that could facilitate better personal access and possibly build to group-based requests, effectively dividing migrant workers who otherwise share grievances and obstacles to access. These stories based on personal experiences run counter to the broader government narrative about eventual incorporation and muddle understanding about rules and procedures while creating uncertainty around whether one can actually access promised services.

A second reason why variation facilitates social control is that it produces a sense of scarcity and unpredictability around public goods. Scarcity may be literal in practice, as when migrant parents receive notice that a cap on the number of students in a classroom restricts the seats available for their children. Or its degree may be perceived when confusing, seemingly ever-changing reimbursement rates for different insurance schemes dissuade a migrant patient from seeking health care at the closest urban hospital to their workplace. This reduces demand-making by migrants because they adapt to this scant provision. While it is not necessarily competitive or zero-sum, there is a perception that there is not enough to go around and that one's efforts to actually get a higher level of insurance reimbursement for medical care or enroll a student for a reputable public school may not be worthwhile if the chance of succeeding is low. And that uncertainty and scarcity is seen as an individual, not policy or group problem, that requires an individual solution such as seeking private substitutes. This form of atomization further fosters divide and rule by reinforcing coping strategies outside the system which should be the provider.

Some conditions make Chinese migrant workers convenient targets of political atomization. Internal migrants are a large group of marginalized people, and their numbers make them more likely to experience political atomization over harder forms of social control such as coercion. Blunt force can be an expensive and ineffective way to regulate this substantial part of the urban labor force, and it is usually unnecessary under day-to-day circumstances. At the same time, when someone shows up in the emergency room of an urban public hospital or tries to enroll their child in school the summer before the start of a school year, some kind of response must be given. More to the point, migrants need the services they are seeking in order to continue living and working in their adopted city. Nor can all migrant workers be kicked out of a city *en masse* because they work in nearly every sector of a city economy. They are, for instance, the factory workers who keep the electronics production lines moving and food delivery drivers who feed office workers at lunchtime. Partial inclusion of some addresses the welfare needs of at least a fragment of the group without foisting a policy of complete exclusion on everyone or requiring the state to make hefty financial commitments for full incorporation.

Devolution of responsibility to city authorities facilitates individualization through two channels, policymaking and funding. When decisions in the policy area are sometimes made by bureaucrats as close to the ground as district officials, there is an opportunity for dissimilar procedures and different levels or quality of benefits across places in the country. In the best-case scenario, services tailored to neighborhood needs, such as more senior assistance in a district with a high proportion of retirees, are possible. Disparities between locations, however, can be used to encourage people who move around for work to choose to go to a rural clinic over an urban hospital for medical care. A lack of a national system that organizes and guarantees interprovincial transfers of social insurance and pensions further ties migrants to one location over the city they may prefer. Likewise, without a centralized financial redistribution and funding scheme to pay for the expansion of urban welfare systems, cities are more likely to be selective about who receives the full menu of costly benefits and who does not. Otherwise, an unexpected influx of workers one year might overstretch a system meant to mostly accommodate native urban residents. Some registered urban residents have their own reservations about sharing hospitals and their children's classrooms with people whom they see as less deserving second-class citizens.

Broad urbanization goals and incorporation directives are centralized, whereas administration (and financing in large part) and implementation are decentralized.[34] Chinese officials refer to this as "the center treats; local governments pay" (*zhongyang qingke, dangdi maidan*, 中央请客, 当地买单), a phrase repeated by many of my interviewees. The central–local gap and fiscal decentralization that generate unfunded and underfunded mandates, to be clear, are neither new nor particular to migrant social policy. Leading cadres face similar constraints within the cadre evaluation system (Edin 2003), whereby local officials must manage unfunded mandates amid competing policy priorities. And efforts to reform the public sector have not yet fixed the underlying fiscal problem for cities either. Incremental government retrenchment in the 1980s and 1990s and inadequate finance broke the intergovernmental fiscal system and undermined public sector reform (Wong 2009). Services can therefore continue to be used as a channel for social control because of continued decentralization in administration and much of the financing of public goods provision.

Decentralization, though not specific only to migrant social policy, enables the deployment of pliable citizenship (Chan 2024). When the provision of public services varies regionally and there is a divide and conquer approach to handling migrant requests for entitlements, the boundaries and categories of second-class citizenship are malleable. Some flexibility is built directly into the system. In situations where regulations can be changed over time, fluctuate between places, and apply differently to diverse groups of outsiders in the city, accommodation and selective inclusion permit cities to create policies according to their respective priorities. These may range from saving money to attracting certain workers toward certain sectors to soothing native urban resentment toward people they perceive as interlopers.[35] Room for maneuvering can be rhetorically described as gradual reform of a complicated system, but so far it is not apparent that these piecemeal policy evolutions are building toward a cohesive national system that would better serve people who move around the country. The tandem marches of urbanization and modernization continue, but uneven development and inequality are not byproducts of the system so much as critical parts of it that keep progress (as defined by the state) steadily moving forward. Flexibility in the system and subnational variations support political atomization.

A move away from political atomization would require a national overhaul in redistribution. Localities would have to coordinate with each other to manage the exchange and transfer of records of people who move from one province to another. Municipalities would need to synchronize down levels of government with district bureaucrats, laterally with their counterparts across the country, and upward with counties, provinces, and the central government. For recentralization to occur as smoothly as possible, Beijing officials would have to marshal political, financial, and social forces. The practical and fiscal benefits of allowing political atomization to continue outweigh the obstacles and costs of a complete revamp. It is tricky to impute intention (especially in what might be viewed as a top-down effort), but it is not necessary to explain why this process persists. The state benefits from individualization whether the system was holistically designed that way or not.

Political atomization carries its own inertia once in existence. It is pragmatic and cost-effective (compared to the alternative of incorporating everyone), and it gives provinces and cities some leeway. Metropolises whose governments assess themselves as already being over capacity and having too many people may opt to limit migrant inclusion. Other municipalities who wish to incorporate migrants more into their public welfare systems can do so. They may be more open for economic or benevolent reasons, but the option is theirs either way. In cities that are more reluctant to integrate migrant workers, the status quo works because the primary goal is not to improve the welfare of recipients. Deliberately or not, patchwork benefits foster political individualization and become self-reinforcing over time because provincial and municipal authorities can exploit them to their advantage. Capitalizing on variation reinforces the underlying political economy of public goods provision that keeps the decentralized, piecemeal system in place. Until and unless the central government finances and administers social services more fully, local governments can make use of fragmentation among them. Both pathways to political atomization supported through variation in entitlements are therefore mutually constitutive in practice.

Individuation in a country ruled by the CCP at first glance appears to share an unlikely overlap with neoliberalism. Since China has undergone decades of market-based reform, that distinction is less clear-cut. The focus on individual responsibility and, with it, individual blame is reminiscent of the underpinnings of neoliberalism,[36] and it is part of the process of political atomization. Decades of a marketized economy and urbanization have improved rural migrants' living conditions and job prospects in the city but also marginalized them, especially the poorest and most vulnerable. Housing reform through the housing monetarization policy in 1998 took a similarly neoliberal approach and created the conditions for more housing inequalities (Lee and Zhu 2006). Before moving away from a command economy, housing and other welfare provisions were seen as the responsibility of the state and not individuals. The CCP is the vanguard of the working class in name, yet privatization has shifted expectations such that individual's shoulder self-responsibility for assistance that was previously provided largely through work units in the socialist welfare system. Coupled with the devolution of responsibility from the central government to municipalities, the pattern of uneven provision is consistent with neoliberal logic. On the surface, deficient or nonexistent services are not the state or system's fault. Attention to the individual obfuscates the sources of systemic shortcomings in providing for migrants' welfare.

Political atomization entails promised services, as opposed to actual services, in exchange for political loyalty. After years of near complete exclusion, central level directives to expand incorporation matched with small openings in certain cities make it somewhat credible that integration is imminent. The creation of new rules and regulations at local levels such as municipality makes it appear as if there is a clear path to accessing these benefits in the city. This perceived exchange works in the short term to assuage migrants who are making demands on urban public service systems. Misplaced blame on the individual and structural constraints buried in bureaucracy extend the grace period during which the government can bide their time and avoid direct blame for lack of fully comprehensive social policy coverage for migrant workers. Outsiders, meanwhile, continue to work and live in urban centers despite empty promises for many while a few receive education, health care, housing, or pensions. In this limbo, undelivered benefits that are supposedly on their way can buy political allegiance, at least temporarily. The framework of embedded inequality underscores how political atomization contributes to our understanding of structural inequality, and it shows why individualization aids social control and saves immediate costs but can eventually be destabilizing for the regime down the road.

EMBEDDED INEQUALITY AND EVERYDAY MARGINALIZATION

Trade-Offs and Risks of Political Atomization

There are risks to relying on political atomization when allocating benefits to migrants and other citizens. Devolution of policy formulation inherently entails relinquishing some measure of central control. The national government is less able to coordinate a uniform policy response to migrant worker issues. On its face, this seems like a straightforward trade-off that makes localities responsible for both successes and failures. Recipients of municipal benefits might attribute incorporation into the city to district and municipal administrators instead of to higher levels of government. Although migrants often mete out blame to local bureaucrats, national officials so far have been able to fend off taking responsibility by promulgating guidelines that present them as the benevolent leaders who are calling for eventual full inclusion of rural outsiders in cities. The long-term sustainability of this gap between central and local policies is unclear because it may provide an opening for rightful resistance (O'Brien and Li 2006).

Another potential downside is that political atomization involves making some concessions. Deflection, phantom services, and individualization differ from complete exclusion. In the case of urban public service provision, at least a few migrants receive some services in certain places. The group of beneficiaries may be limited and narrow, but partial allowances could hypothetically become a slippery slope. That assumes that the forces pushing for these changes have the power and discretion to do so. Officials, however, may not have the incentives to drive these reforms, and migrants who are in favor of them typically do not have adequate resources and are not in a position of power to make them happen. Taken together, a modicum of more political space is available, but the hazards of circumscribed concessions are fairly limited.

Migrants could also potentially knit together their experiences to see the picture of political atomization as a whole. Sheer numbers (in terms of population size) work in their favor, but the ways in which variation aids social control and produces atomization that operates to divide and conquer people hinders cooperative information sharing and the formation of a broad-based collective consciousness. Diluted claims and dampened expectations further hamper the effectiveness of any precursors to collective action that could arise. While a few activists and community organizations that help migrants may recognize the overall pattern, they too are marginalized. Crackdowns on labor NGOs under the Xi administration have made organizing and mounting an effective response more difficult. Even when some do catch on to the pattern, they have little recourse.

A fourth hazard is that decentralized urban public welfare provision and political atomization do not prioritize improving migrant welfare. This is a direct consequence with long-term costs that could be difficult to calculate. There are moral reasons to treat migrant workers as human beings, and there are also economic reasons to maintain a healthy and vibrant labor force in an economy that relies heavily on its export-led sector. Those bureaucrats who are working in good faith to serve their constituents, including people whose household registration is outside the city where they live and work, find it hard to do their jobs. They too are running up against thorny issues within a system that was not designed with migrant interests of equal import to other priorities. Others may engage in bureaucratic incorporation (Marrow 2009) and work to expand services in creative ways within the constraints they have. Civil servants in some places cite their own shared identities with migrants coming from within the same province as them for why they expand urban hospital and public school access to the people they see as their own counterparts. Political atomization has persisted so far, but tensions and trade-offs exist and could erode its effectiveness.

Inequality in Service to the State

Political atomization illuminates how everyday marginalization operates. It reflects the experience of migrants on the ground and reminds us how treating people as peripheral cements structures of inequality. Interviewees reported a feeling of contingency and temporary status (in terms of social rights and other issues) tempered by a sentiment of hope and possibility. Whether this was practicable or a necessary component of survival, many expressed a sense of "next time," "next year," and "I'll try again." Possibility and guarded optimism make the process of political atomization self-reinforcing over time.

The rural fallback option is supposedly always available. People can move back to their home village, farm the land for subsistence, and reunite with their nuclear families if they lose their jobs in the city or otherwise fall upon hard times. Those who have jobs but cannot afford health care or education in their urban destination can depend on clinics and schools in the countryside. However, this cushion is more precarious than it once was. Rural areas have been hollowed out as farmers' land has been expropriated (Chuang 2014), and some migrants are born and raised in the city but still are not registered locally there. These migrants are being squeezed between rural and urban areas in a way that fails to recognize their lived reality. Without this version of a livelihood guarantee, the rural–urban divide and the breakneck speed of urbanization take on a new dimension of inequality.

Social policy toward migrants is itself a set of institutional structures that are formal barriers to equitable distribution. Instead of *hukou* designations alone dictating outsiders' social citizenship, new policies such as eligibility rules and documentation requirements extend structural exclusion to different realms of detail. The hyper-differentiation by, for instance, place of origin and use of pliable citizenship (Chan 2024) within political atomization create cleavages among migrants and block their access. Bureaucratic rules are institutional structures that reduce equality because they force the locus of claims-making for benefits closer to the state's advantage. Instead of making demands based on entitlements owed to them as citizens, migrants must pinpoint their rights within localized bureaucratic guidelines such as proving they meet requirements to enjoy certain benefits. Day-to-day implementation of this social policy also produces informal structural constraints that further entrench migrant inequality. Procedures and norms that municipal and district officials generate in order to decide, for example, what counts as sufficient proof of residence or employment to meet formal documentation requirements on paper can exclude migrants by practice. The higher the bar for meeting procedural norms that are within bureaucrats' discretion, the greater the structural barrier to ground-level access to health care, education, housing, or other services.

Those shut out from public systems due to structural reasons resort to private alternatives, and the formal recognition and regulation (or lack thereof) of these substitutes make them additional institutional hurdles to upward mobility and better well-being. Patients who receive subpar or inadequate medical care from private clinics instead of comprehensive, high-quality care from better-equipped hospitals risk their health and livelihoods, making it harder to improve their family's socioeconomic circumstances in the long run. Private migrant schools that serve as substitutes for public education systems are another example of entrenched inequality via institutions and structures. When these private alternatives are the only practical option and they lack certification, students enrolled in them are unlikely to be able to use them as a springboard toward substantial socioeconomic mobility between generations. Inequity is more than a temporary condition when these kinds of entrenchment embed inequality in complex policy formulations and procedural implementation.

By examining processes of everyday marginalization, this book shows how structures of inequality and social control are linked. Studying protest tells us about one way that state–society relations occur, but it is not the only site of interaction. Protest is often noisy and represents an end of the spectrum in claims-making on the state. Not everyone will participate in a protest in their lifetime, but nearly every citizen will receive some benefit from the state and will need to figure out how to attain it. Political atomization may hamper antecedents to street-level contention. Shifting the focus is important on its own. The frontlines of state–society relations for most citizens are in these mundane interfaces. Structural sources of control affect labor's role in economic development, the well-being of migrants themselves, and public welfare schemes. And it exposes how institutions of social control, such as the *hukou* system, evolve and get updated over time.

CONCLUSION

China's push to integrate hundreds of millions of migrants into its cities has increasingly individualized contention over social rights and situated its negotiation on the state's turf. Collective claims of exclusion and discrimination have been supplanted by one-on-one bureaucratic battles over eligibility and documentation. New regulations that grant social rights to a few while creating different barriers for others make it harder for migrant workers to make demands, much less organize. Local variations and adaptations only serve to further obfuscate the process and make it a complicated patchwork of policies that need to be navigated year to year or any time someone relocates for a job. Many outsiders even blame themselves for not securing the necessary paperwork or meeting the requirements for securing health care, education, and other social services.

This results in the state being able to nudge migrants to do what the government prefers them to do while avoiding being held accountable by those same targets. Cities, meanwhile, get to keep a steady pool of labor to boost local economic development without having to provide the full set of rights to people living and working there. Public services as social control is part of a broader trend of what I argue has been the individualization of Chinese politics and state–society relations. In the Xi Jinping era of authoritarian consolidation and recentralization of power, this remains one area where policy formulation and implementation have remained relatively decentralized and left in the hands of provincial, municipal, and district officials. The institutional structures behind inequality are deeply entrenched in social policy for migrants and its day-to-day implementation. It works as a stopgap but may cause further problems down the road.

New policies have changed the dynamic between state and citizen claimant. Points systems, proliferation of residency classifications, and other policies appear to create a path for migrants to become full-fledged urban citizens. And a select few have been able to achieve this. Enforcement of dormant rules, the establishment of nearly impossible eligibility requirements, and other practices of implementation, however, mean that these benefits remain out of reach for most. These pathways to full citizenship, worse yet, have become endpoints in themselves rather than gradual means to incorporation. Because these policies and practices center on the individual, collective claims of exclusion and discrimination have been supplanted by one-on-one bureaucratic battles over eligibility and documentation. Taken together, political atomization blunts the ability of all migrants as a group to access the public services to which they supposedly have a right.

PART I

PUBLIC SERVICES AS SOCIAL CONTROL

3

Deflecting Migrant Workers

Political atomization pries open spaces between inclusion and exclusion. Migrants are typically considered either incorporated into their adopted cities or not, but they may also be deflected, segregated, or otherwise find themselves short of full citizenship. The next two chapters focus on a top-down perspective of local officials providing public services to migrant workers in China. They expose that complicating how, not only if, authorities provide services allows them to separate outsiders as individuals and differentiate levels of integration using institutions. Cities can channel and stymie claimants through at least four points of service provision: gatekeeping, access, delivery, and regulation. Each of these offers spaces to determine who gets deflected or demobilized and vary the quality of health care and education among the few who do receive benefits.

This chapter focuses on the ways in which municipalities allow (or mostly disallow and discourage) migrants to get services at what is experienced by local officials and migrants at the person-by-person level of provision. Eligibility requirements serve as gatekeeping mechanisms, and for those who qualify, policies and practices limit their access and redirect their use elsewhere. Some workers, such as those who live in company dorms near the factories where they are employed, can use on-site medical clinics, but most seek health care for their families and schools for their children one by one in the city. Through the process of trying to enroll their children in public school or use their social insurance at an urban public hospital, they learn how the state differentiates them from other supposedly equally deserving recipients. Entitlements that appear open to everyone residing in a municipality turn out to be selective in practice. Over time, the state dilutes their claims and dampens their expectations by providing phantom services. The center expands migrant social rights from above and municipal and district officials install new restrictions and hurdles on the ground at the same time.

When faced with pressure to offer migrants benefits, municipal governments have three main options: provide them with services, deny them services, or deflect them.[1] The first choice brings migrants into a city's social welfare system, at least to an extent.[2] For example, Shanghai announced it would accept migrant children into public primary and secondary schools (though implementing this was another matter),[3] while Chongqing and Xiamen let recent arrivals apply for low-income housing (Huang 2012).[4] And in neighborhoods where there is inadequate public education and medical care, many cities turn a blind eye to private schools and health clinics that go into business to cater to migrants.[5] Overall, though, migrant workers' access to social services remains spotty in most cities and generally depends on the locality in which they live and work.

A second approach is to refuse to give them services. This strategy typically relies on household registration (*hukou*, 户口) regulations to keep migrants out of the "urban public goods regime" (Solinger 1995, 1999).[6] In Beijing, for instance, migrant children who do not have local registrations are often blocked from attending public schools. Most cities require high school students to return to their parents' hometowns to take the college entrance exam. And few urban governments grant workers who have rural household registrations eligibility for medical insurance programs or welfare assistance.[7] These and other forms of institutional discrimination systematically exclude migrants, keep them distinct from other urban residents, and turn them into second-class citizens (Solinger 1999).

Beyond these two options, there is a third way to allocate public benefits, which deflects migrants. This strategy of providing phantom services is found in most cities to some extent. Cities or district governments selectively provide benefits to some migrants but exclude others by making it ferociously difficult for them to receive the services they are owed. Authorities may set eligibility requirements that at first glance appear to grant migrants access to public services, but actually do not. Dongguan and Shanghai, for instance, allow outsiders to change their *hukou* from rural to urban, but few migrants are qualified under a complicated points system.[8] In addition, many municipalities, such as Beijing and Chengdu, ask for documents that most migrants are hard-pressed to obtain in order to prove their eligibility for a service. Or city authorities may force them to return home for medical care by refusing to accept their rural insurance in municipal hospitals. Even as urban governments expand access to health care, education, housing, and pensions for some migrants and their children, they deflect many others.

CONTINGENT INCLUSION

The household responsibility system in agriculture has deepened a well-known and stubborn rural–urban divide.[9] After the first major wave of rural-to-urban work migration in the 1980s, members of this "floating population" (*liudong renkou*, 流动人口) became second-class citizens compared to registered urban residents (Chan 1994a, Chan and Zhang 1999, Solinger 1999, Fan 2002, Chan and Buckingham 2008, Chan 2009). Migrants from the countryside were not able to gain access to public services and other rights because they were registered in their home villages rather than in the cities where they worked. Although the *hukou* system has undergone changes in recent years in areas such as residence permits and points systems,[10] these have been gradual and remain incomplete.

Decisions about policies that tether citizens' rights to their registrations are now increasingly left to provinces, counties, and municipalities (Chan and Buckingham 2008, Guo and Liang 2017). Localization of public services has led to the partial extension of rights and benefits in certain places to certain migrants. In contrast to the sharp distinction between rural migrants and urban residents that once existed, new gradations of second-class citizenship have emerged. Highly educated and skilled migrants, for example, usually receive better treatment than less-skilled migrants, and many cities see rural migrants with stable jobs and residences as more desirable than less well settled migrants. These local policies have created new axes of inequality.

Some of the new rules and distinctions are formal and explicit, while others are informal norms generated in the course of policy implementation. The treatment of migrants has become less about complete exclusion and more about partial inclusion for certain people and not others. As access becomes more contingent, claims of collective exclusion and discrimination are often supplanted by individual battles with a bureaucracy over eligibility. Intentionally or not, these new institutional practices have tended to isolate and disempower migrants.

Contingent inclusion is the outcome of combining the assortment of policies and implementation practices. It depends on recipients' individual characteristics, the formality or sector of their employment, their place of origin, destination city, and other conditions. And it can change year to year as they relocate between cities or as their children graduate from primary school to the next level. Without either fully providing or outright denying services to newcomers, municipalities enact political atomization to deflect migrants in a variety of ways within and out of the city. The next section takes stock of the scope of major national migrant policies and the changing demographics of internal migration in China. These put pressures on local authorities to respond to demand for health care, education, housing, and pensions.

MIGRANT STATISTICS AND NATIONAL POLICY

By 2023, about one in five people in China was an internal migrant. Migrants, as in any country, are notoriously difficult to track, and the national census did not begin recording where people actually lived instead of where they were registered until 2010. According to the National Bureau of Statistics' annual survey of migrant workers, there were about 292.5 million migrant workers (农民工, *nongmingong*) in 2021 (National Bureau of Statistics of China 2022). By early 2018, approximately 57 percent of the entire Chinese population lived in urban areas (National Bureau of Statistics of China 2017a). While the total number of migrant workers has increased every year over the last decade, there have been changes in their rate of growth (which declined from a 4.4 percent increase in 2011 to 1.5 percent in 2016) (National Bureau of Statistics of China 2016a)[11] and patterns of movement. Although most migrants are still concentrated in coastal regions, the proportion in western provinces is on the rise (from 14.9 percent of the floating population in 2013 to 16.6 percent in 2015), as more people are moving shorter distances within their home province rather than traveling farther across the country (National Health and Family Planning Commission of China 2016).

The demographic makeup of the migrant population has also shifted. They are becoming older, are more educated, and are earning higher wages. More of them are coming to cities with their spouses and children rather than arriving solo. Over 60 percent of the new generation of migrants who are married are living with family members (National Health and Family Planning Commission of China 2014),[12] and thus more than half of urban migrant households have three or more people living together (National Health and Family Planning Commission of China 2016). The number of women giving birth away from their registered residence is increasing (National Health and Family Planning Commission of China 2014), and the proportion of migrant children born where their parents currently live (not where their *hukou* is) more than doubled from 27.5 percent in 2010 to 56.6 percent in 2014 (National Health and Family Planning Commission of China 2016). About 10.1 million migrant students are enrolled in "regular" primary schools (*putong xiaoxue*, 普通小学), 4.6 million of whom are originally "from other provinces" and 5.5 million of whom are children whose parents are from counties in the same province (National Bureau of Statistics of China 2016b).

Since the 1980s, the lives of migrants have improved in some meaningful ways. Their average monthly income in 2016 was 3,275 RMB, which was up 6.6 percent from the previous year (National Bureau of Statistics of China 2017b). China achieved near universal health insurance coverage in 2011,[13] and according to official figures, 89.3 percent of migrants had at least one form of health insurance in 2015 (National Health and Family Planning Commission of China 2016).[14] A circular of the Ministry of Human Resources and Social Security and the Ministry of Finance stated that the government subsidy for health insurance was pegged to increase by 30 RMB per person in 2017 to 450 RMB (State Council of the People's Republic of China 2017).[15] In another example of how the mobile population's medical care access has improved, there have been pressures and preliminary moves to integrate rural and urban insurance systems and to make them more portable between provinces.[16] The National Health and Family Planning Commission, for instance, issued a circular ordering all provincial governments to launch an off-site health insurance system by the end of June 2017 through which patients could settle their medical expenses without having to return to the location where their insurance plan was issued, but these programs are still in their early days (State Council of the People's Republic of China 2017).

Several policy initiatives in the 2010s made it clear that the central government would like cities to enhance benefits for newcomers.[17] However, thus far the national government has provided few details about how these ambitious goals should be achieved. In order to promote "legal, stable employment and residence" (*hefa wending jiuye he hefa wending zhusuo*, 合法稳定就业和合法稳定住所), the plan allows cities to "implement different settlement policies" (*shishi chabie hua luohu zhengce*, 实施差别化落户政策). Large cities with more than five million people may "strictly control" (*yange kongzhi*, 严格控制) the size of the urban population and set their own requirements for migrants to participate in urban social insurance schemes. Although mega-cities have considerable leeway when deciding how they will integrate outsiders, the burden remains on them to extend services; but they have limited resources and minimal guidance about how to include migrants in their city's public goods systems.

DEFLECTING MIGRANTS WITHIN THE CITY

The combination of central concern and local responsibility often leads to an unfunded mandate.[18] Because migrants are managed locally and support from above is minimal, cities get to choose whom to incorporate and on what terms.

Taking advantage of this freedom, municipal authorities have developed many ways to deflect requests for services. At the district or city level, officials may make it difficult for migrants to send their children to school or to participate in medical insurance schemes by requiring minimum periods of employment and residency. For example, in late 2012 the Beijing Municipal Education Commission announced that migrant children would have access to secondary vocational school entrance exams if they met certain eligibility criteria. But the requirements the Education Commission set up were formidable. Parents were obligated to have been in full-time jobs for three years and to have contributed to Beijing's social insurance program for three consecutive years, while students must have completed all three years of middle school in Beijing. For higher-level vocational schools, parents were required to have had full-time jobs and made contributions to social insurance in Beijing for six consecutive years, and their children must have completed three years of high school in Beijing (The Wall Street Journal 2013). But migrants tend to move around; some go back to their home village for a time and others relocate from city to city.[19] Requiring them to have stayed in one city for a number of years in a row has the same effect as excluding them from the urban benefits regime.

In addition to setting periods of employment and residence that few migrants can meet, a second eligibility requirement involves household registration. Even as it undergoes reform, the *hukou* system can be deployed to tie migrants up in bureaucratic knots and keep services out of reach.[20] Several cities, including Chongqing and Shanghai, and Guangdong Province have introduced points systems for granting residence permits (Dong and Goodburn 2020, Wang 2021).[21] For instance, Guangdong replaced temporary residence permits with residence permits that would supposedly make it easier for non-locals to obtain services, but in reality did not (Guangdong Province Public Security 2009a, 2009b).[22] Candidates' point totals are based on factors such as their skills, education, social security contributions, and criminal records.[23] High school degrees count for twenty points, university degrees for eighty points, and criminal records result in a deduction (Wang and Huang 2010). Sixty points are needed to qualify to apply for urban household registration in the province, and the threshold is even higher (85 points) for a highly desired Guangzhou urban registration (Wang and Huang 2010). One father reportedly went so far as to give blood three times one summer to try to accumulate enough points for him and his son to apply for a Guangzhou *hukou* (Jacob 2011). Many migrants can earn some points, but far fewer are able to amass a sufficient number to change their household registration.

In short, the points system makes it appear that inclusion is possible and that clear rules exist to access services, but it continues to exclude most migrants.[24] Many migrants understand this. Interviewees in Guangdong were openly scornful about these kinds of residence permit reforms. A factory manager and government liaison who employed 160 migrant workers in Dongguan city explained in 2010, "The temporary residence permit and *hukou* reforms don't mean anything. It's still too hard to change your *hukou*. For example, you need to have permanent employment and buy a house." Most of the employees at his factory were from Hunan, Henan, and Sichuan Provinces, and the workers there who were interviewed scoffed incredulously at the mention of *hukou* reform. Many had heard about it but said it would be impossible to rack up enough points. They said they could only afford to live in cheap rentals such as shared rooms and had no hope of being able to purchase a home. The requirement of continuous permanent employment also stood in the way of accumulating points. Many of the workers at this factory, like migrants elsewhere, switched jobs every few years in pursuit of higher wages or better working conditions. Most workers in the construction industry also changed jobs often because their jobs typically lasted only as long it took to complete a building. In most cities, those who have worked for a sufficiently long period in the informal service industry, such as housekeepers, are officially eligible for benefits, but they seldom are classified as permanent workers and so they too are effectively excluded from public goods. Shanghai announced a new points system in 2013.[25] Temporary residents are allowed to apply for a permanent residence permit after seven years if they have amassed 120 points (Shanghai

Municipal Government 2013, Shanghai Daily 2013). A master's degree is worth 100 points and a doctoral degree 110 points (Shanghai Municipal Government 2013), credentials that are out of reach for most migrant workers. Another way to accrue points is to make a major investment in a Shanghai-based company that pays at least 100,000 RMB per year in taxes or has ten or more employees (Shanghai Municipal Government 2013). In short, the points system makes it no easier for most migrants to obtain public services.[26]

Besides creating near-impossible eligibility requirements for *hukou* transfers, the points system requires hard-to-secure paperwork. Even when migrants accumulate enough points, they are often unable to track down the documentation necessary to prove that they are entitled to a service. Municipal and district governments generally require "five documents" (*wuzheng*, 五证) for migrants to enroll in a public school or buy urban health insurance. Typically, these include a household registration booklet, proof of hometown permanent residency, a temporary residence permit, proof of local address, and proof of employment. Some cities, such as Chengdu, may require up to seven documents.[27]

At least three of these documents can be difficult for most migrants to obtain: the temporary residence permit, proof of local address, and evidence of employment. Not everyone has a temporary residence permit because it necessitates registering with the public security bureau. Acquiring proof of local address is also problematic. As the shortage in affordable housing for migrants grows, migrants often share temporary housing and are not always offered leases with their names on them that they can present as proof of residence. Many migrants also do not have labor contracts that they can present as evidence of employment. Informal and low-skilled workers are among the least likely to be on contract. In many small businesses and much of the underground economy, written labor contracts are rare. For example, fruit and vegetable sellers, nannies, and repairmen usually do not have contracts. Even those who are formally employed may be hired as temporary workers despite the fact that their positions are permanent, and so they often do not have the full-fledged contracts that are required.[28] Many other workers who sought labor contracts when they began their jobs are never given them. One feisty migrant worker interviewed in Guangzhou took his boss to court for not complying with the Labor Contract Law. The court sided with the employer and ultimately blamed the worker for not signing a contract, even though the company refused to offer him one after he specifically asked for it when he was hired.[29] A small shop owner summed up the situation well in 2017: "They ask for this certificate and that certificate: proof of housing, social insurance cards, and labor contracts. It's almost impossible."

Additional paperwork requirements have recently been added in some cities, making it harder to hunt down and present all the necessary documents. In Beijing, a new demand appeared in the mid-2010s: at least one parent must now provide physical proof of Beijing-issued social insurance in order to enroll a child in public school.

Even when migrants fulfill all the criteria and can provide every piece of paperwork needed to prove their eligibility for services, they may still be shuffled from office to office in a fruitless effort to get their pile of forms certified. For instance, some officials in Beijing started tightening enforcement of document-checking rules after 2007, and Shanghai did the same: "They always had these requirements. It's just that it's being enforced more strictly now." Previously, the document review process had been more informal, and parents could simply bring their paperwork to a school for administrative clearance when they registered their children and paid their tuition and fees. But more migrants were trying to enroll their children in public schools after the mid-2000s.[30] Once tighter examination of paperwork began, local officials began to step in frequently and send migrants on wild goose chases. Some schools in Beijing now instruct parents to bring their full package of documents to the local government for inspection in order to get another certificate verifying that the documentation is complete. One migrant in Beijing said, "At the local government office, they told me to take the documents instead to the school. By the time they cleared up the document approval, it was too late. The school year had started and I was told to try enrolling my child again next year." With both school leaders and local officials dodging parents and sending them to other offices, migrant students can be left in approval limbo and never make the leap from being technically eligible to actually enrolling in a school.

Deflecting migrants in these ways has two important consequences. First, they must fend for themselves in case-by-case battles over eligibility and documentation, in which responsibility for the provision of a service shifts away from the government and onto migrants themselves.[31] Second, when migrants fail to overcome all the obstacles to buy health insurance or enroll their children in school, they sometimes assume it is their own fault.[32] Individuals navigating their way through this complex and confusing system may not always be able to see that they, like many other migrants, are victims of deliberate local government policies.

DEFLECTING MIGRANTS AWAY FROM THE CITY

By selectively enforcing rules or shutting a service down, urban officials often encourage migrants to seek services elsewhere. In doing so, they divert migrants from urban hospitals and public schools to clinics and schools in other cities or to their hometown in the countryside.

The first way to divert migrants' requests is to enforce dormant rules. There are many regulations that have been on the books for some time but have gone unenforced until city leaders, principals, or hospital administrators decide to apply them. For example, limits on the number of students allowed in each classroom have existed for as long as urban interviewees could remember but were regularly ignored. In the past, as class sizes grew, most schools happily collected the additional tuition fees and crowded more desks into classrooms. In some places, migrants can still enroll if they pay tacked-on charges. For instance, a street sweeper from Anhui Province was told in 2017 that, because she was an outsider, her child could attend a Shanghai public school during the upcoming school year if she paid extra for it. But as more migrant students enrolled and anti-outsider sentiment grew in the mid-2000s, some local officials instead dusted off the classroom size restrictions and used them to exclude new migrant children. In Beijing in 2012, education bureaus, working with school principals, abruptly restricted class sizes to thirty students, while their counterparts in Chengdu shrunk classes to forty-five students, even though classrooms had long held fifty-five to sixty-five children when the additional students were mainly registered urban residents. A former education official in Chengdu explained in 2012, "We're strictly enforcing the limit of forty-five students per class, so we now require parents' *hukou* registration, because now there are too many migrant students."

In Shanghai, most schools first fill their classes with registered residents before allowing in any migrants, lest urban parents complain. Migrant students must get a number on a waiting list and maintain high-enough test grades in the meantime; when they move from elementary to middle school, they must obtain another number and go to the bottom of a new list. In Chengdu, a staff member of a government-organized NGO who was working on a project to integrate migrant children with registered students explained that the waiting list avoided the awkwardness of excluding migrants formally by making their inability to enroll a consequence of classroom capacity, rather than outright discrimination. As one migrant parent in Beijing put it, the school "said it was full, instead of saying that they were not allowing my daughter to enroll." Enforcing previously unenforced rules forces families to send children to private migrant schools or to a school in the parents' home village or city. Relying on existing but previously unenforced rules makes it difficult for migrants to allege discrimination since the rules long predate their claims.

Occasionally officials do not provide any justification at all for deflecting a child. One migrant parent interviewed in 2017 described her attempts to enroll her son in school in Shanghai earlier that year, "They didn't even bother giving me a reason. They just said no; he's not allowed. He should have started first grade already." As outsiders share these stories of frustrating encounters and missed opportunities, and their experiences of being shut out of schools for one reason or another, others are deterred from bringing their children to the city at all. A vegetable seller from Fujian Province working in Beijing explained in 2017, "I heard they couldn't go to school in Beijing, so I didn't even consider bringing them here."

Cities also sometimes shut down the private schools that migrant children attend, as has been common in Beijing, to encourage them and their families to move away, or to dampen opposition to urban redevelopment projects. As China's cities grow and expand into suburban and rural areas, municipal authorities throughout the country are demolishing neighborhoods and evicting residents to make way for more profitable projects, such as luxury malls and residential high rise buildings (Hsing 2010a, Wu 2016). Since the mid-2000s, dozens of migrant schools in Chengdu and various other cities have been torn down as neighborhoods underwent urban renewal.[33] Beijing officials have been particularly adept at getting migrants to leave redevelopment zones with minimal fuss. In Beijing's Fengtai District, for example, local officials put up barriers around four migrant schools and posted signs saying that demolition would begin in one year.[34] There were no other announcements or meetings about the land expropriation or plans for alternative schooling. Migrants did not have the option to send their children to a public school because there were none nearby. A large majority of migrant families in that part of Fengtai decided it would be best to make plans to relocate as soon as possible.[35] They realized that if they waited the full year and demolition began, they might lose out and be forced to move without having found new jobs, housing, or schools for their children.

Nor is education the only service that can be taken away. To encourage urban residents to move elsewhere, officials in some cities have cut off water, gas, and electricity to buildings that are slated for demolition. This pushes "nail households" (*dingzihu*, 钉子户) who are resisting demolition orders to vacate a neighborhood without having to directly confront them or forcibly remove them (Hsing 2010b, The Guardian 2014). Eviction of the so-called "low-end population" and demolition of buildings after a fire in Xinjian Village in the Daxing District of Beijing took away migrant workers' housing in the city (Immel 2020, Morris 2022).

Local authorities and the development companies they cooperate with prefer to avoid direct confrontation with the people they are displacing, since prolonged disputes can lead protesters to dig in, draw the attention of the media, and bring criticism from higher levels (Cai 2008, Chen 2009, O'Brien and Deng 2015). As in Fengtai, urban officials hope to defuse conflict by encouraging migrants to move away on their own, after which they are hardly in a position to mobilize collectively. In addition to thwarting resistance by preventing a critical mass of protesters from forming, withdrawing services lends to the whole process an air of necessary inexorable urban development. As a retired education bureau official in Chengdu put it in 2012: "A migrant school would never be demolished per se. Rather, if there is an issue, it's simply a question of land being bought for development."

The authorities do not always resort to withdrawing services. Urban hospitals are almost always more expensive than rural ones, and differences in out-of-pocket expenses encourage migrants to seek health care outside the city where they work. A combination of lower medical insurance premiums, higher reimbursement rates, and simpler reimbursement procedures in the countryside and in less developed cities make going to a rural health clinic or smaller city a cost-effective choice for many migrants.[36] A restaurant cook from rural Sichuan told me in Chengdu in 2017 that she could use her insurance in Chengdu, but never tried to because the reimbursement rate was so much lower than if she traveled to a hospital in her hometown, where it was 80 percent. At a hospital in the city of Hangzhou, a doctor noted in 2012 that most migrants could only get 10 percent of their expenses reimbursed through their rural health care insurance. Owing to this low rate, a worker in Hangzhou from rural Zhejiang said he planned to wait until he returned to his hometown to have colorectal surgery. He could have received care in Hangzhou but would not think of doing so unless it was life-threatening. Another migrant from Anhui Province who had been admitted to the same hospital was in great pain and urgently needed surgery that day. But she could not afford the 90 percent share of a 5,000 RMB bill, plus the cost of a hospital room, and she and her husband did not want to take time off from work to return to her home village to receive medical care. When the patient suggested she might undergo the procedure at a cheaper, less reputable facility, the doctor said she would likely have to spend more money later to get corrective work done. In the end, the woman left the hospital without scheduling the surgery and hoped her condition would not worsen.

Some migrants who have rural insurance find it impossible to use their coverage at all. Municipal officials sometimes do not work as conscientiously as they might to set up agreements between urban hospitals and rural insurance programs. Without these agreements, migrants have a hard time using urban hospital receipts to receive repayment from rural insurance providers. One migrant family who sold snacks and drinks from a cart had coverage in their hometown in Shandong Province, but, as they explained in 2017, they could not find a way to use that insurance in Shanghai. The mother said, "Everyone we know cannot use it, as it's not accepted here." This conveniently lessens the burden on municipal hospitals.

Urban sprawl and higher health care costs in cities disguise the origins of why it is necessary to go home to receive medical care or to find a school willing to take their children. These factors generate feelings of powerlessness and uncertainty about where to turn. It often seems, interviewees said, like no one in particular deprived them of services; it just happened. When faced with class size limits, development imperatives, and low reimbursement rates, it is hard for migrants to know which institution (the school, hospital, or one of the government departments), which level of government (district, municipal, provincial, or central), or even which person (the principal, hospital cashier, or an official from the bureau of education, human resources and social security, development, or public security) should be held responsible. Without a clear target for their ire, collective contention or even collective consciousness can be difficult to muster.[37]

WHY DO CITIES DEFLECT MIGRANTS?

Municipal officials deflect migrants for many reasons, of which the most obvious is cost: 650 billion RMB (US$106 billion) by one estimate from the Chinese Academy of Social Sciences (Reuters 2013). Given the municipal share of total government revenues, it is challenging for city officials to foot this bill largely on their own. In 2016, the central government collected 50.4 percent of total tax revenue while regional and local authorities received the remainder. But the central government accounted for only 8 percent of the spending on general public services, while regional and local governments had to pick up the other 92 percent. The story was even more lopsided for education expenditures (5 percent by the central government and 95 percent by local governments) and health spending (1 percent by the central government and 99 percent by local governments).[38] In 2016, the national public expenditures budget rose by 6 percent and reached 187.8 trillion RMB (Ministry of Finance of the People's Republic of China 2017), but this still was not nearly enough. In the absence of larger transfers, urban leaders often find themselves financially stretched when asked to pay for better services for migrants. Deflecting demands allows them to benefit from the contribution migrants make to the local economy without covering the full array of expenses associated with maintaining a labor force. Many city governments also face pushback from residents who have an urban registration and whose prejudice against rural migrants affects the integration of outsiders into communities and their ability to make a living (Tse 2016).

But why do local governments not simply refuse to provide services? Deflecting migrants is more politically astute and less likely to cause trouble than denying them outright. When municipal authorities refuse to provide services outright, all non-locals are left out and the government can become a focal point for complaints about discrimination. But when urban officials erect barriers that can be used to refuse benefits selectively one-by-one amid lots of individual paperwork, it is less conspicuously discriminatory *en masse* and buys time to put off overhauling a city's public goods system. For most migrants who are deflected, the source of their exclusion is hard to pin down as they stumble from one obstacle or excuse to another, and from one previously unknown regulation to another.

The central government has placed officials in mega-cities in a difficult spot and has left many feeling hamstrung.[39] Although national leaders are encouraging further urbanization, they do not want crowded first-tier cities to become much bigger.[40] Instead, their goal is to push migrants toward small and medium-sized cities. As a result, *hukou* liberalization is taking place mainly in cities with fewer than five million people. But wages are generally higher and most new jobs are being created in the sixteen largest municipalities with populations over five million (The Economist 2014), and those are the destinations where many migrants want to go. This clash between the central government's urbanization strategy and migrants' preference for bigger cities puts municipal leaders in places like Shanghai, Beijing, and Chengdu in a bind. Policies designed for third- and fourth-tier cities like Benxi and Datong are failing to lure migrants away from China's congested mega-cities. As new migrants appear every day and the national government urges the cities to provide more benefits to outsiders, the authorities in China's largest cities turn to deflection.

Beijing is a good example. In December 2015, Beijing released draft regulations on permanent residence permits that proposed harder-to-fulfill requirements: *hukou* applicants should already possess a non-permanent Beijing residential permit, should be less than forty-five years old, and have paid social insurance premiums in Beijing for at least seven consecutive years (Xinhua 2015). Even if they could satisfy these requirements, they would also have to jump the hurdles of a points system similar to Shanghai and Guangzhou and likely have much the same effect. The vast majority of migrant families will continue to be effectively (if not formally) excluded from urban services despite high-sounding reforms that suggest there is a way for them to gain all the benefits of a Beijing *hukou*.

But the situation is not equally dire everywhere and there are mega-cities where the gap between migrants and officially registered residents is smaller. In other words, even among large, attractive cities, some are more open to outsiders than others, and better treatment of migrants does not solely depend on a city's wealth. Chengdu, for example, has done a particularly good job of incorporating migrant children into local schools compared to Beijing and Shanghai. It has pioneered new ways to manage private migrant schools and allows far more non-local students to attend public schools.[41] Intra-provincial migrants have also been granted substantial access to medical care, and their Chengdu hospital receipts can often be submitted to rural insurers for reimbursement, even while migrants hailing from provinces other than Sichuan continue to face difficulties doing so.

REINFORCING STRUCTURAL INEQUALITY

Being deflected within or away from the city leaves many claim-makers stranded. They are stuck between having a right to an urban public service and being able to access and use it. Individuation makes it so that city governments can provide benefits to a few outsiders while deflecting and denying the rest. When a few are able to use health care and education, it would seem that eventual actualization for everyone is imminent. But instead, phantom services fill that gap and leave rural outsiders without adequate public housing or pensions in the city while also preventing them from having a clear and sufficient basis for complete exclusion as was often the case during early waves of marketized migration in the 1980s and 1990s. Contingency in their urban social citizenship makes this possible.

Phantom services perpetuate structural inequality. Decentralized policies can make someone a full citizen or one of the emergent gradations of second-class citizenship based on their characteristics, the city, and the year. Inequity is baked into the system itself. Any room for discretion for city and district bureaucrats and frontline service providers is limited within the confines of policies, such as prohibitive points systems and reimbursement rates that are more favorable under the New Rural Cooperative Medical Scheme (NCMS) in the countryside than at top urban public hospitals. Over time, this inculcates a sense of being disempowered and disadvantages migrants. Many cannot meet all of the eligibility requirements or accumulate enough points, so they come to expect less from promised expansions of urban welfare systems. Beyond empowerment and agency, they may have a difficult time meeting their basic needs for survival in the city.

Being able to choose from the full menu of service provision is an illusion, and it has consequences for migrants' socioeconomic mobility. The policies, practices, and norms of deflecting them keeps them in the reach of the state while curtailing their agency. The option to use schools and clinics in the countryside belies the trade-off of foregoing higher income to support other family members who have remained in their home village or losing a job altogether. Despite intending to return, they may have to quit to relocate because they cannot take adequate time off, are fired for taking (often unpaid) leave, or find they have no position upon their return to the city. Wages and employment opportunities are too valuable to give up in order to get a minor injury or illness checked out in a rural clinic that likely has inferior facilities and level of care compared to many urban hospitals. Many opt to wait until there is a medical emergency to seek care rather than making regular preventative appointments. Their health and well-being suffer in the long-term in order to maintain a foothold in their urban livelihoods. Migrant children who attend private migrant schools or lower quality public schools will have a difficult time attaining socioeconomic mobility without high levels of education to support it. Though they may survive in the city, they may not all thrive enough to overcome the high walls of systematized inequality.

CONCLUSION

As China becomes less rural, more migrants need and expect urban services. Many municipalities, however, deflect demands for benefits instead of meeting them or denying them outright. City leaders often establish near-impossible eligibility requirements and require paperwork that outsiders struggle to obtain. Municipal authorities also nudge migrants to seek health care or education elsewhere by enforcing dormant rules, shutting down schools and clinics, and encouraging migrants to seek out cheaper options in another city or in the countryside. Urban officials deflect migrants for practical and political reasons. Limiting access is both cost-effective and done in a way that isolates and disempowers migrants and makes it harder for them to protest collectively.

Phantom services change the locus of contention, aid "social management" (*shehui guanli*, 社会管理), and expose new axes of inequality. In today's China, the ladder of citizenship has many rungs and placing a migrant on a higher (or lower) step is a way to control them. Benefits are doled out to favored subgroups or withheld behind a smokescreen of hard-to-contest excuses. The level of inclusion is adjustable and depends on financial considerations or even the personal inclinations of a municipal official or frontline service provider. In an era of phantom benefits, collective claims to benefits that the national government has endorsed are instead regularly supplanted by individual battles. Even when those battles are won, they only generate relief for a single family, while providing an effective lever for local authorities to divide and manage a potentially problematic group.

Migrants are not alone in being deflected. Other people seeking services may also be diverted by a tangle of rules and complications that discourage them from taking to the streets and leaves them with few options beyond negotiating face-to-face with bureaucrats.[42] For example, rural leaders have introduced additional guidelines about which homeowners may receive low-income assistance, which establish new criteria and require evidence that some fail to meet (Chuang 2014).[43] Again and again, deflecting has proven to be a handy tool in the local government's toolbox.

The long-term effectiveness of deflecting remains to be seen. It does work in the short term to prevent migrants from getting health care, education, housing, a pension, or low-income assistance. One study found that, based on policy documents, most cities adopt a rental-based approach to meet migrants' short-term housing needs, and only 12.4

percent of 97 prefecture-level cities take a citizenship-oriented approach to facilitate long-term settlement (Peng and Wang 2023). But these are stopgap measures that may only be keeping an increasingly demanding migrant population at bay without truly addressing their problems. After years or even decades of waiting for a thoroughgoing transformation of the *hukou* system that would bring them more fully into the urban benefits regime, some migrants are losing patience. A number of activists are overcoming depoliticization and individualization and making their frustrations known. Popular action appears to be increasing the most in areas where the migrant population has grown rapidly (Becker 2012), although organizing may be more difficult in the Xi Jinping era. Deflecting is not addressing the needs of China's huge migrant workforce; nor is it clearly serving social stability. It saves cities money but may be pushing other problems down the road and making their ultimate resolution more difficult.

Structural inequality in the form of phantom services disguises the origins of the system and who benefits from it. Central directives about incorporating *nongmin gong* and reducing inequality appear to signal that officials in Beijing care about migrants and are alert to two kinds of disparity that particularly affect them, second-class citizenship in cities and the rural-urban divide. Both separate them from registered urban residents who enjoy full citizenship rights and the greater economic dividends and opportunities available in more developed areas. Simultaneous pushes from the center for deeper urbanization across the country suggest that these processes are part of a larger long-term economic goal. They cannot ignore these cleavages and pursue urban development at the same time. If central authorities seem to support integrating migrant workers (fiscal and tax structures notwithstanding), then they appear benevolent and people left out of urban public services can blame city bureaucrats, district officials, or frontline service providers. Yet they do offer a path to attaining social rights in the city.

The possibility of incorporation, no matter how slim for most, makes it so phantom services benefit the state. Besides administrative costs borne by local governments, migrants themselves shoulder the burden of finding out that there is no easily accessible map for each city's social services distribution system, much less a national one. Individuals zoomed in on their own case find it hard to see that that their inclusion is contingent. Because of political atomization, less clear to any individual navigating the complicated systems that each city operates is that the path to full citizenship is riddled with potholes, missing signage, unlabeled lanes, and dead ends.

4

Demobilizing Migrant Workers

Shanghai declared that it would become the first Chinese city to provide free compulsory education to all migrant children. International and domestic media heralded the announcement in 2010, suggesting an important turning point in making rural outsiders full citizens in their urban destinations. It appeared that local authorities were finally providing benefits owed to these workers and their families. However, this chapter will show how incomplete and under-delivered these reforms are. New forms of separation continue to relegate migrant children to fewer opportunities than their peers with urban household registrations. Their limited incorporation is stuck in these waysides and has not yet led to complete inclusion. Chapter 3 showed how local authorities deflect migrants person by person with phantom services, while this chapter focuses on how they also demobilize outsiders at the higher level of, as perceived by officials and migrants, regulating and managing institutions. Cities' approaches to bringing in (or not) these substantial student populations show how they often privilege maintaining inequality over improving migrant welfare.

Makeshift alternatives to public schools have not escaped official attention, and this chapter turns its attention to municipal governments' policies toward "people-run" (*minban*, 民办) schools for migrant children. As more and more migrants settle long-term into cities, they circumvent the lack of access to state-run urban schools by establishing their own private ones. However, these schools are often in dilapidated buildings with worse conditions and less qualified teachers than urban public schools. While some local governments begin to integrate rural migrants into city services, they simultaneously attempt to regulate the private substitutes that spring up to fill the educational need. In the name of reasons such as safety concerns, they use this as an additional channel to use public services as a tool of social control. Their corresponding policies for integrating children into urban public schools reinforce inequity.

How, not only if, services are delivered and regulated is central to entrenching inequality. The rules and practices represent another way to suspend migrants between exclusion and complete inclusion. Accessible services are nonexistent in some cities, but in others the degree of incorporation can be limited to more desirable migrants and lower quality benefits. Whereas deflection is a gatekeeping mechanism for eligibility and access, the nexus of public and private school regulations is most uneven at delivery. The patchwork of service provision, as in the previous chapter, fractures migrant workers into different gradations of second-class citizenship and further disempowers them in ways beyond exclusion.

A PRIMER ON MIGRANT SCHOOLS

As I entered the principal's office, which also served as the vice principal's office and faculty meeting room, he motioned for me to wait at the conference table while he tended to a teacher's request in another room. "Have a seat. Sorry for the chairs. They were donated," he sheepishly apologized as he grabbed a folder off his desk in the corner before heading down the hall. As I sat down in the closest chair at the table in the center of the room, I nearly fell to the cold concrete floor. I looked more closely and realized that the chair, like the other twenty-three in the room, was only about six inches from the ground. The tabletop was at my neck level. When the principal (who was taller than me) returned for our conversation and sat down across from me, the table at least reached his armpits.

Though the school staff and children were in good spirits, the school building was lacking. The rolling black office chairs had been donated to the school because all of the pneumatic pump mechanisms were broken, rendering the seating useless in any typical office setting. They were otherwise destined for the dump. Students' desks were likewise in poor condition and noticeably old. We kept our heavy winter coats on to fend off the November chill, worsened by the lack of heating in the building. As we walked the halls to meet teachers and students, I noticed out of the corner of my eye that a screwdriver handle functioned as the doorknob for one of the classrooms. I volunteered with migrant schools as a token of my gratitude for the generosity and time they shared with me for my interviews and daylong stays gathering ethnographic observations, and these conditions were not unusual.

Private "people-run" migrant schools like this one I visited in Beijing popped up in the mid-1990s.[1] They multiplied elsewhere as more migrants brought their children to the cities. From the start, most of these people-run schools were deemed illegal. The local government in Beijing excluded migrant children from public schools and neither recognized nor supported private migrant schools (Kwong 2004).[2] Since then, local governments' role in this form of migrant education has become more proactive as it has increasingly contracted out private social services and regulated them. According to national policy, the Compulsory Education Law of 1986 requires a system of free nine-year compulsory education for children (National People's Congress 1986). An amendment two decades later adds that no tuition or miscellaneous fees should be charged for mandatory schooling (National People's Congress 2006).

These alternatives are substantially more accessible than urban public schools for migrant students. They are conveniently located a short walk or bike ride away from the homes of migrant families in concentrated pockets of the city limits where they live. For many parents who commute toward the central business district for their jobs, this shortens the time spent dropping off their children at school for the day. Were it not for these nearby schools, the fortunate few who can get into a public school might have to walk and take multiple bus lines to arrive in time for school-wide morning exercises. Migrant schools are also financially more reachable. In general, the schools' funding comes from student fees. Short-term sponsorships from Chinese companies' corporate social responsibility programs support a lucky few. Student fees can range from, for example, approximately 350 to 1,000 RMB (US$56 to 160) per semester, and teacher salaries start at 1,500 RMB (US$240) per month.[3] Many receive additional support from domestic and international NGOs.

While these migrant schools are more affordable than public schools for families, many cannot offer a high-quality education. Teachers at migrant schools tend to be enthusiastic but under-qualified, since their better trained and more highly educated counterparts have local household registrations and teach in public schools for superior salaries. A pair of teachers recounted that some of their colleagues were so poor that they sold vegetables under a bridge and on the side of the road at night and on weekends to supplement their meager incomes.[4] There is high turnover among these teachers, many of whom are migrants themselves. They may also see their position as a stepping stone to a job at a better equipped school, which contributes to more churn year to year. One teacher I spoke with was hired as a gym instructor, but he became an English language or math teacher depending on what the school needed each year.[5] Enrollment numbers and standardized test performance reflect barriers to high-quality education for migrant students in the city. Rural children who do not migrate with their parents, known as "left-behind children," are more likely to enroll in school than children who migrate to the city with their families (Yang and Duan 2008), suggesting that these students continue to encounter roadblocks to enrolling in urban schools. Migrant students who attend the poorest Beijing public schools still significantly outperform students in migrant schools (Lai et al. 2014). Surprisingly, left-behind children in rural schools in Shaanxi Province outperformed migrant students in Beijing migrant schools on standardized tests for a 2008–2009 school survey (Liu 2010). Though rural schools are notoriously poorer than urban schools, their students still did better than students in urban migrant schools.

Besides inadequate financing and staffing, migrant school facilities are also rough-and-ready. They may be in converted buildings with relatively low-rent payments and rely on donated furniture and materials as much as they can. One school I visited in Chengdu was located in a building that formerly housed a restaurant. Rooms that previously served as elegant, intimate private dining areas meant to seat eight to ten people were converted into classrooms. Some rooms were L-shaped or more like parallelograms than traditional squares or rectangles. While this was an architectural feature of the restaurant, it made for difficult classroom management, cluttered seating and desk arrangements, and awkward chalkboard viewing angles for students. Without heating in the buildings, students and teachers bundled up in the winter. Schools that receive company donations or sponsorships tend to be in better shape. Though conditions were poor and proper teaching materials were in short supply, principals reported that basic building safety was not an issue in the schools I visited and that they had passed safety checks before. Local officials use a magnifying glass approach to assess the structural integrity of schools and other issues when they seek to regulate them.

Just as the overall migrant worker population is difficult to track, their children who accompany them (and their education provision) are also hard to monitor. According to the 2018 National Education Statistical Bulletin, the number of children accompanying migrant workers in cities totaled approximately 14.2 million. Among them, about 10.5 million were enrolled in primary school and about 3.8 million were enrolled in middle school (Ministry of Education 2019). The National Bureau of Statistics reports the status of migrant children's education based on their survey data. In 2019, 99.5 percent of children of compulsory education age attended school. Of them, 83.4 percent of primary school age children and 85.2 percent of middle school age children were in public school. Both percentages were increases over the previous year. Others attended government-funded private schools. The same survey says that 11.9 percent of children of primary school age attended government-funded private schools (a slight increase over the previous year) and 8.8 percent of those of middle school age also attended government-funded private schools (a decrease over the previous year) (National Bureau of Statistics 2020).

But these numbers paint an optimistic picture. Children born to migrant mothers are four times more likely to be unregistered than registered (Vorthems 2019). One estimate calculates that 1.74 million migrant children of primary school age and 550,000 students of middle school age are excluded from urban public education systems (China Labour Bulletin 2020). Official numbers belie the number of migrant children and their actual participation in urban welfare systems. Examining the modes of private regulation and public integration reveal how atomized and inconsistent migrant children's enrollment in urban public schools is.

THREE MODES OF REGULATION AND INTEGRATION

The state plays two roles in social service provision: as provider of public institutions and as regulator of private alternatives. Local governments have adopted three main strategies to regulate private migrant schools and integrate migrants into urban public schools: (1) suppression and exclusion, (2) selective absorption and segregated inclusion, and (3) certification and full inclusion. Three city cases exemplify each pair of approaches, but they are not necessarily exclusive to these locations. Dual roles allow them to create matching policies that together serve goals of social control rather than prioritizing the education and social mobility of rural migrant students.

Each method of regulating makeshift alternatives has a complementary incorporation strategy for public schools. In suppression and exclusion, local governments close and demolish private schools and block migrants from enrolling in public school. Through a segmented approach, selective absorption and segregated inclusion involves closing down small, unlicensed schools and taking over the rest while allowing some migrants into public schools but often segregating them from urban students. The implementation of certification and full inclusion is an innovative tactic that best preserves existing access channels that are convenient for migrants to get to by legalizing and certifying private schools and also allowing migrants to attend public school. This chapter considers the progression of these policies over the last decade and shows that bounded inclusion ultimately helps to atomize and demobilize migrant workers in Chinese cities.

Beijing launched a second, widely criticized wave of closures of migrant schools in 2011. Shanghai had recently announced it would provide free public education to all migrant children, while Chengdu certified the quickly growing number of private migrant schools. Chengdu also welcomed migrants into public schools more openly than Beijing and Shanghai. Wealthier coastal cities that have relied on migrant workers the longest and are experiencing labor shortages provide worse services than poorer inland cities. This section establishes some of the major differences across these cities in wealth and education provision before breaking down the patterns of private regulation and public integration they exemplify.

Providing public services is expensive, and the most desired and best quality ones are often in more developed cities. Extending them to citizens who were not previously included is costly in terms of setting up systems, expanding bureaucratic capacity, and delivering the benefits themselves. Around the time these changes were introduced, Beijing's GDP per capita in 2010 was US$11,218.[6] Many of the country's top hospitals and universities are in the capital city, and it is sixteen times easier for a Beijing student to earn admission to top-ranked Tsinghua University than a student from Hunan Province.[7] Moreover, a Beijing *hukou* is among the most sought-after in China, another indication of the substantial benefits registered Beijing residents receive. Despite these numerous advantages bestowed on Beijing residents, migrants in Beijing do not fare so well. The city carried out major crackdowns on private migrant schools. Without alternatives for their children to attend public school, migrant parents withdrew their children from school or moved out of Beijing. The percentage of migrant children who do not go to school is higher in Beijing and Shanghai than the national average.[8]

Shanghai is another desirable, long-standing migrant destination, but outsiders there have more access to formal education. According to Chinese and international news coverage, Shanghai is leading the way in providing services for migrants.[9] Like Beijing, it is a cosmopolitan first-tier city on China's prosperous coast. State-owned enterprises in Beijing and

Shanghai lure the best and brightest students from other parts of China with the promise of a local *hukou*, showing how desired the benefits that accompany one of these registrations are. As the financial center of China, Shanghai's 2010 GDP per capita amounted to US$11,238, slightly higher than Beijing's (Cao 2012, Zhang 2012). Shanghai stated it would provide free education to all migrant children and is generally perceived to be more welcoming to rural migrants than other cities, but practices on the ground are more circumscribed. Some integrated migrant and public schools actually operate as segregated schools with different hours, curriculum, and teachers for migrant and local children.[10] The policy also only covers compulsory education and excludes high school admission for migrant students.

In comparison, Chengdu is the less-developed capital city of a province better known as a migrant-sending location than destination. It has fewer resources than Beijing and Shanghai, and municipal authorities there face rapidly growing demand on its public services from migrants as factories chasing cheaper labor costs move inland across China and toward Southeast Asia.[11] Yet migrant students have the most access to education there among these three cities. Chengdu's 2010 GDP per capita was US$6,466, just over half that of Beijing and Shanghai (Chengdu Statistics Bureau 2011). Though Chengdu is poorer and further inland, migrant children have long had an easier time enrolling in public schools, and the number of migrant schools is increasing.[12] Not only can migrant schools remain open, but the local government also certifies them. Migrant children who graduate from certified schools can at least present a certificate verifying that they have finished middle school, which employers often require. Surprisingly, Chengdu provides better education services to migrants than Beijing and Shanghai.[13]

The three case cities adopted different strategies for regulating private migrant schools and integrating migrant students into public institutions: (1) suppression and exclusion, (2) selective absorption and segregated inclusion, and (3) certification and full inclusion. Together, they represent a fairly comprehensive menu of ways to regulate the educational opportunity of those who transplant to the city. While this list may not be exhaustive, it shows a range of policy responses and how they show government aims beyond educating migrant children or helping them achieve socioeconomic mobility. They can serve as examples from which other cities can model their own policies.[14] To understand how the last set of approaches stands out, we first need to examine what comparatively less-welcoming schemes encompass.

SUPPRESSION AND EXCLUSION

Suppression: Shutting Down Private Schools

Suppression of migrant schools in Beijing has come in waves. In 2006, Beijing launched a major campaign to crack down on illegal migrant schools in the districts of Chaoyang, Daxing, Fentgai, and Haidian under the auspices of "The City of Beijing School Board Notification Regarding Strengthening the Management of Schools Operated by the Floating Population." Another surge of closures followed in 2011, garnering much international attention. While municipalities may close schools at other times, these swells of action affected many migrant families across the city at once and left them with few other private schools in the neighborhood. Transfers to public schools were not on the cards for most either because of the complementary policy in that realm.

The government cited concerns about physical safety and poor education quality for shutting down these schools.[15] In particular, they said they were wary of possible injury to children in schools located in unsafe buildings. According to formal policy, "there is a list of criteria for migrant schools to meet. If schools meet them, then the government gives a per student subsidy. Otherwise, they shut down the school."[16] The sudden and coordinated closure of schools in waves suggests that more is at stake. School safety is a legitimate concern that should require regular inspection, such as on a yearly calendar, rather than when it serves as a convenient reason to get rid of an imperfect but viable education option for these children. Nor does it do much to improve the quality of schooling they receive at these institutions. This same NGO staff person who worked with migrant schools in Beijing and Shanghai said, "This has been good for ensuring the physical safety of schools and their facilities but teaching and education quality remain poor."[17] If excellent education for these students is the goal, hiring more qualified teachers and adequately funding these institutions would be policy priorities in addition to occasional crackdowns. Involuntary shutdowns and the expected consequences of them discourage migrant workers from settling in the city or force them to move out of a neighborhood.

The severity of migrant school crackdowns in Beijing varies by district each year. In 2009 and earlier years, Daxing District had the reputation of being stringent in shutting down migrant schools, especially kindergartens. Haidian District was especially tough in 2010.[18] At the time, only sixty-four schools out of approximately 400 had been able to obtain legal licenses.[19] District discretion is high in this fragmented environment of policy implementation. When municipal and district level authorities are both involved in making decisions, the landscape for migrant parents appears more complicated and patchier. They may hear from a family member or friend from the same home village as them that a particular city is welcoming and allows their children to attend school, only to realize later that these opportunities are confined to certain districts. Where they live depends on, for instance, where affordable housing is available, if there is public transportation between their dwelling and their work, or in which part of the city their social network enabled them to land. District discretion is another manifestation of the decentralization and localization of social policy for migrant workers.

If or when officials will close a school also appears capricious to migrant families. An unexpected wave of closures makes it difficult for parents to plan in advance or adjust afterwards. It is not just a matter of their local school closing but often of nearby ones (to which they might potentially transfer) facing the same fate, too. As a researcher, I encountered the same problem, though with less serious consequences than parents whose livelihoods might be in danger if they do not have a place to send their children when officials announce changes seemingly overnight. In 2012, when I asked to revisit one migrant school in Beijing that I had gone to two years prior, the school administrator said the school had been demolished. A year before the closures, officials quietly put up walls and signs indicating the school would be shut down. He also reported that the local government closed down three other migrant schools in the same neighborhood within a year. The survival of makeshift schools depends on local authorities at least tacitly allowing them to stay open, and migrant parents have little recourse when the government decides to intervene.

Exclusion: Keeping Migrants out of Public Schools

To compensate for closure of private migrant schools, Beijing public schools are supposed to allow displaced children to enroll. The reality of migrant children being able to attend public school falls far short of this goal, and most migrants continue to be excluded.

Public school options are often far away or nonexistent for migrant families. In order to enroll their children in public school, parents first have to find a public school within the educational district where they live. Many migrants in Beijing reside in outlying migrant villages far from the city center. Housing, food, and other living expenses are much cheaper outside the Fifth and Sixth Ring Roads away from the city center. However, for many migrant families, there are few or no public schools nearby to accommodate their children. As a result, migrant families are forced to let their children transfer between three or four public buses to get to school or else uproot.[20] The few public schools that are close to districts where migrants congregate are especially under-resourced compared to their counterparts in the city center, but they also carry the heaviest burden in absorbing students from migrant schools. A Beijing education official said, "The good schools keep getting better. They have better students, better teachers, etc. The poor schools keep falling behind."[21] Moreover, local officials are reluctant to take on the cost of building entirely new schools in predominantly migrant neighborhoods to serve these students. This is a consequence of the unfunded mandate that cities have across migrant social policy.

Those who find a geographically accessible school frequently run into other barriers. This is consistent with a study that has found that urban governments provide quality public education to those who need it least, such as nonlocals with high levels of economic and cultural capital (Friedman 2022). When migrant parents find a public school that should accept their child based on where they live, some report that they are still being shut out. Many migrant parents are unable to gather required documentation in time or pay for registration fees.[22] Enrollment in public school requires the presentation of five documents (*wuzheng*), consisting of a temporary residence permit, proof of a Beijing address, proof of employment and hometown permanent residency, and a notice from authorities in their place of origin stating that there is no one to care of their children back home. Proof of employment is especially difficult to acquire for some migrants because their bosses do not provide employment contracts, or they work in the informal economy.

In addition to burdensome documentation, many schools ask for extra fees in the form of required donations.[23] Such fees have been banned since 2006.[24] Nonetheless, one migrant from Henan Province reported that the local private migrant school cost 500 RMB (US$80) per semester, whereas the local public school she wanted to send her daughter to charged ten times as much, not including hundreds more that would be required in "additional fees."[25] In Beijing, one migrant mother from Hebei Province paid a so-called "voluntary donation" of US$4,800 to enroll her daughter in a Beijing primary school; school officials made her sign a document stating the fee was a voluntary donation (Levin 2012). According to a National Bureau of Statistics study on migrants' quality of life, 49 percent of respondents who brought their children with them to the cities had to pay an average registration fee of 1,226 RMB (US$200) in addition to regular tuition. Additional financial outlays make it hard for migrant families to secure a place for their children.

Parents who can cobble together documents and fees may face a different kind of hindrance. Municipal and district authorities report pressure from urban constituents to avoid bringing in registered rural students. Complaints range from reluctance to share resources to grumbles about the character and academic ability of migrant students, showing these particular parents' intolerance of their fellow citizens. When a representative of a Haidian District educators' organization was asked why the district's officials did not approve or register more migrants in schools, she said, "Because it brings down the overall quality of education in Haidian. Urban parents don't want their kids to go to school with migrants."[26] Sometimes public schools claim that there are no openings left for additional students in order to exclude migrant children, though separate spots are reserved for local urban students.[27] "With more local economic development in our district, migrant children enrollment has steadily increased in recent years. Because of this, we have had to reserve spots for local students in public schools. Otherwise, urban resident parents complain to us," said a government official in Beijing.[28] Discrimination is an obstacle outsiders cannot easily overcome with bureaucratic prowess or financial means and makes it clear that they are receiving unequal treatment.[29]

A trickle-down effect shapes teachers and parents' decisions.[30] The weight is not only seen in high school when the college entrance exam is taken, but also in middle school because that is where teachers prepare students for the high school exam (*zhongkao*) and to a lesser extent in primary school.[31] One migrant cigarette seller lived apart from his son in a different province because significant differences in exam materials precluded them from moving together to the city. He said, "[My son and I] live apart so he can graduate high school and hopefully go to college ... My son goes to school in Henan [Province], while I work here [in Beijing]. He is currently in his second year of high school and will take the college entrance exam there in two years."[32]

Although many migrants are banned from enrolling their children or face insurmountable obstacles in the form of documentation and extra fees, a small number of migrants said that in recent years their children have been able to attend public schools for free.[33] According to a public policy scholar, Beijing has a few, but not many, public schools designated specifically for migrant children that were established around the mid-2010s.[34] There are not enough to accommodate everyone. "While it's technically possible, it's become harder to get our children into public schools. It's become harder. The paperwork is more onerous. Sometimes they ask for more than five documents. And they require more serious checking and verification," said a fruit and vegetable seller in Beijing originally from Shandong Province.[35] However, this appears to be the exception and not the rule.[36] Her son was able to enroll in fifth grade at the beginning of the policy, but the paperwork was complicated and another migrant parent from the market where she had a stall had to help her navigate everything to get it right. "I still don't know how to explain the process," she added glibly. Several public school principals and administrators stated that the central government paid the tuition and fees for migrant students via the school, though this only worked if migrants were able to enroll in the first place.[37] Each year, school staff count the number of migrant students they enrolled and apply for per capita support from the government for books and other supplies.[38] Nonetheless, many migrants continue to be shut out of the urban public school system. A teenage daughter of another fruit and vegetable seller in a Beijing covered market stared at her smartphone and watched videos online as she nonchalantly said, "I stayed in my hometown in Fujian to go to school, because I could not go to school in Beijing. My grandparents took care of me."[39] After finishing her compulsory education elsewhere, she accompanied her mother to Beijing to work.

Lack of accessibility and availability of seats in classrooms, difficult documentation requirements, levies of onerous fees, and discrimination often keep migrant students out of Beijing public schools. When students' private migrant schools are closed and their designated public schools are out of reach, some families ultimately leave Beijing and return to their home villages in order to secure some form of education for their children. Suppression and exclusion represent one end of the spectrum of strategies.

SELECTIVE ABSORPTION AND SEGREGATED INCLUSION

Another approach is more welcoming than complete exclusion but falls short of full incorporation. It combines selectively absorbing private schools and separating migrant children from their registered urban peers in public schools. Shanghai is an example of this middle ground, but there are many variations on which other cities can riff to leave migrants in quicksand between exclusion and inclusion. These distinctions suggest that partial incorporation is neither a straightforward path to nor the same as full integration. Quality of incorporation fluctuates across cities and districts in China and shows that simply not being outright barred is insufficient for the most meaningful improvement.

Selective Absorption: Taking over Private Schools

State takeovers of private providers seem preferable to closures at first glance. Shanghai sought to first close down private schools that were unlicensed or deemed too small, and then take over the remaining ones. Unlike in Beijing, the plan did include several further steps to ensure migrant access to education after the policy change. The formal plan was to integrate migrant children into existing public schools and waive their fees, build new public schools in outlying (predominantly migrant) neighborhoods where previously there were none, and renovate some of the better private schools. After the policy change, three types of schools were available for migrant children in Shanghai: schools where migrant and local children were fully integrated, schools where they were segregated, and migrant-only schools.

Officials touted the benefits of taking over "people-run" schools. Since 2014, the number of migrant schools has gone down in Shanghai, totaling 145 in 2015 and 137 in 2016 according to official numbers.[40] Shutdowns such as those in Beijing are hostile and antagonizing to outsider families. Closing down small or poorly functioning schools should set a baseline of minimum quality.[41] Taking over existing ones should ensure geographical proximity for migrant students and secure steady government funding for them.[42] Moreover, building on current resources should prevent an influx of migrant students into urban public schools who are often reluctant to take them in.[43] For example, some were able to keep their old principal to maintain continuity of leadership. The process appeared to work in theory, but implementation, as it often is, was more complicated.

Many of the schools that the municipality took over are at a disadvantage. They tend to become migrant-only schools, which are typically poorest in quality compared to other schools.[44] This is in part a product of the fact that these schools are located in far-flung areas of the city, where migrants live. To improve them, Shanghai gives subsidies and sends principals or vice principals to turn these ostensibly private schools into people-run, government-subsidized (*minban gongzhu*) schools.[45] Unlike Beijing, where schools report that the central government pays for migrant student subsidies, the Shanghai municipal government foots the bulk of the bill.[46] In one district, schools receive subsidies ranging from 2,000 to 4,000 RMB (US$320 to 640) per migrant student.[47] But migrant schools receive about 25 percent of what public schools receive in public funding from the local government.[48] Teacher salaries sometimes come from district budgets.[49] Although their tuition is subsidized, migrant parents are responsible for paying their children's fees for books, lunches, and activities. In 2017, a family from Shandong Province who operated a mini cart store on a street corner said, "We would like our son to go to primary school here in Shanghai, but he cannot. They won't let him. So, he has to return to our hometown in the fall to go to school ... Neither public nor private schools have allowed him to register."[50] Many migrant parents find the results of the reforms to be underwhelming.

Segregated Inclusion: Separating Migrants in Public Schools

Shanghai public schools did move to bring in migrant students. After the overhaul and reorganization of people-run schools, more migrant children are able to attend public school in Shanghai than in Beijing. And some public schools are fully integrated, but fees have not disappeared despite being illegal.[51] The methods and forms of incorporation, however, converged on separating migrant students (and usually treating them worse than their classmates). Their inclusion is therefore segregated and incomplete.

Public school teachers routinely treat migrant students differently than their urban registered peers. The reasons are largely structural due to the incentives they have for attaining professional promotion and procuring funds for their school. Some teachers favor local students, in part because they want to prepare students for the all-important college entrance exam (*gaokao*). Test scores determine where they will go to university and how bright their future job prospects will be. Migrant students registered elsewhere cannot take the exam in the city, so teachers are reluctant to devote extra tutoring or other resources to them. Because the curriculum for the exam differs by location, migrants who have to take the test elsewhere need to study different materials than Shanghai students. For migrant students wishing to remain in Shanghai to further their education, they can only attend vocational high school (Organization for Economic Co-operation and Development 2016). Neither teachers nor students, especially those who are striving academically (ironically and unfortunately), have enticements to reward either side's efforts under these circumstances.

The segregation is more pronounced in some schoolhouses. When migrant children were integrated *en masse* into public schools, some districts and schools segregated schools.[52] "In Shanghai, there were segregated schools which separated migrant and local students. They went to school at different hours and had different lunch times. They even had different teachers and studied different curricula," said a staff member of a migrant education that operated in several cities.[53] Moreover, they were spatially separated into different classrooms (Lan 2014). Migrant children are technically allowed to attend school, per the law, but their education is subpar compared to that offered to local children in the classroom down the hall. "Shanghai has a figurative 'door card' which restricts migrants from fully entering public schools and wants to preserve its higher level of culture and moral quality," said a teacher who had been on exchange between schools.[54]

The discourse offered by school administrators around the segregation emphasizes the interests of migrant students. Government officials defend the practice as a practical solution. Principals and teachers justify the segregation by saying that, since only students with local *hukou* can take the entrance exams, their schooling and preparation should be different from migrant children's.[55] Because local children's test scores determine the school's ranking and reputation, school staff and teachers channel more resources to local students than migrant students.[56] The resolution of problematic segregation within the same school has been to separate rural migrant students into different schools. These schools mostly have retired teachers of lower quality than those in public schools for urban registered children.[57] Although media coverage has portrayed Shanghai as a leader in integrating migrants into public education, "Shanghai is like Beijing. They both represent cities that are stricter toward migrants and provide worse services."[58]

CERTIFICATION AND FULL INCLUSION

A third approach is more inclusive than the previous two. By certifying private schools and fully including migrant children in public schools, Chengdu meets migrants where they are. This pair of strategies is comprehensive and ensures that rural migrant students receive education in the city regardless of their registration status and the location where their parents were able to find an apartment or shared room. Municipal authorities legalize private schools and incorporate outsiders into urban public schools. Their full inclusion puts these students in the same classrooms as their urban peers and aims to provide the same treatment to everyone. Resources and certificates of documentation help bolster the legitimacy of private migrant schools for newcomers who prefer this option.

The contrast shows how different migrants have come to possess multiple gradations of second-class citizenship in many of China's metropolises. The difference between this approach and the combination of suppression and exclusion is clear, but the more interesting juxtaposition is against the pair of selective absorption and segregated inclusion. A significantly more open and welcoming method of certification underscores why it is important to interrogate the quality and extent of inclusion, not only whether migrants are no longer out-and-out excluded. In comparison to full incorporation, partial inclusion (through segregated classes and separated schools) adds a new layer of inequality rather than contributing to overall equity. More substantive integration is possible.

Certification: Legalizing Private Schools

"We are legal," proclaimed the principal as he proudly beamed. When entering the office of his migrant school in Chengdu, the first thing visitors see is the prominently posted certificate from the local government. It is framed, complete with official stamps and seals certifying the school. Established in 2004, the school started with around 200 to 300 students and grew to include over 1,200 students eight years later.[59] Unlike in Beijing and Shanghai, where migrant schools are being eliminated, the number of migrant schools in Chengdu increases each year. In 2003, there were about ten migrant schools in Chengdu, and their existence was precarious (Froissart 2003). There were more than fifty of these informal substitutes in 2012, approximately sixty to seventy in 2017, and the number is climbing.[60] Rather than deeming private migrant schools illegal or demolishing them, the local government is endorsing them.

Certifying existing schools has several advantages for migrant workers. With the authorization, schools can grant diplomas that students are able to present to future employers as proof of having finished middle school or high school.[61] These schools are already operating in neighborhoods where migrants live, so they are highly accessible. Parents do not have to uproot their families to find an open spot in an existing public school in the city, and students can easily commute to and from school safely without having to travel to a faraway district. Although they are still private schools, the quality of education is relatively better than migrant schools in other cities. This is partly because teacher wages and school fees are higher in Chengdu than places such as Beijing; school fees range from 1,000 to 1,800 RMB (US$160 to 290) per semester.[62] Instead of being makeshift substitutes, certification legitimizes them as viable alternatives for migrant students who need to take their compulsory education in the city. This method is not only beneficial for migrants.

Certification of migrant schools is also good for the local economy and the agendas of government officials who are responsible for fostering development.[63] The ability of young people to earn diplomas that serve as proof of education level is increasingly important as more and more employers require proof of education to determine eligibility to work and wage levels. As Chengdu and other inland cities and provinces continue to develop and attract more industry, they need workers who have the right skills and are willing to stay in the region to work. Furthermore, government officials do not have to worry about building new public schools or squeezing migrant children into existing public schools that are fully enrolled. Instead, they follow the natural development of the schools and their proximity to migrants, which contribute to migrant welfare, local service provision, labor force development, and the possibility of socioeconomic mobility.

Full Inclusion: Incorporating Migrants into Public Schools

The complementary policy from state-run providers is notably favorable for city outsiders. Authorities incorporate migrant students directly into urban public schools with fewer obstacles. Outside laborers, including a restaurant cook and street sweeper, with grown children recalled a time when their children went to school in their rural hometowns in another part of Sichuan Province because they could not attend in the city.[64] Around the mid to late 2000s, all migrant children were supposed to be allowed to attend public schools free of charge.[65] According to the Chengdu municipal government, unlike in Shanghai, "migrant children go to public schools, with the same teachers, curriculum, and so forth as local students."[66] Funding is more decentralized than in Beijing or Shanghai, and the district government subsidizes public schools that enroll migrant students.[67] In this case, resources flow in to help meet needs and deliver financial support for directives.

Not every migrant has been incorporated, but many more can attend than before and access continues to increase. A migrant mother who recently arrived in Chengdu was in an open-air labor market looking for a job that involved cooking or doing housework. Without stable work or any knowledge about the integration of migrant children into education services in Chengdu, she decided not to bring her children with her to the city and left them in the care of their grandparents in their home village.[68] For her and others in the same situation, the incorporation would allow them to keep their families together as they pursue employment in the city. "Although not all migrant children can go to public school here yet, approximately 90 percent can attend right now," said a government official in Chengdu.[69]

Not only are more migrant students eligible to go to public schools, but the barriers to enrollment are lower than in other major cities. "The public schools around here have many migrant students, especially in primary and middle school. If they live in the district, they simply take a number and earn good enough test grades to get into the school," said a government-organized nongovernmental organization (GONGO) staff member, whose organization served as a resource for the district and neighborhood to connect residents with services.[70] Parents take a number once to get in line to enroll in primary school and a second time later to attend middle school. If nearby public schools are full, the government sometimes allows migrant children to attend schools outside their district.[71] This stands in stark contrast to the demolition of migrant schools coupled with de facto exclusion from public schools in Beijing or the segregated inclusion of migrant students in Shanghai. Chengdu provides migrants with the most reachable access to education services compared to these other cities. It also serves as an example of how quality of inclusion shapes migrant workers' social rights in the city and in turn their welfare.

DEMOBILIZING DEMAND WITH POLITICAL ATOMIZATION

Cities' approaches to migrant education demobilize migrant workers' demand for public services. The ways in which they regulate private schools and integrate rural students into public schools contribute to political atomization. And they do so through both similar and different mechanisms as deflection. Here the city-by-city approaches of paired strategies demonstrate how authorities use the process of political atomization to divide and conquer migrants as outlined in Chapter 2: differentiate migrants, distribute services selectively, dilute claims, and dampen expectations. The process of political individualization is interwoven in a variety of regulatory schemes. Local officials differentiate migrants by disaggregating them, which is another form of dividing and conquering them into subgroups within and across cities. Unevenness self-reinforces inequality by differentially allowing migrant children to enroll in schools that vary by geographical location in the city (corresponding to convenience and accessibility), management ("people-run" or state-run), shades of legality and legitimacy, and quality of teaching and learning opportunities.

Dispersing children across schools allows municipalities to differentiate among migrants by choosing where to place them. In effect, those whom they perceive as deserving go to better schools. Their choices include private migrant schools, migrant-only public schools, segregated public schools, and integrated public schools. A pattern in Shanghai, for example, is that local policies deem which migrants are the most preferred and place them in the highest quality public schools. Schools there have a points system (Wan and Vickers 2022), which is similar to but separate from the *hukou* points system, based on factors such as parents' age, education, type of permit (long-term or temporary), labor contract, rental housing, and whether they are registered with the police. After parents accumulate points, they then apply to the Education Bureau. The bureau assigns the "best" candidates to integrated public schools, "middling" candidates to migrant-only schools, and the "worst" candidates to no schools.[72] This accords with the firsthand experiences of many interviewees who had applied through proper procedures but were denied for unknown reasons. Those left empty-handed were usually informal or hourly workers, not the preferred, highly educated professionals such as investment bankers or lawyers.

Education policies also distribute services selectively across other divisions. Private schools scattered across cities receive different treatment, as officials shut them down, take them over, or certify them. "People-run" schools in certain districts of Beijing are more likely to be targets of crackdown and demolition than others. Migrant-only public schools in Shanghai are usually less equipped with high-quality teachers and adequate state funding than those that primarily serve registered urban students. Comparisons among cities within a single region and across the country reveal how inconsistent education rights are for migrant children. More hospitable treatment in Chengdu shows what meaningful and complete inclusion can look like in practice. On an optimistic note, the combination of certifying private schools and integrating migrants fully into public ones could serve as a model for meeting migrant workers where they are rather than shoehorning them into middle ground alternatives or excluding them. It has the effect of increasing migrant welfare instead of primarily serving goals such as preserving inequality and social control as some of the most developed (and wealthiest) Chinese cities are doing. Despite Chengdu's innovations, selective distribution typically means that highly desired migrants enjoy urban social services while outsiders whom officials desire less or perceive as easily replaceable encounter impediments. As one government official from a municipal development bureau said, "Those with high-level skills and senior talent are encouraged to come and have no problem accessing services."[73]

After hyper-differentiation and selective distribution comes the diluting of migrant claims. Newcomers to the city perceive a false choice between having to leave their children behind in the countryside and taking a chance on (the largely undelivered promise of) urban public schooling. Just as deflected migrant workers blame themselves when they cannot access phantom services, those who encounter closed and segregated schools find it hard to square their lived experiences with the fanfare around integration policies and supposed central empathy for marginalized groups. After a brief moment of agency when they submit an application, they end up feeling disempowered when they are denied. Private schools as an implicit fallback option are no guarantee either, as their fees can be substantial. A migrant from another part of Guangdong Province operating a small shop in Guangzhou sent her daughter to private school after not being allowed to enroll in public school. She pays approximately 7,000–8,000 RMB in tuition, 800–1,000 RMB for books and supplies, and a few other fees that bring total expenses to 10,000 RMB per year.[74] Repeated disappointments like these demobilize migrants as they learn firsthand about the gap between promised reform and their own experience on the ground. They expend energy and time to chase documents and points when they are facing a system which permits only a few to become part of it.

Lived experiences and diluted claims dampen migrant workers' expectations over time. The choices they sense are available to them are an example of this consequence. Parents send their children to private schools knowing that they risk lack of certification or, worse, abrupt closure. They live apart from their children and leave them in the care of elderly grandparents in their home village. Self-selection year after year demobilizes demand across the entire mobile population. Some continue trying to enroll their children in public school, and of them, a few succeed. But most forego urban public schools altogether because of cost or lack of available spots for migrant students. The phenomenon is the same in other large cities where services for migrants are contested. In Guangzhou, for instance, a fruit and vegetable seller with an outdoor stand in an "urban village" (*cheng zhongcun*, 城中村) said that her children stay in their hometown to school because she cannot enroll them in either public or private school in the city.[75] She added that, even if they were allowed to attend, it could cost too much money. Answers to basic questions of whether their own children are permitted in public schools in Guangzhou varied widely across interviewees, reflecting a paucity of clear and uniform policies and procedures for them.[76] In some of the cities that seemed the most open, migrants saw a small opportunity at the start of policies but have since found those closed off. They expect that gradually more will open as incremental reform progresses, and not to be deflected and demobilized.

The paired strategies complement one another in aiding political atomization. Between the regulation of private schools and integration of public schools, the degree of exclusion and inclusion that cities offer to outsiders is consistent across the duos. Where private schools are shut down and demolished, public schools are exclusionary. Where private schools are taken over, public schools are segregated or separated. Where private schools are certified, public schools are inclusionary. The consistency of municipalities' approaches, regardless of whether they were coordinated from the top this way, to migrant education provision uncover their general stance toward those they consider to be outsiders. The decentralized hodgepodge is a characteristic of the system because it emphasizes constituents' movement through bureaucratic processes and regulations over claims of discrimination in social rights or exclusion. Social control of a marginalized group remains a priority over effectively providing high quality and obtainable public education for migrant students who accompany their parents to the city. The effect, most importantly, is to control rural migrants to keep their labor while limiting their demand on urban public services.

Pushing Visible Results and Avoiding Blame and Criticism

How and when municipal governments introduce changes to migrant education policy provides information about their priorities. Local officials are motivated to get credit for visible results and avoid blame and criticism for bad outcomes. In each of the approaches to regulating migrant education, officials' different orientations shape what constitutes tangible results and ways to avoid blame and criticism. Unlike politicians in other countries with electoral motivations who sometimes avoided blame for unpopular actions rather than claim credit for popular ones (Weaver 1986), Chinese officials generally want to claim credit for good changes and avoid blame for problems when they provide or take away benefits for city outsiders. They are aware of how these reforms look to higher level officials, who are in a position of power to decide their future promotions for career advancement. Their incentives are intertwined with social control because both support stability maintenance and social management, which are overarching policy priorities for the government.

Local authorities are interested in social policies that yield quick, positive results. In public service provision for the mobile population, this is directly related to social control. In the lead up to international events such as the 2008 Summer Olympics in Beijing and the 2010 World Expo in Shanghai, visible results meant shutting down and taking over migrant schools to remove eyesores during the municipalities' time on the global stage. Local authorities are inclined to implement policies better and faster when highly visible results can be seen quickly, because good outcomes that cannot be seen within the official's tenure will not benefit their performance review in time. An official in city management said, "The question is incentives – for the government and for local people ... when results can be seen almost immediately, within a year ... officials can report good results."[77] He contrasted this with attempts at social security reform, which had stalled because it involved long-term planning and required decades of people paying into the system for high-level officials to see progress and for ordinary people to reap benefits from the system. A wave of crackdowns in private migrant schools and demolitions of buildings is immediate and visible.

Besides trying to get credit for noticeable results, local officials also seek to avoid blame for bad outcomes. Grassroots cadres use discursive strategies to avoid being blamed, such as by delegitimating performance standards, reattributing blame, and transferring blame risk (Li et al. 2021). When I asked an interviewee about why migrant school safety had suddenly become the focus of municipalities, she whispered, "Because of the earthquake."[78] We were not in a region known for high seismic risk, so I assumed I misheard her and had a puzzled look on my face. But I had heard her correctly the first time. School building safety became a nationally politicized issue after the 2008 Sichuan Earthquake. According to official figures, 4,700 students died when more than 7,000 school buildings collapsed in the earthquake disaster zone (Choi 2013). Some parents argued that twice that number of children died. Grieving parents alleged that local governments and construction companies used substandard materials and took cost-saving shortcuts to pocket the difference. An official 700-member taskforce found that substandard construction had caused the buildings to fall. The corruption scandal sparked public outrage over the collapse of the "tofu-dreg schoolhouses" (referring to the shoddy construction). Local governments suppressed dissent as parents' protests targeted higher levels of government and gained more media attention within China and abroad. The state did not want to risk being blamed again for the deaths of any schoolchildren.

After the school building collapses in the earthquake, the regulation of migrant school safety gained prominence. Local officials and principals admitted that this policy came down from higher-ups, and it became tied to their prospects of promotion.[79] They realized that if any children got hurt in any of the unregulated private migrant schools, people would blame the local government.[80] Migrant school closures came before there were real alternatives for migrant children to attend public school, suggesting that regulation of private schools was a reaction to politics rather than part of broader social policy reform. Even in areas where earthquakes are not common, no calamities involving schoolchildren could occur under local governments' watch. In more restrictive Beijing, they shut down migrant schools altogether. An NGO staff member who worked closely with local officials in slightly more open Shanghai confirmed, "Shanghai built the new public schools for migrant children to standard. They had learned their lesson from the Sichuan earthquake."[81] In Chengdu, where migrant integration was better, building checks were part of the certification process.

Local officials do not only seek to avoid blame for the deaths of school-age children,[82] but they also want to avoid public criticism from the central government. When the media picked up on the demolition of one principal's migrant school in Beijing during the annual "two meetings" (*lianghui*) of the National People's Congress and Chinese People's Political Consultative Conference, a period of political sensitivity, the central government criticized the local government for closing the school. With this critical momentum and time-sensitive support, the school administrators sued. They won their legal case and were able to reopen the school. However, later, when outside attention about the demolition subsided, the local government resumed hassling the principal.[83] They waited only long enough to avoid additional public blame and criticism from the central government before continuing with their original plans. The timing and manner of shutting down this school and others indicate larger twin concerns of social stability and control of marginalized populations.

CONCLUSION

The local state plays two main roles in migrant education services. As regulators, municipal authorities shut down, take over, or certify private, "people-run" migrant schools that serve as informal substitutes when rural students cannot enroll in urban public schools. At the same time, as providers they exclude, segregate and separate, or include those students in public schools. Three main approaches to regulation and integration are (1) suppression and exclusion, (2) selective absorption and segregated inclusion, and (3) certification and full inclusion, as exemplified by Beijing, Shanghai, and Chengdu, respectively. Cities can demobilize demand through partial and incomplete inclusion, exploiting the wide range of options between outright barring and full incorporation. These local variations leave most migrants marooned and politically individualized in the hodgepodge. A few can enroll their children in urban schools, but many are left with less traction on discrimination claims and less uniform marginalization experiences around which they can organize. Municipal and district officials use migrant social policy as a means to achieve other concerns, such as cleaning up their image before international events or avoiding blame from below and criticism from above.

Their approaches to private regulation and public integration are complementary. Each pair shows a general orientation on a continuum of more or less embracing outsiders who work and live in their adopted cities. Those willing (and able) to take on the onus of extending benefits to them do so by meeting migrants where they are by, for example, certifying existing private schools that are convenient and accessible for families they serve. Cities that are less inviting find reasons at convenient times for them to close and demolish these same makeshift alternative institutions. They demonstrate how public services can function as a tool of social control, which is more apparent when improving people's welfare is not the primary driver of policy changes.

Time wasting is its own form of social control. Engaging people in the process of accumulating points, gathering paperwork, verifying documents, shuttling between offices, saving money for additional fees, determining the rules of any given district or city, moving after schools are closed, and more are the procedural components of phantom services and migrant social policy. This is another difference between deflecting and demobilizing versus simply denying migrant workers. Outright exclusion is a quick and direct outcome. For many, they may not attempt to seek urban entitlements at all if they know it is impossible. Deflecting and demobilizing, though, require citizens to spend time, energy, and resources to make their case according to policies that, on the face of them, should help them. One study found that targeted disadvantaged groups, including migrants, are systematically excluded from public services due to disproportionate administrative burdens placed on them (Wang et al. 2023). Many migrants work long shifts six to seven days a week, sometimes spend hours commuting between their low-rent shared apartments on city outskirts to the central business district where they work, and live frugally to save a substantial portion of their wages to remit to family back home. Few have the luxury to hire out the work for practical and financial reasons, so they are stuck running through the list of administrative tasks. They are among the people with the fewest resources in terms of spare time or money to expend on these enervating endeavors, and their ability to send their children to urban public school or access other entitlements depends on it. The carrot often dangles just out of reach.

Part I of this book focused on how local governments use public services as a tool of social control. Chapter 3 highlighted the ways in which deflecting migrants person by person at points of eligibility and accessibility grant urban entitlements in health care and education to a selective subgroup while keeping them unattainable for most. Chapter 4 showed how this same process works at the institutional level to demobilize demand in the regulation and management of migrant schooling in the city. Both contribute to the process of political atomization of migrants over time as deflecting and demobilizing help to divide and conquer among this large, marginalized group of people in China. Their presumed and actual mobility makes them susceptible to these forms of control by the government. Bureaucratization and an emphasis on procedures such as paperwork verification and points accumulation channel them into navigating access on the state's turf instead of being able to claim collective exclusion and organizing around universal discrimination. But migrants are not entirely helpless and have found ways to subvert social control.

PART II

MIGRANT WORKERS BLUNTING CONTROL

5

Playing with Institutional Leeway

"If you die, you die. No one cares," said Mr. Zhao as he and his fellow construction workers lamented their lack of accessible urban health care at the outdoor labor market where I met him.[1] The pavilion provided shady reprieve on another hot, humid summer day in the capital of Sichuan Province while they waited to be hired for the day. His succinct sentiments about his lack of health insurance and any kind of social protection are one example among many of the ways in which migrant workers perceive their own circumstances and access to urban benefits. Firsthand experiences like his are often absent or muted in announcements about progress in social policy reforms. While many outside observers might assume that incremental integration will eventually eradicate the well-known exclusion that characterized the past, most migrants must continue to find ways to survive in cities where they are deflected and demobilized instead of becoming fully incorporated.

Across the country from Chengdu in Beijing, migrant workers tell their own story in the Culture and Art Museum of Migrant Workers I visited in 2019. Located in Picun in the outer suburbs, the railroad-style rooms housing the museum showcase a number of displays that center migrant workers' voices. Each room has a dedicated theme, and subjects of the museum supplied the artwork, injury accounts, uniforms, and other objects that represent aspects of their daily lives. The museum has limited hours and arranging a visit involved calls to several people to schedule a time with the key keeper to unlock the front door. A long white banner with red characters and words stretched across one of the main rooms reads, "Recording Workers History, Respect for the Value of Labour" (*jilu gongren wenhua lishi changdao laodong jiazhi zunzhong*,

记录工人文化历史 倡导劳动价值尊重, their translation). Part II of this book adopts a similar approach by making the stories of Mr. Zhao and others the focal point. It shows migrants' experiences, challenges, and adaptations in urban public service provision, including the downstream effects of political atomization from their own perspective.

Part II examines how Chinese migrant workers are able to subvert social control and gain some benefits in the city. Part I presented a more state-centric view of the aims and functions of managing the floating population by demonstrating how they deflect and demobilize members of this marginalized group. The next two chapters take a more bottom-up approach, challenging the monolithic view of city transplants as constantly helpless in their vulnerability. They marshal resources available to them, playing with liminal spaces within institutions and sometimes sidestepping the state altogether in moves of pragmatic survival and improvisation. Chapter 5 stays largely within the urban welfare system and the informal institutional substitutes intended to replace what newcomers cannot receive from the state. Chapter 6 moves farther outside and away from the formal system as migrants devise strategies that rely less or not at all on the state.

This chapter focuses on migrants finding and making institutional leeway. They do so by working with the bureaucrats who administer and deliver urban entitlements to gain access through their discretion. Frontline service providers are the faces of the fragmented urban public service system.[2] Like "street-level bureaucrats" elsewhere, they operate in the space between organizational guidelines and client needs and demands (Lipsky 1980). Street-level bureaucrats can assist constituents as they navigate the bureaucratic morass of eligibility, enrollment, paperwork, and payment. They interpret and adapt national directives to formulate policies that regulate public service access and delivery for registered residents and those who are not registered but are living in their cities. Recipients learn from their routine interactions with service providers and government officials and gain a realistic understanding of how and when, for example, they can use their health insurance in an urban hospital or qualify to apply for public housing. Hospital administrators, doctors, principals, and teachers may be more willing to assist them in accessing urban public hospitals and schools when they have a shared regional identity or co-migrant empathy. In local systems where benefits are individualized, city newcomers can try to squeeze into what openings there are. When formal institutions are unavailable or insufficient, enterprising citizens establish informal substitutes such as "people-run" schools. By using these spaces, migrants are able to blunt elements of political atomization.

Their informality, however, is also a source of precarity and dulls the ability of migrant workers to escape the local state's grip.

PRACTICAL PRIORITIES AND RESOURCEFULNESS

Unmet need alone does not fully explain the existence of social service substitutes. On the other side is the underlying political economy of a marketizing post-socialist public sector and the emergence of opportunistic business ventures. Since the 1980s, health care and education services have undergone market-oriented reforms as part of China's economic transition.[3] Before reform, the finances for public health and public education institutions were highly centralized. The decentralization of funding and fragmentation of provision changed the political economy of the public sector in China and the priorities of service providers, including hospital administrators, doctors, principals, and teachers. For rural migrants, there is an additional level of fragmentation between their rural health insurance providers and urban public hospital caregivers. Out-of-pocket payments for health services as a percentage of annual household consumption has risen since at least 2000 (Long et al. 2013). A fragmented health care delivery system further contributes to inequality. Marginalized migrant workers are seeking services from providers who feel squeezed by financial pressures that advantage wealthier patients. The post-socialist public sector led to more inequality in services but also cracked open some space for frontline providers to exercise discretion in their delivery of services.

Migrant workers have to be pragmatic in claiming citizenship in the city. Most cannot afford to spend much money or time or be overly idealistic in trying to expand their access under urban welfare schemes. Focus on work demands a short timeline for making plans and day-to-day decisions. The more immediately they need health care, education, housing, pensions, and other entitlements, the more time and money they are likely to devote to finding them in the city. When the imperative arises, they are more willing to dedicate resources to finding an urban hospital or school that will accept them and their children. For practical reasons, health care helps them sufficiently heal from an injury or recover from an illness in order to get back to work. Seeking medical care is often reactive, not preventative or proactive. In turn, ensuring that one pays into insurance they can actually use or has it through employment can become an afterthought until their coverage gets tested when they become hurt or sick. Housing is a necessity which is provided to many factory or construction workers, and pensions are desirable but seem out of reach and far in the future. While they covet social protection, attaining it in the city may range from difficult to near impossible. A municipal street sweeper from Anhui Province wearing a powder blue uniform and holding a push broom said that her work provided health insurance she could use in Shanghai, but two children could not accompany her because she could not afford the education fees.[4] Further up the street at an intersection, a husband and wife team from Shandong Province who ran a cart selling food and drinks were informal workers who had no company that could provide them with any kind of insurance.[5] Their six-year-old son and one-year-old daughter were with them during the summer, but the older child would have to return to their hometown to attend elementary school in the fall.

Being resourceful helps migrant workers identify and seize opportunities. Many know generally not to rely on the local government but are glad for opportunities to enter the urban welfare scheme when they can. They often seek to minimize immediate, out-of-pocket expenses unless they are absolutely necessary. It is hard to frontload paying for costs such as high insurance premiums and yearly school fees when they are carefully budgeting their monthly wages (or payment that comes only once per year for those in industries such as construction). They have demands, and they have learned from years of marginalization and individualization that mobilization efforts are rarely rewarded with consistent government responsiveness. Being resourceful comes in handy in these uncertain circumstances where a few can capitalize on, for example, enrolling their children in an urban public school, but most must find other ways to get medical treatment or use other necessary services.

The juxtaposition of their simultaneous need to pounce on openings and feelings of powerlessness was apparent during a day I spent interviewing migrants seeking work in Chengdu. There was no shortage of people willing and interested in speaking with me because they were waiting for new job postings on the bulletin board or for someone to come and hire them. Suddenly, dozens of construction workers surrounded me. They were desperate to tell their stories of wage arrears to someone because neither their company nor the government had been receptive to aiding them in solving their problems. Although they knew I was a student researcher, they hoped I could help them communicate their issues to higher level officials who could intercede on their behalf. They were eager for a sympathetic ear because they had found little traction in getting the backing of local officials to confront the subcontractors who had run off without paying them and help with other issues outside their control.[6] But, later that same day, another woman suggested I was a fellow migrant worker posing as a researcher because she said she could not imagine why someone outside her own community would be invested in listening to her talk about her life as a self-described marginalized person in society. Her skepticism waned after we sat down next to each other on the closest concrete ledge and I earned her trust while interviewing her and other migrant workers around the site.

Rural transplants find and make institutional wiggle room to get some form of social services in the city when they need them. They do this for practical reasons to keep working for the higher wages that drew them to the city in the first place, to deal with pressing problems when they get sick or need a place to send their children to go to school, and to deftly jump on chances to fulfill their needs when they arise. Strategies of survival allow them to find and make services just in time, but they are shaky solutions for a system that, at its core, atomizes them.

WORKING WITHIN EXISTING INSTITUTIONS

One approach is to find institutional leeway and work within existing formal institutions. Newcomers locate a place in the system or someone who can help them navigate the bureaucratic process to get a spot on the school roster for the academic year or to get help with making a payment plan treatment in the hospital. Because a few people are able to avoid being deflected and demobilized, there is at least some flexibility and discretion (even if they are less than expected or optimal) in local systems. Getting paperwork certified, demonstrating eligibility, enrolling family members, and paying still involve interacting with another person at each step of the way. These doctors, teachers, and school and hospital administrators are potential allies in a bid to snag a classroom seat or hospital bed.

Bureaucrats confront the intersection of class and migration status as they make mundane decisions. Low-skilled migrants make up the marginalized class of migrant workers, who some callously characterize as uncultured farmers and country bumpkins. High-skilled, educated migrants comprise a different social class and are not typically called "migrant workers," though many are not originally from the city where they live and work. For native urban residents who discriminate against rural migrants, these two social markers of class and migration status are denotations of second-class citizenship. However, service providers who are themselves high-skilled, educated migrants may not draw such a sharp distinction between themselves and their clients who are low-skilled migrants and sometimes identify with them.

Providers have discretion to exercise in their delivery of public goods and benefits. Doctors and teachers are not only gatekeepers to services, but they also determine the quality of care they provide to different patients and students. Room to maneuver may depend on the sector, available resources, and the bureaucrat's position, but they still have an impact on someone's quality of medical care or education. On top of sometimes using moral judgments in their provision of services (Maynard-Moody and Musheno 2003), many doctors, teachers, and other providers' identities relative to their clients influence their treatment of migrant workers. Their attention enables some migrant workers to access additional services over the baseline, even as other providers restricted others' level and quality of care. This differentiation in service provision to various clients exemplifies the degree to which street-level authorities can sometimes expand or restrict migrant services.[7]

In health care, doctors have discretion over tests, referrals, diagnoses, treatments, and other dimensions of care for patients. From the moment patients enter a hospital, doctors and patients can make various medical decisions that affect the final billed amount. At each step, doctors use their expertise to decide what is medically appropriate, but often interviewees explained there were several options. A patient can begin by choosing traditional Chinese or Western medicine. According to some doctors, traditional Chinese medicine is cheaper per visit and is more suitable for treatment of chronic conditions, whereas Western medicine is more expensive, high-tech, and appropriate for short-term illness or emergency situations.[8] Doctors in one area can also recommend a doctor who practices the other type of medicine. Patients can then see a general physician or someone they think is in the appropriate specialty (e.g., orthopedics for a suspected broken arm), either of whom can refer them to another doctor with a sub-specialty who often charges more money. How each of these physicians tests, diagnoses, and treats patients is not always a single pre-determined outcome based on a checklist of symptoms. Rather, there is some leeway in how thorough an exam is and whether the symptoms or underlying conditions are treated.[9] Many migrants prefer private clinics (see Chapter 6), for which they can afford to pay in cash upfront, compared to receiving more expensive treatment in a top-tier public hospital and where they can obtain dispensed medicine quickly.[10]

School administrators and teachers, too, have some latitude over services they offer. They control the general level and content of their daily curriculum, classroom management, and after-school tutoring. In their daily curriculum, teachers often teach to the top of the class in order to push high achievers toward better grades in standardized tests that are used to measure teacher effectiveness and determine their bonuses and reputations.[11] Therefore, the curriculum closely tracks the local high school and college entrance exams (*zhongkao* and *gaokao*) content with little regard for the students' actual backgrounds, levels, and previous content studied.[12] Likewise, while managing classrooms, teachers can favor certain students and pay particular attention to them by gearing review and answers to questions toward them. This can make a big difference in the educational trajectory of a vulnerable student with fewer opportunities for educational preparation and without extra support outside the classroom.

Using a more selective tactic, teachers can choose to tutor some students after school and not others.[13] These regular tutoring sessions can be the deciding factor in a competitive education system where students contend for limited spots in top high schools and universities. The standardized test system that was supposed to open the playing field for entry to all students regardless of background inculcates a practice in which the majority of students take after-school tutoring to remain competitive with their classmates who are doing the same. Migrant students' parents are less likely to have the disposable income to pay for private tutoring to compensate. Additional help in the aggregate can change the arc of students' education, particularly those from more disadvantaged backgrounds. A clear pattern has emerged in which the best migrant students go to public schools based on the district-level education bureau's assessment of factors such as their parents' age, education, type of permit (long-term or flexible and temporary), labor contract, rental housing, and whether they have registered with the police. Students in the middle of the pack tend to go to private migrant schools, and the worst performing or least desirable do not get to go to school at all.[14] These spaces of discretion are important because the interaction and relationship between migrant clients and service providers can shape the quality of services delivered.

Migrants may encounter bureaucrats who exercise discretion in acts of co-migrant empathy, an original term. Doctors and teachers, who are sojourners themselves and often identify with their migrant patients and students, can opt to give their clients medical care or education services above the bare minimum. The difference is detectable in quality and attention, as noticed and recounted by providers and recipients. They need not necessarily hail from the same village or be part of the same network, separating the effects of those more personal familial relationships and social connections. Often, the same cities that low-skilled migrant workers flock to for the highest wages and best prospects for setting the foundation of a better life for their children are the same cities where highly educated, high-skilled professionals from smaller cities or less developed provinces are also likely to settle with similar hopes and dreams. Many of these local bureaucrats recounted seeing versions of their same struggle and sacrifice in migrant workers. High-skilled and low-skilled migrants face similar restrictions, but the former can buy access to services, procure them through their employers, or change their household registration to the city where they now live and work.

Newcomers may at first stumble into co-migrant empathy that greases the wheels of accessibility before knowing to recognize and possibly look for it. Sympathetic providers feel a sense of affinity, and respondents said "we" are all deserving of health care and education, dissolving the insider–outsider line that sharply divides native urban residents and rural migrants. Migrant workers in Chengdu, for example, can enlist the aid of a GONGO responsible for connecting them with public services in the city. A staff member, who herself is from Sichuan Province but is not a native of Chengdu, described her position as the migrants' advocate in the system. She said, "Migrant workers move around a lot, so it's hard to give them services. By the time I get all the information and resources, the migrant client has moved out of the district."[15] Despite the fact that clients who move away are no longer in her jurisdiction, she took extra efforts beyond her job responsibilities to develop personal relationships with these migrant clients and retain their personal cell phone numbers to follow up and ensure they are able to access urban social services even after they move away. Her organization also worked closely with the district government, allowing her to serve as a crucial link between her clients, service providers, and the local state.

In public hospitals, migrants may find that health care providers who are themselves outsiders better heed these patients' vulnerability. They may, for example, be more willing to squeeze in an additional migrant worker for an appointment or otherwise help them get appropriate care. This is in the context of a system where it is not unusual for people to use their personal networks or give gifts and cash to get a timely appointment or more attentive medical treatment from a doctor in a public hospital. Besides the usual hospital gurneys and waiting chairs, duty-free airport shopping bags packed with bottles of imported whiskey, foreign chocolates, and high-end perfumes and skincare are common sights in hospital halls. A doctor originally from Hubei Province practicing in Beijing said, "The informal system of giving gifts and *hongbao* [red envelopes] to doctors to get better, faster treatment and appointments further disadvantages migrants, who cannot afford to do this."[16] As a fellow outsider to Beijing, she said she tries to compensate for most migrants' inability to offer expensive items or large amounts of cash by noting who is a migrant worker and keeping their place in line for appointments even if they do not have enough money on hand for a deposit when they initially visit the hospital. Migrant patients take note of this latitude and can share this information with others in their factory or construction site who may end up in the same hospital one day. The courtesy and familiarity with their specific spots of vulnerability may seem small, but the cumulative effects for marginalized groups add up over time and make a difference to recipients' livelihoods.

Migrants who meet empathetic doctors can receive care attuned to their needs. These medical practitioners seek to provide additional care on the spot because they fear migrant workers might not have insurance or access to advanced care in the future. A doctor in Shanghai went out of his way to remind his migrant patients that they could "pay a deposit first. If that turns out not to be enough, then they can get an allowance and pay more later."[17] Some of his previous patients assumed they always needed to pay the full bill up front for medical services and therefore avoided seeking treatment until their injury or illness became severe or they had collected enough cash to cover the cost of any contingencies. A smidge of give in the system is valuable to anyone accustomed to being deflected or demobilized.

Doctors with co-migrant sensibilities aim to incorporate migrants' mobile lifestyle into their medical care. For example, in a hospital in Hangzhou, a doctor from Hunan Province advised her migrant patient to borrow the money necessary to undergo surgery at her current hospital rather than at a rural clinic in her home province of Anhui. Because her patient was a migrant worker, she encouraged her to seek care here and offered to speak with hospital administrators about different payment plans.[18] She offered concrete options such as a sharing a three-bed hospital room with others to save money. A deposit would secure this 20 RMB per night (approximately US$3 per night) room, which was a more affordable option than the 600 RMB per night (nearly US$100 per night) room overlooking a famous landmark. Having a provider who offers to assist with deciding and negotiating payment plans and not just prescribing medical procedures helps migrant workers in a time of high stress and need.

Other empathetic practitioners try to fundraise to help their patients pay for procedures. One pediatrician, for example, asked her friends who are businesswomen or sometimes placed ads in newspapers asking for charitable donations for her patients when they could not afford an installment of payment.[19] At her hospital, an overnight stay in the intensive care unit (ICU) cost approximately 5,000 to 10,000 RMB, stays for her migrant children patients often lasted about a week, and it could cost as much as 30,000 RMB per day in the ICU. These costs add up quickly, and she admitted that this was an important part of her individual medical practice. However, not all doctors partook, nor were they expected to, as part of their jobs.

Migrant parents can turn to another group of frontline service providers to enact co-migrant empathy. Teachers may devote more personalized teaching and make a longer commitment to migrant students with whom they identify. Though some native urban residents reported being fearful of going to the countryside or teaching rural students, teachers who were migrants themselves said they were more comfortable in these settings. More importantly, they felt an obligation to extend educational opportunities to migrant students to improve their future prospects of employment and upward socioeconomic mobility. When nominated for a program to work with rural students, some teachers needed to be incentivized with an extra 300 RMB/month (about US$50/month) in salary.[20] In contrast, another participant who was an outsider to Beijing said, "I volunteered on my own. I myself come from the countryside."[21] Principals and teachers reflected on their treatment of these marginalized students.[22] Migrant students who find such teachers receive more support in their educational attainment with possible payoffs for their future opportunities. They can build long-lasting relationships that support the students' education.

Rural students studying in cities may also receive extra tutoring from migrant instructors. Sympathetic educators see themselves as allies of rural students in overcoming the additional obstacles they face as migrants. One teacher said, "College entrance exam problems have increased in the last few years. Teachers need to stay to help students prepare for two years."[23] She felt an obligation to provide extra help to migrant students to study for the important exam, especially as their parents were unlikely to be able to afford the fees for cram schools that are popular among urban residents. Chinese parents spend on average 120,000 RMB per year for six hours of additional tutoring outside school, and some spend as much as 300,000 RMB per year.[24]

While "other teachers often left to develop their own careers in better schools," one teacher who taught in a neighborhood dominated by migrant students said, "I came from a rural school … I am still in touch with them."[25] For teachers who enact co-migrant empathy, they see education as the best opportunity for migrant students to propel themselves into a better life as they themselves were able to become teachers instead of staying on the family farm or joining the factory production line as many of their hometown peers did.

Migrant workers may find that local government officials with whom they share a regional identity make extra efforts to support them. As they explained, the connection lessens the distance between them, and they may be more inclined to attribute different socioeconomic statuses to circumstances and luck and less as a judge of character. A migrant and local bureaucrat may bond over coming from the same province or speaking the same local dialect. A person who worked closely with government officials to connect new migrants with public services said about their shared identity, "In Chengdu, there is no local/insider versus outsider. We are all Sichuanese."[26] Though most of the government bureaucrats I interviewed in Chengdu considered themselves bona fide native residents of the city, many spoke of how their grandparents or friends were migrants from other parts of Sichuan Province. "Chengdu is a different kind of city. It is unlike Beijing or Shenzhen. Chengdu has always had people from the village," said a researcher of urban planning.[27] They see themselves as further along an almost inevitable trajectory of rural migrant to urban resident, which helps create a small institutional opening in service provision.

It helps migrants who are on the receiving end of co-migrant empathy to remain in the same political jurisdiction. Officials are able to make their access to public services more seamless and set up intra-provincial transfers. For example, public hospitals in the city of Chengdu can accept insurance from other cities within Sichuan Province if they establish mutual agreements in advance.[28] Migrant workers find medical care more accessible when they do not have to shuttle back and forth between places to get the highest reimbursement rate possible or weigh up whether to take unpaid leave to seek health care in their hometown. The mindset helps decrease the perceived gap between bureaucrats and migrants. A researcher of public administration said, "Municipal and local-level cadres, as compared to provincial-level cadres, are local people. They have local sentiments."[29] Local systems of public service provision often do not lean in the favor of migrants, but what room for discretion there is creates an opening for officials and service providers to sometimes accommodate them and their particular needs.

MAKING AND USING INFORMAL SUBSTITUTES

Frontline bureaucrats' sympathy is often not enough to overcome systemic individualization. A fruit and vegetable seller from Shandong Province said about public services, "I don't expect to have them, so I don't use them. We don't get any kind of that helpful treatment from the local government."[30] Migrants who still find themselves excluded can turn away from trying to squeeze into public institutions that are unavailable to them and look for other alternatives. Because their jobs and desires to continue earning higher wages in urban areas limit their geographical spread, they cannot simply move back to the countryside for these services without sacrificing other opportunities. To deal with these constraints, they establish and use informal substitutes in lieu of state provisions.[31] Making and using institutional leeway therefore also entails replacing formal benefits, such as urban public schools.

Self-made substitutes, no matter how imperfect or inadequate as complete alternatives, are a point of pride for some. As we visited a migrant school in the Changping District of Beijing, a former migrant worker-turned-activist emphasized, "We prefer the term 'self-managed' [*ziban*, 自办] school. We make them for ourselves. We manage them ourselves."[32] For him and teachers and principals in the school and others like it, calling it "people-run" or private eluded the key feature that these informal institutions served a marginalized group within society. The remade term evinces a sense of survival and independence in an urban environment that fails to provide education for their children or support these alternatives. The number of subway line changes and the black cab ride we needed for the last leg to get there alone represented the distance between the state in the city center and these citizens in the northwestern suburbs of the capital.

Many hospital directors, principals, and administrators in similar positions elsewhere face pressures to prioritize finding new revenue streams over maintaining quality of care.[33] With less state support, the focus on financial viability and emerging market competition results in some hospitals and schools turning away low-income migrants, who cannot afford extra fees. Yet, at the same time, other entrepreneurial administrators see an opportunity to provide private services to migrants through money-making business ventures, filling the gap between too expensive public services and no services at all in the city. At the point of service delivery, these reforms also affect doctors and teachers. Many are underpaid, must find other ways to support their incomes, and learn to exercise what discretion they have in providing services to their clients.

Decentralization of public services and changes in funding structures resulted in unintended consequences. Market-oriented financial reforms led to the overprovision of unnecessary services and the under-provision of socially desirable services, such as the reduction of communicable disease transmission (Liu and Mills 2002, Blumenthal and Hsiao 2005).[34] There is little coordination of care among providers, and health care providers repeat tests unnecessarily or keep patients who should have been transferred (Yip and Hsiao 2009). In response to problems in health care provision, patients and their families have engaged in disruptive or violent behavior (known as health care disturbance, *yinao*, 医闹) toward medical personnel and workplaces (Huang 2021).

After devoting a significant number of years to acquiring medical knowledge and training, many Chinese doctors work long hours and feel they are underpaid. Doctors' low base salaries are set according to a government workers' pay scale. Hospitals can pay bonuses, but few do since they are underfunded. A doctor fresh out of medical school in Beijing makes about the same as a taxi driver, 3,000 RMB (US$490) per month including bonuses (Takada 2013). An experienced doctor at a prestigious first-tier Beijing hospital earns 10,000 RMB per month (US$1,600 per month).[35] As is typical elsewhere, many doctors in one Hangzhou hospital where interviewees were staff worked seven days straight on duty, and they had to remain within five minutes of travel time to the hospital. Unless they were lucky enough to live nearby, they spent much of their time in their offices or hospital sleeping quarters waiting for patients.[36] With little time available for moonlighting in second jobs or private clinics, doctors squeeze out any supplemental income they can while on the job. Like hospital administrators, they contend with fiscal incentives to over-test and over-treat to charge more fees for each additional medical service and prescription. By putting the focus on generating revenue, market-oriented reforms of the public health care sector make high-quality health care less accessible for the mobile population.

Health care is not the only public sector to undergo market-oriented reforms. The education system also met with financial decentralization and the subsequent need to diversify revenue bases.[37] According to a Euromonitor survey, per capita annual disposable income in China rose by 63.3 percent from 2007 to 2012, while consumer expenditure on education jumped by nearly 94 percent (Sharma 2013). Urban households nationwide spent on average 11.9 percent more on education (including culture and recreation) and 11.6 percent more on health care and medical services than the previous year, and rural households spent on average 13.8 percent more on education and 14.6 percent more on health care in 2019 (National Bureau of Statistics of China 2020).[38] And these conditions further disadvantage migrant parents. In a competitive environment where many believe college entrance exam scores can determine a person's entire career and, therefore, life trajectory, they vie for educational advantages for their children. Inadequate resources limit their ability to pursue aspirations for socioeconomic mobility and financial stability for their children through their educational attainment.

In public schools, increased competition in education means that administrators push teachers to raise test scores and outperform other schools. Many teachers earn relatively low incomes and report that they feel education is important and find their work gratifying, but they are frustrated by the emphasis on standardized test scores and lack of opportunities to advance their careers.[39] However, they also encounter professional constraints and requirements that tie promotions and school funding to student test performance. Schools compete for reputations and are ranked according to the previous year's student test performance. A Shanghai public school, for example, receives 20,000 RMB per student per year in funding whereas a migrant school in Minhang District receives about a quarter of that amount, or 5,000 RMB per student per year.[40] Teachers face resource constraints that limit the time and energy they have to distribute among students, which induces them to focus more on local students' and less on migrant students' trajectories. Because migrant students tend to come in with poorer educational backgrounds and are less likely to score highly on standardized tests, teachers concentrate in-class help and after-school tutoring on the students who are more likely to earn higher grades, registered urban residents.

For private schools, high demand for migrant education in the city and low supply open a market for private schools as money-making business ventures. Entrepreneurs make private education available to migrant parents who want their children to go to school (both for the education and for a place to send their children while they go to work) but cannot enroll them in public schools. Wealthy migrant parents, such as one family from Jiangsu Province, pay as much as 400,000 RMB (US$64,000) over three years for their children's schooling in Beijing so that they can test into the country's top schools, Beijing University or Tsinghua University.[41] "Non-resident outsider parents are a source of revenue for principals and education officials ... so it's difficult to reform," said an NGO representative.[42] Principals attract students by allowing migrant children to enroll and charging fees that are lower than those of high-end private schools that are financially out of reach for them. Private migrant schools can charge around 1,000 to 1,500 RMB per semester for each student, depending on the grade level. At a school in Chengdu, elementary school costs 1,300 RMB per semester and middle school cost 1,550 RMB per semester.[43]

Profit-seeking principals take advantage of these opportunities to establish schools. While collecting thousands of dollars in fees from families, they employ low-cost, vulnerable teachers who cannot find work in other schools because of their rural household registration status. It is difficult to hire teachers for these schools and they may be under-qualified, leaving a teacher who did not speak any English, for example, to instruct the English language class.[44] Teachers in migrant schools make 800 to 1,200 RMB/month, five times less than public schools teachers' salaries of 4,000 to 6,000 RMB/month.[45] Though many of these schools' principals have substantially higher standards of living than their teachers and own cars, some teachers are so poor that they must work side jobs to make enough money to cover their basic expenses.[46] Parts of education, like other public sectors in China, have become a business.

Migrant workers are therefore both beneficiaries and victims of China's brand of a socialist market economy. Those who move to the city seek economic prospects, and entrepreneurs make institutional wiggle room and land on a business opportunity. More settled and financially stable migrants can provide these in-between services for those newcomers who typically have not yet laid roots in the city and have shallower pockets. Mutual appreciation of their outsider status engenders sympathy with the others' challenges. Nonetheless, this creativity and resourcefulness belie a deeper structural problem. In describing that formal places were blocked off and informal substitutes functioned precariously, one migrant activist said, "They lost in health care; they also lost in education reform ... It's all money-driven."[47] Private schools and surrogate legal aid clinics therefore do not fully help migrants attain all necessary health care, education, or other kinds of help in order to sustain healthy lives in the city or increase their socioeconomic status. Stand-in institutions remain just that and are insufficient.

DOWNSIDES: DISCRIMINATION AND DEMOLITION

The same spaces of institutional leeway that allow for frontline service providers to exercise their discretion to help migrants can also be used to discriminate against them. Not all administrators are sympathetic to outsiders, and some bureaucrats closely follow procedures that produce atomization and thereby reproduce biased treatment. They may avoid accommodating them based on assumptions about their clients' appearance or spoken dialect. Judging migrants on their appearance, for instance, interviewees said, "you can tell who are migrant workers by their tan skin, ripped or worn clothes, etc."[48] A doctor who routinely treated migrant patients said that teenage "factory workers tend to look young and skinny" compared to their peers living in the city.[49] In the city of Dongguan in Guangdong Province, some residents traveled on roads reportedly segregated between local natives (*bendi*) and outsiders (*waidi*).[50] One downside of small openings in bureaucratic discretion and service provision is that they can work against migrants and have tangible consequences for their well-being. Opportunities for co-migrant empathy and other moments of flexibility that aid city outsiders are liminal and contingent.

Migrant patients may be in the care of public hospital doctors who assume they will not be interested in long-term care or have the ability to come for a follow-up visit. Onsite observations of doctors' differential treatment of patients show how conditional empathy for migrants is. A Beijing doctor criticized, "Migrants' character and morality are unacceptably low. They need more education."[51] Over the course of three hours, two patients entered his office with similar ankle injuries but vastly different appearances. One was a young man dressed in name-brand athletic wear who hopped into the office on one foot with the aid of his friends, one of whom cradled a basketball while the other held his injured friend's shoe. The doctor sat him down, joked about their basketball playing skills, and palled around with the patient's friends. Then he proceeded to slowly examine the patient's foot and ankle, pressing on different areas to assess pain levels and whether the injury was in the bone, tendon, or ligament. Afterwards, he offered to send the patient to have his ankle X-rayed and discussed various options for treatment from resting the ankle to setting it in a hard cast until they settled on an air cast.

Service providers, such as this same doctor, are not always sympathetic to migrant patients' needs and may prematurely foreclose appropriate treatment options. Later that day, another young man hobbled into the room with what looked to be an injured ankle, but he received noticeably different medical treatment from the same doctor. Unlike the first patient, he wore torn, slightly dirty clothes and was accompanied by an older man who was the labor subcontractor who hired him. His companion clutched a stack of cash in his pocket in anticipation of paying for tests and treatment. The doctor asked a few curt questions before suggesting applying ice or heat and staying off his foot for a few weeks. The patient inquired about a cast, but the doctor dismissed it as an expensive procedure that required follow-up care. After the patient left, the doctor turned to me to explain the difference in treatment for the same injury and said succinctly and disparagingly, "You can tell who's a migrant." As was typical of justifications I heard for this differentiated treatment, he couched his advice as being in the best interest of the client and said he was actually doing the patient a favor because he could not afford the pricier options nor comply with follow-up care.

Patients may find what slivers of discretion they have to be closed off by hospital administrators, too. Some urban medical centers are reluctant to treat migrant patients because they believe work-related injury disputes are common to their cases and that the migrants' employers will not pay. Hospital administrators worry about nonpayment when there is a dispute about whether an injury was sustained on or off the job. A doctor at a Beijing hospital said, "If the hospital provides treatment and the patient runs away without paying because they cannot afford it, the hospital has no way of chasing them down."[52] Regardless of their personal stance on the workers' compensation case, health care professionals like him think the battleground should be in the company or local government's office, not in the medical facility. In addition, workers' compensation cases are complicated by the fact that construction and factory workers often live in company trailers or dorms, where it is less clear if injuries in these buildings count as on the job. These administrators would rather forgo beginning intake and treatment for a patient if it seems likely that a protracted battle over payment or fairness may ensue.

Migrant patients also have to be careful to find institutional openings in a way that does not appear disruptive. Besides concerns about nonpayment for services performed, many hospital administrators and doctors thought workers' compensation disputes are troublesome for hospital operation. When an injury could become a worker's compensation case, migrant NGO staff in Guangzhou and Dongguan warned, "Sometimes employers do not want their workers to go to the hospital. And sometimes the hospital, public or private, does not allow legal aid providers to enter the hospital because they are in cahoots with the factory or company to keep migrant patients and compensation disputes out."[53] As a result, these organizations purposely accompany migrant patients to hospitals to ensure they receive treatment and to fend off any possible employer intrusion. As hospitals become the site of contention for NGOs assisting migrants, many hospital administrators and doctors are more likely to perceive some migrant patient cases to be potential nuisances and disturbances to the orderly functioning of the hospital.

The need for migrants to demonstrate orderliness and obedience exists in urban public schools as well. Some principals are loath to admit migrant students, since they assume their families may be unable to pay fees and that they are more likely to drop out within a few years. When offered the chance to participate in a national teacher exchange program, some native urban teachers are reluctant because they perceive the countryside and the people living there to be dangerous, a characterization which they extend to their rural migrant students.[54] Other teachers see migrant children as more likely to have poor study habits and behavioral and truancy problems in the classroom. Some assume migrant parents would be absent from any attempts to work with educators to help their children succeed in school because they are too busy working long hours or are lazy and disinterested.[55] "Parents themselves are not well-educated, so they don't encourage their kids to study in school," said a teacher.[56] Comparing the amount of work needed to monitor an urban student versus a migrant student, another teacher said, "We must tell migrant students when to study, when to rest, etc. We must tell them what to do by the hour in the lead-up to a test."[57] Commenting on what he believed was migrant parents' low character and the difficulty of teaching migrant students, another teacher said, "A significant problem occurs when migrant parents don't pay attention to their kids' education. It's hopeless."[58]

Competition for school rankings encourage urbanite teachers to support urban students over migrant children, and many teachers face pressure from native urban resident parents to keep migrant students out of the school. This is more common in middle school and high school, where competition between schools for high test scores and district rank becomes more intense than in primary school. "Local parents don't want their kids going to school with migrant children. So, if a school starts to accept many migrants, local parents will start to pull their kids from the school. Eventually, that public school has only migrant children," said a scholar–activist focused on education.[59] Since it is common for migrant students to have studied different curricula as they moved between schools, most struggle in their studies. Many public school principals and teachers are anxious that migrant students' grades will bring down the overall average for their schools, which could tank their ratings in comparison to other schools. "Average grades are their only measure of how the school is doing," said a principal justifying the greater attention paid to high-performing urban students.[60]

The college entrance exam further discourages teachers from prying open institutional space. Even when teachers have high-achieving migrant students in their classrooms, they have little incentive to support, tutor, or mentor them. Because exam eligibility is geographically limited for these learners, the system produces a perverse outcome in which the proportion of low-achieving students increases as their cohort of students graduate from middle to high school. The best migrant students tend to return to their home villages, where they are eligible to take the college entrance exam, in hopes they can continue onto higher education. One teacher explained, "If a migrant student's grades are high, parents tend to send them back to their *laojia* [hometown] because their expectations are higher for this child to succeed in school ... Sometimes we [teachers] even suggest to parents of migrant students with higher grades to go back."[61] Regardless of whether migrant children in Shenzhen went to state vocational school, private migrant secondary school, or state high school in the city or attended a rural school, they tended to end up in low-skilled urban service work (Goodburn 2020). Informal substitutes are not necessarily a path toward upward mobility or better career prospects.

Meanwhile, teachers' jobs become harder as the percentage of struggling migrant students in their classroom grows with each passing grade level. "Students with poor grades tend to stay in Beijing, so the average grades of classes drop, and classroom management gets harder each year," said teachers in a public school in Chaoyang District, Beijing.[62] For teachers, this drains their energy and motivation to invest in migrant students since the best of them will likely leave the school district before long. Alluding to a fixed pie of resources to be split between urban residents and migrant workers, a researcher said, "Shanghai's Local People's Congress protects local interests. There is still only free migrant education for primary and middle school because (1) they want to limit college entrance exam opportunities to local residents only and (2) [there are] limited education resources."[63] Due in part to public service system designs, there are doctors and teachers who effectively discriminate against migrant clients when delivering health care and education services.

Approaches of working within existing institutions enable migrants to gain access one by one, but there are shortcomings. Those looking to survive and keep their jobs in the city are able to benefit from high-quality urban public hospitals and education. A patient who gets prenatal care preserves the health of herself and her baby, and a child who finishes primary school can continue on to high school and possibly the college entrance exam. The hitch is in the lack of widespread systemic change. Singular strategies help individuals who are largely powerless, but they fail to help others get the same access in the future. For the fortunate ones, a victory one day does not portend permanent access in the coming years. A small shop owner from another part of Guangdong Province operating in a Guangzhou "urban village" said, "My life isn't stable, and I can't count on government services. My work is temporary. My shop might make enough money next year, so I can't plan to stay long enough to prove long-term residence and pay into social insurance to be eligible for any of the services offered to Guangzhou outsiders."[64] Full social citizenship in the city remains provisional and potentially fleeting.

CONCLUSION

Migrant workers in China have to be practical and resourceful in making and finding institutional wiggle room. Frontline providers who exercise co-migrant empathy and discretion within formal institutions help them sidestep the lack of widespread urban public service provision, enabling workers to keep their jobs when they get sick or bring families to their destinations. Informal alternatives such as makeshift "people-run" schools further fill the gaps on the outskirts of cities, but they remain imperfect substitutes for formal institutions. While subverting control is possible, downsides exist and opportunities for discriminatory treatment can occupy the same liminal spaces. Carving out leeway in formal channels and seeking informal alternatives are precarious ways to secure services and access contingent citizenship.

Filling the holes in urban benefits enables migrants to undermine elements of political atomization. Specifically, members of the floating population dodge being differentiated by making and pursuing their own private substitutes for schools and other services. They take selective distribution at face value by working with bureaucrats to be the beneficiary of what discretion they may have. By finding other ways to organize collectively without making new demands on the state, they do not have to overcome the problem of diluted claims. And they avoid the time-wasting elements of social control via individualization. Dampening of expectations has less teeth when city outsiders do not expect much in the first place, especially in terms of systemic overhaul and complete inclusion.

The effects of deflection and demobilization, too, are less consequential. When they are able to use informal substitutes, phantom services do not force them to move to another district or to another city based on the whims of local government. They can build some consistency and predictability in a lifestyle marked by constant mobility, necessary flexibility, and sudden change. It is possible to live long-term in the city despite restrictions on their becoming full citizens and new forms of second-class citizenship. While they accept piecemeal gains by default, they can try to use them as temporary lifeboats as they await more permanent and larger reforms. Institutional wiggle room essentially helps migrants dodge the trappings of being deflected or demobilized by squeezing into whatever flexibility there is or avoiding the formal system altogether with replacements.

Finding institutional leeway works because of, not despite, the effectiveness of political atomization. Differentiation of migrants continues in effect as people deal with municipal or district bureaucrats only in their specific circumstances instead of tackling systemic change. Selective distribution occurs because the wiggle room is relatively small aside from cases involving highly desired migrants who usually sail through the requirements and do not need to negotiate with administrators. Others' claims are thinner, and their expectations diminish when they fail to pry open additional room. In the end, this approach reinforces the procedures and practices of political atomization by hewing alongside them.

6

Making Do and Muddling Through

"Pay first." Mr. Li hobbled into the emergency room for his intake and consultation, and this was among the doctor's initial instructions. He was a migrant in his fifties from Henan Province who had injured his left foot and ankle. While running with a wooden shoulder yoke and balancing baskets of fruit, he had fallen and twisted his ankle. The doctor advised him to first visit the cashier's office downstairs before getting an X-ray, which cost 109 RMB per scan, and recommended an air cast for now. If any bones were broken, it could be a serious injury and require a lengthy healing process.

He needed surgery, unfortunately, and his story exemplifies how important having readily available cash is for medical emergencies. An initial estimate put the price range from 10,000 to 20,000 RMB, and he had no health insurance, workers' compensation, or any other form of insurance. The injured worker turned to quietly consult his so-called relative (calling him this granted him access to the room), who appeared to be his boss based on their conversation and differences in appearance and clothing. He visibly became increasingly worried about the doctor's orders to come back on Friday for the orthopedic surgeon to give him an exact cost for the surgery. Without enough cash to cover the medical expenses or any form of insurance to offset them, he knew he would likely be forced to manage the pain at home and not return to the hospital for treatment or surgery. His eyes dropped.[1]

A thick stack of 100 RMB bills, snacks to nibble on, and maybe a colorful plastic folding stool for waiting in line to pay were the things migrant workers advised others to bring if they were sick enough to need to go the public hospital. "I have seen patients' families counting out their coins and small change to scrounge up enough money to pay their hospital fees. I see them standing in line," said a doctor describing countless observations of her migrant patients over the course of her career.[2] At the hospitals where I spent the day shadowing medical professionals, a sign for "Pricing Cashier" hung over a wall of glass barriers between cashiers and clients where patients paid for their tests and procedures before anything could be done for their medical care at the hospital. Clutching slips of paper and doctors' referrals detailing their ailment and the treatment, up to around two dozen people stood in a haphazard line snaking through the waiting area and hallway. The majority knew the importance of paying as soon as possible when the cashiers' windows opened and came equipped to make the long wait more comfortable and ensure they would not miss their spot in line. Long before an illness reached that point of severity, most had visited a local "black clinic" (*hei zhensuo*, 黑诊所) to self-treat at home with medicine while they continued to go to work.

Such modes of survival in the city focus on migrants making do to meet their needs rather than solely gaining access to institutions. Unlike the resourcefulness that drives them to find institutional leeway, the pragmatic strategies in this chapter do not necessarily depend on access to formal benefits. From a migrant's perspective, formal institutions and informal substitutes are uneven and therefore not always reliable. The state is only sometimes involved in any administration of services during the process, and some approaches involve evading or at least minimizing state attention and regulation. Migrants find other ways to fill holes in entitlements left by localized service provision and political atomization, and these strategies do not require the luck of encountering frontline service providers exercising co-migrant empathy or offering other sympathetic treatment. But neither are they entirely informal alternatives meant to simply replace formal benefits embodied in urban public schools and social insurance schemes widely accepted by city hospitals. They are different from institutional replications of exclusionary establishments, such as private migrant schools intended to stand in for government-provided education. Opting entirely out of the formal system altogether is among the tactics, despite notions that nearly all migrants are trying to gain and keep access to urban welfare systems. These are key differences between the needs-based approaches identified here and the more service-based ones central to making and using institutional leeway.

The effects of political atomization are therefore muddled. On one hand, individual and group-based efforts to get basic essentials blunt the consequences of social control. Migrant workers who sidestep the formal system and do not come to rely on expectations for shaky benefits can work and live where they want regardless of their unmet demands on the state. But on the other hand, their muted or complete absence of requests to local governments reinforces the system overall. Structural elements of individualization remain intact without overt calls for full citizenship and the requisite systemic overhaul, much less one-off entreaties at the margins for beneficiaries. While registered rural workers can eke out an existence in their urban destinations, the larger edifice of inequality endures.

SCRAPING TOGETHER NEEDS

A spirit of self-reliance underpins migrants' flexible urban existence.[3] When their child is old enough to enroll in primary school, they get sick or injured, or other necessities arise, they react depending on the situation's urgency and their resources. They often pursue whichever option is readily accessible and affordable before escalating to the more expensive solution as a last resort. This may require foregoing the best or most preferred route, such as securing a spot in a government-run school or seeking treatment from a top specialist doctor at a public hospital. For many people, doing what gets them back on the manufacturing line or in the restaurant kitchen for work more quickly trumps chasing comprehensive, long-term benefits that may end up out of reach for them anyway.

Meeting needs differs from attaining social citizenship and full inclusion in the city. Pragmatic decision-making in the day to day lives of rural migrant workers dominates because uncertainty and transience are features of their work lives and urban existence. Changing jobs within the same company, switching factories, or moving to another industry or region of the country is not uncommon. When one is accustomed to being treated as replaceable and therefore disposable labor, timelines for planning livelihoods inevitably shorten. One agent who employed migrant workers said that a nanny who cut her hand while chopping vegetables to cook a meal for a client would not qualify as having suffered an injury on the job. When asked whether the agency provides insurance for workers, she said within her employees' earshot, "If the nanny gets sick, the client can just exchange for a new one."[4] A woman in her thirties from a village in another part of Guangdong Province arrived in the provincial capital three days ago for onboarding and training only to find out that neither the agency nor her client would provide health insurance.[5] Instability creates problems for those seeking permanence, but it is also the possibility of earning more money or finding a better job that propels many to leave their home village in the first place. By stringing together medicine when they fall ill or keeping cash on hand, they retain flexibility that fits their routine compared to the rigidity of localized entitlements that usually cannot be transferred between rural and urban systems and among cities. A robust safety net, except perhaps for subsistence farming on their family's land in the countryside, is lacking whether they sidestep the formal system or experience individualization.

The more that mobile populations employ strategies outside the formal system, the less they depend on the local government. The consequences for the broader relationship between migrant citizens and the state are twofold. For those individuals whose direct experience causes them to opt out of participating in government-provided entitlements altogether, they make fewer requests and cause less hassle for municipal and district officials charged with incorporating them. Even the scrappiest newcomers may give up on pursuing benefits from a system that appears on the surface to be opening up but largely excludes them in new ways instead. "Other public services? What other government services? I don't expect to have them, so I don't use them. We don't get any kind of that helpful treatment from the local government," said a fruit and vegetable seller.[6] The flipside of this decreased burden of migrant expectations is that their reliance on the state corrodes over time. This weakens the entire group's demands for structural change and eventual inclusion, but it simultaneously curtails the reach of the state into this already amorphous group and makes social control of the floating population less effective.

There are two main categories of ways in which Chinese migrant workers scrape together their needs. One is a largely individual-focused responsibility of covering essentials. This may help them fend off more costly use of social services, both in terms of money and time. Going to black clinics for expedient medical treatment, for example, enables them to continue working without worrying about insurance reimbursements and unaffordable out-of-pocket costs for hospital admission. The government may shut down clinics out of safety or other concerns, so this method of minimal health preservation is efficient but precarious. Visiting clinics that are unregulated and taking medicines they dispense can be dangerous to patients' well-being and generate their own prolonged medical problems as well.

A second category is composed of community-based solutions, wherein groups of city outsiders band together to meet their needs. Some are impromptu while others are more planned in anticipation of potential problems to come. The arrangements themselves are distinctly informal, though they may at times interact with formal institutions. Construction workers from the same village who share a dorm room next to their build site, for instance, may agree ahead of time to have a certain amount of cash on hand to contribute whenever a medical emergency arises among one person in the group. Improvisations like these conform to the lifestyles of mobile groups of people, but they are as limited in scope as they are creative.

The small scale keeps these solutions flexible and convenient. Their feasibility depends on the voluntary participation of members of a group who must be physically nearby and available to join. Accountability rests on their familiarity and trust with one another and the realization that they can rely on each other when times are hard and they are far from much of their immediate family and hometown friends. Because they are user-friendly with reasonable contributions and fast turnaround when an emergency comes up, they work well for people for whom unforeseen circumstances can upend their work schedules. They can turn to their bunkmate for cash instead of risk their employer firing them for taking time off to file paperwork for eligibility, shuttle between government offices to jump through bureaucratic hoops, or take a trip to the countryside to use their rural insurance. Paying into a system for which pensions are not transferrable between different regions can become less of a concern. And so can the thorny issue of making contributions into entitlements that seem to never come to fruition as migrants are deflected or demobilized at each turn.

The ephemeral nature of community problem solving is double-edged. Accessibility and immediacy are hard to beat, matching migrants' year to year timelines for work and mobility. If they leave their job, they take their resources with them with little concern for unused benefits. Not paying into government social insurance schemes frees up their disposable income. Having fungible cash reserves in their pockets builds in an elasticity to their ability to respond to unexpected emergencies at work or home. The shared lived experiences of those participating in group-based schemes adds a social element of understanding to what is essential in the moment. And yet because these arrangements are short-lived, they cannot provide long-term protection, a lasting sense of security, or transferrable help. In the direst emergencies, pooled resources among community members may not be enough to cover the costs of long-term hospital stays or months and years of recovery and rehabilitation. Nor do they encourage preventative care or other approaches that would support their sustained well-being over time.[7] Despite these limitations, they are helpful cushions for those caught in the space between alleged eligibility and actual access or those shut out altogether.

Combining individual and community means to meet demands gives migrants agency. They grant some autonomy back to workers whose choice is often discounted in the accounts of them as completely vulnerable second-class citizens or of them as beneficiaries of the country's economic growth rate and supposedly extensive *hukou* reform. Piecing together these techniques does not require waiting for structural reforms. They need not negotiate with frontline service providers to get forms verified, pull numbers to get a place in line for enrolling their children in school, or compare complicated insurance reimbursement rates for medical procedures across county and provincial borders. Saving time and increasing cash reserves are benefits themselves for registered rural residents working in cities.

IMPROVISING BY THEMSELVES

The first way of meeting needs focuses on individual problem solving instead of seeking substitutes for formal urban institutions. The public system, for the most part, does not accommodate mobility or take into account the multiple moves that many migrants make throughout their lifetimes. A State Council white paper on China's public health as a human right simply stated, "An increasing number of the floating population now have better access to basic public health services" (State Council 2017). The Healthy China Action Plan (2019–2030) emphasizes supply-side reform in health care services (National Health Commission of the People's Republic of China 2019), but it still promotes the residency-based urban and rural medical insurance system that does not serve much of the mobile population's needs.[8] Transience is a defining characteristic, and their impermanence, whether it be after a couple of months or several consecutive years, in a city makes it difficult to pay into a localized system and then reap benefits from their contributions. Without flexible or easily transferred benefits that follow their journeys crisscrossing a province or the country, they may be left empty-handed when they arrive at each new location. The place-based patchwork system, moreover, means that every job relocation requires having to figure out new sets of entitlement schemes, eligibility and documentation rules, and informal replacements. For many, the hassle of keeping up eventually outweighs any small chance of receiving benefits. Some migrants do not feel a sense of entitlement in the first place, because they have experienced being deflected or demobilized one too many times or they understand the reality of degrees of second-class citizenship. They therefore default to relying on themselves instead of the seemingly fickle formal system.

One common strategy exemplifying this approach is to use illegal private clinics for health care. For workers who put in long days and fastidiously save their wages for remittances, private clinics are affordable and convenient. A clinic visit can cost approximately 50 RMB, compared to 1,000 to 2,000 RMB for a hospital visit.[9] Many have flexible and late-night hours that suit the schedules of those working during the day, and some even allow migrants to buy on credit. Concentrated in predominantly migrant neighborhoods, they are usually in accessible locations and do not have lines. And they save migrant workers a long trip home to go to the village clinic, township health center, or county hospital, even if their rural health insurance might cover part of their visit.[10] Most are reluctant to seek any medical attention at all and only visit clinics after waiting and realizing that the ailment will not resolve itself. "When you don't have insurance, you hope it's not serious and go to the clinic or pharmacy," said a migrant worker in Chengdu who worked three hours away from her home village.[11] If they self-diagnose their illness as minor, what rural transplants describe as "being a little sick," they hope a quick trip to the clinic that results in them leaving with medication in hand that they can administer themselves in their shared apartment or dorm suffices.

Speedy trips to private clinics are a convenient option for those in the informal economy. Self-employed dumpling sellers, fruit and vegetable vendors, and others do not have a labor contract that can show proof of employment to meet eligibility requirements for government services. One migrant in her forties said, as commonly uttered by others, "I don't have social insurance or any other kind of insurance. I've never had any of these social protections or services ... I am just looking to find a job doing some housework."[12] Few have any expectation of ever getting health insurance because "past employers have never bought any of kind of insurance for [them]. Not health insurance, work-related injury, pension, etc."[13] Even for older migrants who might be facing more medical problems in the near future, health care means treating common colds, abrasions, or sore muscles rather than seeking primary care or addressing chronic injuries or illness. Years of working as, for example, temporary construction workers or independent housekeepers for various households have reinforced a habit of cobbling together health care from clinics since they assume they will never have insurance coverage.[14] Despite the lower quality of medical care and possibly dangerous conditions, most migrants still frequent these clinics.

Seeking treatment at illegal clinics is expedient but may not be safe or dependable.[15] Facilities can be hidden down alleyways, range from a single room to a table set up outside, and are often not staffed by licensed doctors or medical professionals. "If a clinic has government certification, then some insurance companies will accept the receipts. However, the rules and standards for getting certified are tough to achieve. Not many private clinics meet these standards," said a doctor at a hospital in Shanghai.[16] During a crackdown on illegal clinics in Harbin, Heilongjiang Province, officials found clinicians operating without a license, using expired pharmaceutical drugs, and generally in unsanitary conditions (Health Commission of Heilongjiang Province 2015, People's Daily 2015). Furthermore, they reported that garbage and drugs were being stored in the same place and that disposable medical devices were being repeatedly reused between different patients. The National Health and Family Planning Commission announced that they cleaned up 6,626 black clinics one year (National Health and Family Planning Commission of the People's Republic of China 2013). According to government figures, the Beijing government shut down approximately 1,000 black clinics per year between 2010 and 2013.[17] The Beijing Municipal Health and Family Planning Commission cracked down again on these clinics in another strike-hard campaign (Xinhua News 2015). Unregulated clinics dispensing counterfeit drugs is a potential problem as well, but demolition of closed sites leave migrants with no other alternatives.[18] After publicized campaigns against black clinics, clinics that were shut down usually reopen nearby as there continues to be a market for their services.[19]

The decision to visit private clinics in itself limits the kinds of treatments patients may receive. By their nature, one-room establishments of this sort usually offer therapies such as pills or intravenous fluids. They do not have the capacity to prepare a patient for emergency surgery, run a magnetic resonance imaging scan or other diagnostic tests, or refer someone to an in-house specialist. Owing to related cost concerns, migrants may turn to cheaper traditional Chinese medicine instead of more expensive Western medicine when they have health problems. Herbs, pills, and other traditional Chinese medicine typically cost less than extensive contemporary medical tests, procedures, and surgery.[20]

Relying on clinics may not only have consequences for their wallets but also their health and wellness in the long run.

If such clinics are their first stop, visiting the public hospital is their last resort in the city. Usually, only in cases of emergency do they take this potentially expensive trip that could require an unaffordable cash deposit and overnight stays that would peel them away from the construction site or factory floor. Many migrants know that hospital bills can be astronomical and avoid hospital care altogether, even to seek preventative care or check for an early diagnosis and prognosis that could stave off more expensive care that may be required to treat a progressed illness or chronic injury. A fruit and vegetable seller from Shandong Province working in Beijing for more than ten years in various forms of informal employment said, "You have to have the Beijing-issued insurance card. Without the card, you can't access anything. When I get sick, I pay out of pocket to go to the hospital here. I gather a bunch of cash before I go, because I know I'll need to pay myself. I don't have the Beijing insurance card."[21] Calculating whether they can afford out-of-pocket costs is crucial to their health care decision-making.

Finances are important but they are not their only concern. For registered rural residents, the option to return to their home village for medical care is a possibility. The time they need, however, to take off work in order to hop on trains and buses home traversing the country may force them to forego wages and possibly lose their jobs if their employer deems the leave too long. "If I get a little sick, I rest at home. If I get very sick and must go to the hospital, I bring several thousands of RMB in cash to pay," said a migrant who worked in construction in Guangzhou and Beijing. He continued, "Since I can only use my rural health insurance in my home county, I save cash for emergencies in the city so I do not have to request time off work and possibly lose my job."[22] An informally employed migrant worker said, "It's so much money. And here in Beijing, every day you have to pull a number and wait ... One visit is never enough. It takes at least a few days to resolve anything, but I don't have time to return to my hometown. There's no one available to look after my fruit and vegetable stall if I leave."[23] So, migrants frequent these clinics as go-to points of medical care and not merely temporary bridges until they can get more advanced care at the public hospital.

There is a need for private alternatives in other areas, including legal aid. Local entrepreneurs, who may be migrants themselves, step in to create these replacements and keep them running. Their quality is often subpar compared to urban public versions but they are better than nothing.

And prices are set accordingly; migrants pay him 500 RMB instead of 3,000 RMB to a lawyer. The explicit goal, as one person running a more informal legal aid clinic said, is to offer something between zilch and unaffordable, inaccessible formal institutions.[24] He himself was not a trained or certified lawyer and insisted that his wealth of experience and reading up of policies and previous legal cases could provide a leg up for his clients who otherwise had no time or resources to gather the received knowledge themselves. Justifying his work, he said his clients could never afford the fees of a lawyer and were grateful for services from someone who only charged several hundred *kuai* (块) and, further, understood their plight as another sojourner from a different province himself. Word of mouth often brought them to his doorstep, or cell phone number and website as it were, and his makeshift services stood in contrast to the establishments he was trying to approximate. Professionalized legal aid centers offer printed booklets and training for their migrant clients, and they have staff with deep knowledge of the laws and experience with advocacy.[25] Yet there continues to be demand for informal surrogates for these legal advice services.

A second personal strategy involves straddling the rural–urban line and is separate from using health clinics for self treatment. Individuals improvise by strategizing to work in a city that is closer to their home village so they may access rural services if it becomes necessary. A manager who employed forty-four migrants out of fifty-six total workers confirmed, "Many migrants from Sichuan who work in the provincial capital Chengdu try to keep and use their rural health insurance by not venturing too far away … Workers do not have to go as far as Beijing or Guangzhou. They can just stay closer to home."[26] Economic development is no longer as concentrated on coastal areas of China, making it possible for more people to move within their home provinces or at least stay closer to them. Demand for and contention over public services are still concentrated in mega-cities where higher wages and social networks continue to dominate incentives to move, but local migration is growing. By retaining their participation in more affordable rural insurance schemes and working within reasonable traveling distance to those public benefits to which they have access, these migrants try to reap the wealth of city jobs and retain the safety net of the countryside. They can also worry less about transferability and ever changing, localized eligibility requirements decided by each municipality.

Other workers stay within a one- or two-hour-long bus ride of their hometowns. By working in a city close to their home village, they can go home for medical care on their day off from work without having to take unpaid leave and risk losing their jobs. Other migrant workers with families who bring their children to the city can live and work in the furthest outskirts of the city, where they can be within commuting distance of a rural school.[27] A teacher who was a migrant herself transferred jobs and moved schools to live closer to her hometown outside Beijing where her family was covered by insurance, said, "I moved because I wanted to be closer to my child since he was sick."[28] A community NGO staff member describing these migrants who worked near their home villages said, "They are all close to their hometown, so if there's an issue, they can talk to the boss and go home if someone's injured in the family, etc. There are two kinds of migrants: the first who go far away from home. The second stay near their home [and] go home frequently."[29] Migrants staying within shorter travel time to their village is consistent with the trend of more intraregional and local movement.

Working closer to their hometown is a small but personally significant way for them to push back on the forced distance of moving for work. Previous generations often left their children in the care of grandparents in hollowed out villages, and this is a way to buck that norm.[30] Nor do they have to chance being left out of urban public schools year to year or counting on private migrant schools that may not be certified or high quality. Rebuilding and keeping these family ties that they know to be tenuous based on their parents' experiences are a valuable way of hanging on to a bit of agency in a process that, while profitable, can be dehumanizing and come with high personal costs. Although, for example, the second generation of migrants has higher demands, "they only have two choices: stay in jobs where they are treated poorly or quit and rely on their parents until they get married."[31] Having some choice, if limited, is empowering for vulnerable people who are subject to political and economic structures that continually shut them out.

Besides catering their work location to be closer to their hometown, migrant workers can try to pinpoint services that are closer to where they work. A trend has emerged since at least the mid-2010s in which parents send their children to boarding schools in townships close to the outer edges of the cities where their jobs are. Parents working in Shanghai, for instance, enroll their children in boarding schools in nearby Anhui or Zhejiang Provinces, and their children commute into and out of the city or board at the school during the week and visit their parents in the city on the weekend.[32] These schools are a viable solution for migrant families because they are neither public schools in Shanghai nor ones in their rural hometown. During more extended breaks, they can bring their children for a visit into the city itself and enjoy some semblance of life together as a family unit. Those who put their children in the care of grandparents in their home village must wait until Lunar New Year to reunite with their families for their one chance each year. Boarding schools in townships provide a halfway point option when migrant students are deflected or excluded from public schools in the city.

A third individual strategy for meeting needs is to selectively opt into and out of schemes. The fragmented nature of public services usually disadvantages people with mobile livelihoods, but migrant workers sometimes take advantage of it to finetune the trade-offs between having access to benefits and cash on hand. Many migrant workers are inclined to only buy workers' compensation out of the five kinds of social insurance available. By doing so, they can avoid paying into schemes for other kinds of insurance that they will likely not be able to use when they move to another city for their next job. According to an annual report on migrant workers compiled by the National Bureau of Statistics, approximately 26 percent of migrant workers had work-related injury insurance, whereas only about 18 percent had medical insurance in 2014 (National Bureau of Statistics of China 2015a). With an increase of 0.98 million over the previous year, this amounted to 73.6 million migrant workers who had work-related injury insurance in 2014 (National Bureau of Statistics of China 2015b). There has been a consistent gap between coverage for work accident insurance and medical insurance coverage since at least 2008.[33] Often, migrants who have this kind of insurance have employers who routinely pay for it or can be convinced to take on the expense. "I had work injury-related insurance before through my company, but I don't anymore. I do not plan to buy any on my own, either in the countryside or in the city," said a migrant worker about the advantage of workers' compensation being paid by her boss when she worked at a factory.[34]

For those workers whose employers do not provide insurance, they can purchase bare-bones catastrophic coverage with financial assistance from the company. Although some are barred from participating in urban insurance, others can buy workers' compensation, especially since an injury on the job in the city that requires emergency care is likely serious and expensive to treat. A factory worker in Chengdu from another part of Sichuan Province who made about 1,000 to 1,500 RMB per month including several hundred for overtime work said, "I decided to buy insurance for myself, although it's voluntary and not required by anyone. I pay about 50 RMB per month, and I think my company puts in another

100 RMB per month ... I must go to a pre-determined hospital in this district that works with my insurance company."[35] A study in Wuhan found migrant workers were willing to pay about 30 to 51 RMB per month for basic health insurance, especially if it protected against substantial financial losses due to the need for catastrophic care (Bärnighausen et al. 2007). They prefer insurance coverage for costly worst case medical issues that require advanced care at urban public hospitals.

Migrant workers also get access to insurance through their employers by negotiating insurance, housing, and food costs separately from wages. In construction and factory jobs where workers live in dormitories on site, employers often quote payment amounts that bundle all of these together. "There are many misleading or false ads. For example, I saw an ad that said wages were 3,000 to 5,000 [RMB] per month. In reality, they deducted 2,000 for housing, 10 per meal, etc. In the end, your total wage would only be about 1,000 per month ... Now I know to check and negotiate," said a construction worker in Chengdu.[36] By discussing deductions for benefits such as insurance separately, workers can choose to pay only for workers' compensation or decline location-dependent insurance from the company and earn higher wages which they can put toward other services or expenses.

If companies are unwilling or unable to provide insurance or pay for medical care, vocational schools provide insurance while their students and recent graduates work in factories. A group of workers I met at a factory were not allowed to buy insurance from the large multinational company for whom they worked but were able to have their old school purchase it for them.[37] Although they were working full time, the company called them "interns" instead of employees so they would not have to provide benefits. Many complained about the company's buck-passing for insurance coverage, but one intern agreed with the company line that put her in a separate category from other migrant workers even though she was a non-local who performed the same tasks on the same production line and had the same vulnerabilities in terms of public benefits as them. She said, "I am not a common worker. I am not an ordinary migrant worker like those others who work on the factory line."[38] Other researchers found similar practices being used at Foxconn factories, where they cut labor costs by employing student workers at sub-minimum wages and without having to pay into government-run insurance schemes for them (Pun and Chan 2012). Minimal coverage from vocational schools is better than none at all.

The spirit of resourcefulness evident in these individuals making do by themselves shows migrant adaptability. During fieldwork, respondents were eager to glean information from others' experiences through our conversations. They were curious to learn how their peers in different industries or other cities were meeting their needs, which helped them piece together emerging gradations of second-class citizenship. (Government officials, too, in their interviews with me pondered borrowing ideas from other cities facing similar challenges and constraints as them.) Others I interviewed, such as a group of construction workers in Chengdu, hoped I could be a conduit for their concerns to those in power, even after I explained my role as a researcher. Migrant parents organizing a protest over college examination restrictions for their children in Beijing worried about outsiders potentially disrupting their meetings. As adaptable as they were being, these moments of resourcefulness also signify their untenable position and the difficulty of overcoming structural barriers as individuals.

IMPROVISING WITHIN COMMUNITIES

Migrant communities help make up for their members' lack of political power and status. They can improvise group-based solutions to cobble together their needs in municipalities which deflect and demobilize them away from the urban public entitlements scheme. In contrast to institutional pathways, community solutions tend to be small scale, self-designed, and sometimes impromptu. Ten construction workers who share a company dorm room may participate, or outsiders hailing from the same village and working in the same city may band together. Because many migrants share apartments or dorms to save money, some store emergency cash with the labor subcontractors for whom they work. Subcontractors handle their wages anyway, and a level of dependence is part of that relationship. A cluster of sojourners can do the same within their migrant neighborhood on the urban edges where they sleep at night and rest on the weekends away from the central business district where they work during the day. Rural migrant men who worked as porters in Chongqing have created their own cooperative labor groups (Zhang 2020). Need sparks ingenuity to come up with a way to solve whatever problem is at hand, such as a member's sudden illness. Informal agreements may last months or years depending on how long the group stays in the same physical proximity.

The first step toward relying on group-based solutions may be exiting from public welfare as a strategy. Opting out of the formal system allows them to avoid paying into social insurance schemes that they perceive to not serve them. They may negotiate with employers to forego these payments to garner higher wages or other benefits they prefer. Construction workers from Henan, Sichuan, and other provinces working in Chengdu complained about the unclear accounting of deductions from their monthly wages and were often unsure whether they could ever benefit from supposed monthly deductions for insurance and other living expenses.[39] Because they lived on the construction site in dorms provided by the company, they had few options unless they could manage to negotiate wages separate from these costs up front when they were hired. A number of workers in the informal economy and other migrants I met did not bother to register with the local police or apply for official temporary residence permits.

Much-hailed household registration system reforms likewise may not be as anticipated or tempting as previously thought. While collecting ethnographic observations and interviewing migrant workers at an open air labor market in Chengdu, I noticed a bulletin board near a municipal government official's outpost. Dozens of paper job ads with employers' cell phone numbers were posted over a splashy announcement of new local *hukou* system policies for those interested in changing their household registration. I only observed one person, out of hundreds who passed through the area over the course of that entire day, lift the work posts to read the full copy of the text and learn about land-related requirements and other details. A number of rural residents do not want to change their household registration because they would have to give up their (possibly valuable) land that also provides a safety net; though migrant waves have risen, they do not have guaranteed job stability and live in urban precarity, especially without transferrable government services.[40] Such choices run counter to the common perception that all migrants are trying to enter the urban entitlements system and, more to the point, that incorporation into public services alone would draw too many rural workers into cities. Migrant workers navigating a largely immobile, localized public service provision system seek what choices they do have to meet their needs.

Some small- and medium-sized factory owners agree with these workers' solutions. Giving out discretionary payouts for medical visits can be in their interest, and they say they cannot afford to pay for insurance because of already low profit margins and increasing demands for higher wages. "We do not offer health insurance to our workers. The company cannot afford social insurance for every worker. When they have a minor illness, the workers take pills or go to the local clinic. When they are seriously ill, they can go to their hometowns and use their rural health insurance," said a factory–government liaison for a factory in the city of Dongguan in Guangdong Province.[41] An official labor representative in Chengdu explained the practice in more detail, "Often, businesses make a 'deal' of sorts: The company will deduct 100 RMB per month from wages to buy insurance, or the more popular choice is to give them [migrant workers] 500 to 600 RMB when they actually get sick or injured toward paying bills."[42] It was a popular win–win choice, because companies save on labor costs and migrant workers earn higher net wages while keeping a source of funding for dire medical problems.

Storing cash that is convenient to access is a popular strategy. In addition to medical expenses, non-medical costs, such as for caregivers, travel, food, and family members' accommodation can also result in catastrophic health payments and health payment-induced poverty (Yang 2020). Money (in the form of cash or the equivalent in mobile payment accounts) is more useful than vague promises of institutional access. Immediate enrollment of children in school or high reimbursement rates for urban public hospital use are desirable if they are widely available and attainable, but the reality of supposed incremental institutional change has little meaning for someone who has a chronic health condition or medical emergency that requires immediate attention. Nor is it practicable for the parent whose child is of age to enter elementary school but cannot begin and who must suddenly find care for the hours they are working. While they could keep cash on hand just for themselves, many find other ways to fund backup plans and pool resources for safekeeping.

Migrants already work for subcontractors, rely on them for cash flow, and often sleep in the next bed over or bunk above in the same dorm room as them, so they can function as depositories of makeshift health savings accounts for their workers in the city. In the construction industry, the hierarchal layers go from workers at the bottom to the "small" subcontractor, "middle" subcontractor, "big" subcontractor, and finally the company.[43] Because the workers often follow subcontractors and headhunters from their village to city, "trust matters a lot for getting work."[44] State-owned construction companies function similarly to private industry; pay goes from the company to subcontractors, not directly to workers.[45] Moreover, subcontractors usually only pay their workers once a year, just before Lunar New Year or when the project is finished. When I spent the day celebrating Mid-Autumn Festival at a construction site, it was the labor subcontractor who let his workers off early and gave everyone a bonus for the holiday.[46]

Informal insurance groups are another self-run community scheme to meet members' needs. They provide a pool of readily available cash for participants who require going to a hospital for serious medical care instead of winging treatment at a clinic. A construction worker in Chengdu said, "No company has ever bought me any kind of insurance ... The company does not care. They don't ever buy coverage for workers' compensation."[47] Instead, he pools risk with other workers from his home village. Everyone in the group keeps some cash on hand or with the labor subcontractor who serves as the group leader, but each person's money alone will not suffice to pay for an emergency hospital visit. A member of the group who needs to go to the public hospital can then collect from everyone and will then have enough money to bring with them to cover various medical contingencies and procedures.

A sense of community permeates the arrangement between group members. With dampened expectations from having been individualized, informal insurance structures provide a modicum of relief that they are not alone and unprotected in the city. Ties based on shared hometowns or work positions are sufficient for understanding peers' predicaments when they require emergency health care. A doctor in Shanghai described the strategy from his point of view, "Most migrant patients borrow money first from friends and family before going to the hospital. Once they've collected enough cash, then they go see the doctor."[48] Others rely on their informal insurance groups and similar regional networks within the city when they seek to change industries or jobs but stay in the same municipality. Workers, for example, can move from hammering and sawing on construction sites to manufacturing shoes or metal pans and bowls in factories through their communities.[49] In positions where they are vulnerable to market forces as laborers and state control as members of a marginalized population, their ability to rely on others is invaluable. And the willingness to contribute to another person's welfare and protection has its own self-perceived benefits, too.

But informal insurance does not always work well. Many households in low-income countries deal with economic hardship by participating in informal insurance within their communities rather than through public or market-provided insurance schemes, but the arrangements are often weak because of idiosyncratic risks and lack of enforcement for reciprocity (Morduch 1999). Sometimes migrants pay back their group members when they can, but other times they do not or instead pay it forward to the next member with a medical emergency. According to the migrants participating in them, these groups are relatively informal but provide some relief when they cannot afford to keep a large stash of money aside in case they have a medical emergency and do not want to be forced to return to their hometown to get care. They thus create a version of insurance outside the government-sponsored social insurance schemes.

Other approaches skirt the bounds of rules and regulations or are illegal, such as by sharing social insurance cards. One migrant explained, "You can lend your card to a friend. Hospitals are happy to take any card because they can make money off patients."[50] A Chinese researcher confirmed the prevalence and success of this strategy, "If they don't have rural insurance, they can borrow their family or friend's cards … A few clinics can even accept insurance cards."[51] Migrants who had passed off friends' cards as their own were open about the practice, claiming that it was a small pushback on a system that excluded them. According to them, the doctors who treated them did not check too closely or turned the other way as long as someone paid for the services. "It's not that hospitals care whether you have insurance. They only care if you can pay. To protect against non-payment, they require a cash deposit. If you can't pay the deposit and you're not about to die, even if it's very serious, the hospital will not accept you."[52] Card sharing serves as proof the migrant patient could pay and therefore get treatment in the public hospital. As a migrant worker quipped to me, if the state treated them as indistinguishable members of a marginalized social group, then they could all share one face, meaning one insurance card. In effect, migrant workers converted their societal anonymity and status as outsiders into an ill-gotten benefit.

However, insurance companies are becoming more aware of card sharing and have begun to track use more vigilantly. "This is a problem – cheating and getting around the system. Some companies buy work-related injury insurance for one person. Then a bunch of workers use the same insurance card," said a senior doctor at a hospital in Beijing.[53] Complaining about the spread of the practice, he continued, "Hospitals and doctors should check identity cards more carefully for their name and especially their picture. Insurance companies check more strictly." Inside a fragmented system with imperfect coordination between public insurance, hospitals, and the administrators of government-issued cards, these migrants break the rules to share insurance cards and reduce costs.

Insurance cards can be shared for health care, but acquiring access to public education without the proper documentation requires a different strategy. Some migrants purchase fake papers to try to meet the burdensome documentation requirements for enrolling their children in public school in many cities. "Documents are so important that fake certificates and packages of certificates are available for purchase," said a Chinese scholar–activist who knew migrant parents who had purchased and used them.[54] Fake identification cards, diplomas, certificates, and licenses are readily available for purchase, and migrants use them to enter the urban labor market (Wu 2010). Not only are fake papers available, but sellers even bundle them into convenient packages that fit the documentation requirement, such as the "five documents" needed for public school enrollment in Beijing. It is easy to identify the cheapest fake documents as counterfeit, and the all-inclusive, more believable packages of papers are more expensive and therefore less affordable to the migrants most desperate for them.[55]

Community solutions are designed by and for migrant workers. They tailor them to their means and resources available to them to scrape together needs. Because they are often short-lived, they fit their mobile lifestyles insofar that they do not have to make irreversible commitments to contribute. Their participation grows out of a shared struggle and accessible solution that is among their dorm mates, within their own neighborhoods, or through their social networks. Informal improvisations do not tie them to a place in case they change jobs or relocate to another city. A migrant who owned a small shop in Guangzhou had bought insurance for a few years in the past but she was never able to use it, so it went to waste according to her.[56] As prices for her rural insurance rose from 15 to 20 RMB per year to 80 RMB per year, it seemed less worth it to her. The lesson she learned was not to pay fees for an inflexible program that does not suit her lifestyle, though she said she would reconsider it if it were more customizable. Informal insurance, by contrast, provides migrants like her with cash on the spot when an emergency arises and does not dictate that she return to her hometown for treatment.

Migrants can cooperate privately yet experience political atomization. The key difference is in migrant individualization vis-à-vis the state specifically, as qualified by "political" in the term. While different forms of cooperation could be seen as similarly situated, political atomization stymies mobilization against the state but does not go so far as to eliminate all collaborative behavior among people who work together and live in migrant communities. The degree of hyper-differentiation by local officials in practice does not typically align with how migrants perceive themselves and their communities. A sojourner from the Inner Mongolia region might be likely to identify more with another person from there than someone from Fujian Province, but they are unlikely to sort their community members by housing lease or proof of employment contract (which the state does). The concomitant selective distribution of benefits by the state and resulting dampening of expectations plus dilution of claims are parts of the atomization process that do not inhibit private cooperation. Collective claims against the state and collective class consciousness are undermined, while person to person connections within neighborhoods and other communities remain intact. By banding together to meet needs and fill gaps, they may actually somewhat relieve the state's burden to provide health care, education, and other services to them.

A major downside of informal group schemes is the lack of an institutional safety net. They cannot disperse risk in the way that larger and more formal insurance arrangements can nor can they can guarantee adequate resources. Workers who live together on a construction site face similar injuries and illness may spread through the group through their close physical proximity, and the same applies to neighbors who congregate together in shared apartments. The group, moreover, cannot handle simultaneous emergencies that affect everyone participating or that are beyond the scope of an initial cash deposit. Continuing treatment for a chronic condition, for example, would overextend the group's shared stash of money. Still, they can help cover a visit to the hospital for an immediate emergency.

Nor do they solve recurring problems. Educational access, unlike emergency medical care, is an ongoing issue as students grow older. In one migrant family from Shandong Province working in Beijing, the mother sold vegetables during the daytime while her husband sold them at night to ensure there would always be someone available to watch their children since they could not attend school. She said, "I have lived in Beijing as a vegetable seller for ten years and have gone without health insurance ... Only people with a state-owned enterprise work unit have it ... I brought my kids to Beijing to watch them."[57] And parents hope not only to enroll their children in primary school but also set them up for a chance at higher education. "My child cannot go to school in Beijing, despite the new policies that say they can go to public school ... Going to a small, not famous college in China is the same as working temporary jobs now. So you might as well not go to college if it's not *Qinghua* or *Beida*. Work experience is more important any way for migrant workers today," said a migrant worker frustrated with the exclusion from public services.[58] Migrants making do within communities are able to cobble together resources to meet some members' needs but not everyone's.

UNDERMINING OR REINFORCING POLITICAL ATOMIZATION?

Political atomization can increase migrant reliance on making do by themselves or within communities. Those outsiders who have previously been deflected from urban public goods and demobilized one too many times learn to turn to other sources to meet their needs. While informal insurance or storing cash may not be new survival strategies, they are also byproducts of a system that individualizes instead of incorporates them. Patchy, uneven distribution tends to inculcate self-blame and a sense of powerlessness, especially when not every migrant feels a sense of entitlement to services in the city. With diminished hope and no sense of opportunity in formal structures, exiting from the public welfare system or at least lessening reliance is sensible. Seeking care at an illegal private clinic that is affordable and accessible then becomes a serviceable option. Those who are more hopeful understand the futility of being overly optimistic and fall back on illegal health care clinics, too. In some ways, therefore, strategies of cobbling together needs undermine political individualization when migrants cooperate to make self-regulated solutions. Informal insurance payments ultimately go to the public hospital when a participant lands in the emergency room. Nor do these approaches generate new collective demands on the state, which political atomization deters. They are synergistic insofar as they all dampen migrant expectations of inclusion and focus on person-level responsibility.

Officials continue to announce reforms as momentous changes in policy and give hope to migrants. When news spread that Shandong Province would soon allow migrant children to take the college entrance exam regardless of their household registration status, many migrant workers rebuffed the idea. "Starting this year in Shandong Province, outsiders, including migrant workers, can take the college entrance exam there," heralded a government official of the imminence of the reform.[59] While she praised the change in policy as the first in an inevitable wave of migrant education policy reform, she also said, "The Chengdu Education Bureau is not discussing this yet. This is because there are too many students."

An education researcher noted, "The college entrance exam in Shandong is one of the country's most difficult for getting into college, so there are no real results or gains from allowing migrants to take the exam there."[60] According to him, because of education deficits and the popular opinion that earning admission to university from taking the exam in Shandong was particularly difficult, migrants are unlikely to even take up the chance to take the test there. Frontline service providers have their own reasons to be skeptical. A principal of a school in Beijing with a 90 percent migrant student population said, "Last year in October, Beijing talked about outsiders taking the college entrance exam here – but there were no results."[61]

Hearing about other migrants' stories of political atomization can have the same effect as being individualized themselves. When someone learns about a peer's experience with being deflected, they themselves can lose morale and become demobilized from even attempting to prove their eligibility, enroll their child in school, or use their social insurance in an urban public hospital. "I didn't have time to take care of my children. I'm always working and I heard they couldn't go to school in Beijing, so I didn't even consider bringing them here," said a fruit and vegetable seller from Fujian Province working in northeastern China.[62] Workers like her need to be certain their children can attend school for, at a minimum, the practical reason that they can work during the day. Her expectations lowered because of the uncertainty of formal inclusion into urban public benefits and of the reliability of individual or community solutions. The effectiveness of political atomization in this way continues apace as the self-assigned responsibility sticks to the person instead of to faults in the system.

Yet making do also reduces migrant workers' dependence on the state. As a single outsider or a group of newcomers create solutions to fulfill their needs, they effectively inch away from the pull of promised structural reforms. Political atomization works through a refined grasp over marginalized people, and it cannot function without enough reach into these citizens' lives. The local state's looser grip and shorter range undermine political atomization by pushing mobile people further from mechanisms of social control. Complete exit from the welfare system weakens government domination over migrant workers, who gain some freedom and agency through improvisational problem solving. They need not be concerned about losing a spot at the municipal public school when their child advances grade levels or changes schools, nor do they have to worry about segmented reimbursement rates at rural clinics or urban hospitals when they use private clinics in the city instead. Too little enmeshment with the state presents its own set of governance and population management problems for districts, municipalities, and the central government.

CONCLUSION

Chinese migrant workers can make do and muddle through instead of depending on prying open institutional access. By focusing on meeting their needs, they devise strategies that diverge from gaining full citizenship or entirely replacing, for example, urban public hospitals and legal aid clinics. Cobbling together health care, education, and other needs on their own tends to be small scale, flexible, and convenient but also ephemeral. They may do so by making do by themselves, as many do by relying on illegal private clinics instead of navigating social insurance schemes at the urban public hospital. Other times they opt out of formal entitlements and choose to participate in informal insurance or other methods in which they make do within communities. Individual and group improvisations are byproducts of political atomization that reinforce some elements of the process while undermining other parts of social control.

The gap between migrant problem solving and state policy toward them shows the difference between each stakeholder's aims. Expansions in urban entitlements need to better meet city transplants' needs on dimensions such as accessibility (in terms of physical proximity and eligibility) and mobility in the way that informal innovations do. Though short-lived and imperfect, the improvised solutions reside in the same dorm or neighborhood as participants, remain open after employees get off work, are affordable for those with lower or less dependable incomes, and are otherwise convenient. Most migrant workers seek public goods in order to support their employment in the city or improve their children's future prospects, and scraping together needs allows them do so when they cannot overcome being deflected or find a suitable substitute institution. Central directives and local policies, however, effectively privilege goals of social control and political atomization over user-friendly and widespread incorporation. Because of this divergence, migrant welfare needs are underserved in the current patchwork of municipal social policies.

Another important implication of an improvised existence is that the focus remains on individual solutions for a systemic problem. But one-off solutions will never completely overcome what is a fundamentally structural issue of social control that extends beyond exclusion into demobilization and deflection. Illegal health clinics cannot treat an undiagnosed autoimmune disorder, conduct regular and routine preventative wellness check-ups, do an appendectomy or other emergency surgeries, or provide high level medical care that a top-tier urban public hospital can. Informal insurance likewise is insufficient in the long run and cannot provide adequate protection or risk-sharing among vulnerable groups whose livelihoods and work are already precarious. Nor do they help push for an overhaul of the formal system to better accommodate those who most need welfare or support reforms toward that goal to solve the larger problem. Improvisations may do the opposite by serving as a safety valve to release some of the pressure to do away with contingent citizenship rather than effectively building in new gradations.

Making do solves immediate needs as they pop up but can be detrimental in other ways. The conditions which generate them ultimately hamper economic development and industrial upgrading while hurting the labor force and migrant welfare. Being treated as disposable and workers feeling that way will not help sustain a healthy, robust labor pool as China tries to escape the middle-income trap. Breeding new structures of discrimination that become enshrined through municipal policy implementation may aid social control but undercut other policy priorities in development. Migrant survival that depends on them filling gaping holes in entitlement schemes in cities dotted across the country will not solve the equity issue or other deeper systemic problems arising from inequality.

This chapter examined how individuals improvise around authoritarian control in everyday circumstances. Most migrants are relatively powerless vis-à-vis the Chinese state, but nevertheless they have found ways to meet their needs. Newcomers have devised strategies of survival so that they can keep their jobs, save their disposable income, and attain a higher quality of care than would otherwise be available to them. These practices and informal institutions suggest that migrants have found ways to curtail some of the effects of social control, but it is mostly at the margins. The state's use of public service provision as a tool of social control remains largely intact.

7

Conclusion

Political atomization is a tool in the state's control toolbox in China. Local governments use political atomization, aided by variation in public services for migrant workers, to maintain social control and inequality. This book examined approaches to state control of migrant workers beyond coercion and sources of disparity within social policy with a focus on education and health care services. Softer approaches complement other practices of social management and indicate that how, not only if, governments provide benefits is a tool of everyday control in authoritarian governance. The lived experience on the ground of rural-to-urban migrants shows how this embedded inequality and everyday marginalization play out in day to day household decisions and interactions with bureaucrats and frontline service providers. A patchwork of localized benefits entrenches inequality for hundreds of millions of Chinese migrant workers through public service provision by enshrining new forms of contingent citizenship and precarious labor to divide and rule them.

After a long day spent at a teahouse with representatives from across several different bureaus in the city of Chengdu, an official from the local public security bureau waited until a group of his colleagues descended the stairs to use the restroom and others went for an after-dinner smoke to pull me aside. In hushed tones as we approached the lobby, he said, "In the next few years, the question of how to manage migrants will only become more important. It will be one of, if not the most, important issue for public security."[1] Local governments' approaches to managing migrants have diversified, expanding to include the use of the welfare state to bolster stability. This is in line with a trend of securitization of social governance policies through which the party-state patronizes and polices the new urban underclass (Thornton 2017). Chinese scholars corroborate, "There is a strong relationship between public services and social stability,"[2] and "stability maintenance is not just about reducing crime and resistance. It's broader and includes social welfare."[3] The knitting together of urban entitlement schemes and stability maintenance in social policy reveals government officials' perceived association between them and how this lens shapes regulation of migrants.

Political atomization is the process by which the state creates policies that structurally treat marginalized people as individuals to enact selective inclusion over group-based exclusion. The state differentiates migrants, distributes services selectively, dilutes claims, and dampens expectations through policies and practices that undermine outsiders' claims to benefits owed to them. The process effectively makes migrant workers responsible for benefits owed to them by the state. Persisting for practical and political reasons, atomization emphasizes personal responsibility over systemic problems, undercuts collective consciousness, and obscures who is to blame. Counterintuitively, governments such as that in China selectively deflect and demobilize marginalized groups of people instead of only plying them with entitlements to generate loyalty or obedience.

Many cities deflect migrant demands for services within and away from their localities instead of meeting them or denying them altogether. Municipal authorities create eligibility and paperwork requirements that are almost impossible to meet and acquire. They enforce dormant rules, shut down private schools and clinics, and incentivize migrants to seek less expensive benefits elsewhere to encourage city outsiders to seek education and health care in another city or in the countryside. A few migrant workers, often the most desired by the state, receive benefits while others are left to navigate channels to eligibility and access one by one on the state's turf. The effects of phantom services isolate and disempower migrants and make it harder for them to organize collectively.

Besides deflecting migrants, local governments demobilize them through piecemeal partial inclusion. Municipalities determine migrant education opportunities primarily in two ways, by regulating private migrant schools and incorporating them or not into public schools. Suppression and exclusion, selective absorption and segregated inclusion, and certification and full inclusion are three main approaches to regulation and integration. Officials can demobilize demand through incomplete inclusion, wherein a few families can enroll their children in urban public schools while many are left to fend for themselves to find spots for their children in private schools or send them to their home villages to attend rural schools. Strategies of private regulation and public integration for demobilizing migrants are complementary and part of the approach of dividing and conquering them.

Migrant workers can subvert elements of the process of political atomization to somewhat blunt social control and attain a form of health care, education, and other services. Though they are relatively powerless, they can make and find institutional leeway by depending on pragmatism and resourcefulness. Frontline service providers, such as doctors and teachers, at the point of delivery may exercise co-migrant empathy and discretion within formal institutions to help them enter urban public entitlement schemes. Informal organizational alternatives such as "people-run" schools and makeshift legal aid clinics also fill institutional gaps. Migrants carve out institutional leeway within the systemic bounds of political individualization to make their way into the narrow but available channels through which they can get some education or health care. They also risk being reverted into a target of the state when sudden crackdowns and other government interventions occur.

When prying open institutional access does not work, migrants make do and muddle through in order to at least meet their needs. By scraping together forms of medical treatment and other social services that do not require institutional access, they improvise to eke out an existence in the city without having to uproot their lives based on the whims of changing social policy. By themselves, migrant workers seek out treatment at illegal private clinics instead of dealing with complex social insurance scheme rules at the urban public hospital. Within communities they may ask to opt out of formal entitlements, showing that not everyone wants incorporation, or participate in small, self-made informal insurance groups. While migrants can undermine components of the process, it is difficult to overcome broader systemic atomization. Individual and community-based innovations are byproducts of individualization that also reinforce some parts of the process. Taken together, Parts I and II of the book show why public services can contribute to social control and how migrants can subvert elements of political atomization. But the process still has limits.

LIMITS OF POLITICAL ATOMIZATION

A number of perverse outcomes, unintended or not, result from the accumulated effects of individuation. One consequence is that years of this process may push migrants too far out of the reach of the state. Softer modes of social control involve a delicate grasp that is between overwhelming force and a grip too tenuous to be effective. While violence can be costly and generate backlash, a hold that is too loose or distant could hobble state efforts to manage migrants and other groups through social policy or other similar mechanisms. Targets who are completely depoliticized may escape from the state altogether,[4] but workers are an essential part of the Chinese economy and authorities cannot afford to ignore or be unable to manage them. Mobility, then, may be at the core of the state's problematization of this group of citizens and defines the governance challenge for them. Outsiders' strategies of relying on substitute institutions like private schools and making do, such as devising informal insurance groups, curtail the effects of political atomization and nudge migrant workers away from a dependence on the state.

Making migrant workers deal with the state one by one is at once sophisticated and imprecise. Providing contingent rather than universal benefits, steering migrants away from using services in urban areas, regulating private substitutes, and withdrawing services are not suitable for achieving every policy aim. Despite official policies offering the promise of benefits in an attempt to attract migrants to small, more recently developing cities, these strategies of less overtly coercive social control cannot overcome a more fundamental obstacle to excessive urban concentration in China's largest cities. Most rural-to-urban migrants continue to select destinations based on economic opportunities and social networks. And although local authorities can grant household registrations and concomitant benefits to wealthy, highly educated migrants, it is difficult to use municipal-wide guidelines for social service provision to target workers needed for a specific industry or company that is experiencing labor shortages. Subtle political control through softer means reflects a refined approach to authoritarian social management, but the decentralized nature of public service provision and difficulty of exact targeting restrict its usefulness in governance.

The procedures and practices that make up individualization are costly for migrants and government officials themselves. Although it is cost-effective compared to the complete extension of benefits to everyone, it is considerably more resource-hungry than doing nothing. Insofar as time wasting contributes to social control, those seeking access who are fruitlessly shuttling paperwork to prove eligibility for their children to attend urban public school or other services or pursuing informal replacements for medical care lose out in multiple ways. They forego wages or risk their jobs, do not receive formal benefits, and are no further along on a clear path to full social citizenship. For municipal authorities, developing and maintaining new residency points systems, checking documents and verifying eligibility, and determining access down to the level of frontline providers' offices drain resources, too. Incoherent policies and unfunded mandates between national directives that promise inclusion and municipal and district policies that incorporate only a few migrants are inefficient compared to outright exclusion and, more importantly, unsustainable.

Weighing near- versus long-term consequences exposes how shortsighted political atomization is.[5] In the short run, it works to contain and channel migrant workers' demands while retaining their labor locally. A persistent mismatch, however, between state-driven urbanization and migrant movement dogs policymakers up and down different levels of government and across various bureaus, especially those responsible for policy implementation and local development. It does not resolve the undertow that pulls rural migrants toward mega-cities that offer the lure of higher paying jobs. No single municipality or district can solve the problem alone, because migrants move around and political individualization exploits the gaps between different localities' provision. More inclusive and generous cities need to fund their policies and deliver on benefits, and more exclusionary ones must ensure there is a steady supply of labor while managing demand on services. The process works as a stopgap but may cause further problems in the future because of these kinds of contradictions.

Political atomization creates new cleavages and sources of inequality instead of eradicating the stubborn rural–urban divide in China. The welfare state is supposed to be a safety net and protective barrier, but in this case it reinforces and spawns new forms of discrimination. Private schools and clinics address immediate problems for those who need to secure a spot in school for their child or to recover from an injury or illness so they can return to work. Yet they fail to address the underlying inequity that Beijing claims to want to reduce. Education is among the channels for social mobility, but rising wealth inequality is constraining opportunities for those who are not affluent (Wang 2019). Other economic issues besides inequality and hampered socioeconomic mobility are of concern.

A few are beginning to see through onerous requirements for eligibility for and actual access to urban social services. A migrant worker from Henan Province who sold vegetables out of a cramped storefront in a migrant neighborhood, for example, heard that property ownership would help fulfill the residency requirement for her adopted city. She said, "Beijing housing prices are too high. I looked, and the average price I found was 10,000 RMB per square meter. When I only make a couple thousand to 10,000 RMB per month, there's not much left over after paying rent for my house and store and for food. For example, one head of bok choy only sells for five *mao*."[6] Formal policy dictates her child is eligible for enrollment in Beijing's public schools if she meets the requirements, but she is also aware of how many of the eligibility requirements are near impossible for her to meet. Migrant participants organizing a protest about education access adapted quickly even as the location of their meeting had to change multiple times up to the last minute. While it is difficult for migrants to organize resistance against political atomization, it is possible more activists will notice the pattern and its effect in the aggregate as years pass.

Other stakeholders are learning from their brushes with the fallout of political atomization, too. The demolition of private substitutes for public services is becoming less of a surprise to the leaders of informal substitute institutions. After they are closed, migrant schools and black clinics often reopen in the neighborhood and continue to serve the local population. "Migrant schools are always being relocated, not completely demolished, in land grabs," said a Chinese researcher with extensive personal ties to the migrant school community in Chengdu.[7] Principals adapt and relocation becomes an anticipated part of their tenure as leaders of migrant schools. They typically rent buildings for their schools and learn not to immediately panic when demolition notices for their schools are posted. "Which schools are demolished does not seem to depend on the quality of the school nor providing a real, better alternative," said a migrant activist who worked closely with principals of migrant schools in Beijing.[8] When he first received news that the main school he worked with was to be demolished, he was frustrated but accepted it as he knew that illegal migrant schools' existence was always uncertain. He walked around the neighborhood to alert others in the same boat. Uneven regional development across the country, an unhealthy and under-educated labor force, and unhappy migrant workers who have the potential to organize in large numbers are among potential issues on the horizon.

IMPLICATIONS FOR CHINA

The persistence of political atomization has political, economic, and social implications for China. Its second major economic transition from an export-based economy to an industrially upgraded, consumption-driven one will require an educated, healthy labor force. In the last four decades, the government has been able to capture the benefits of mobile workers in a marketized economy while consolidating their authoritarian rule. However, these same solutions to today's problems may gradually corrode regime stability and the underpinnings of a pliant pool of labor. By shifting the focus of contention from group-based claims about discrimination to individual negotiations in the offices of street-level bureaucrats (Lipsky 1980), local officials have enacted policies and practices that incorporate some migrants while leaving most people behind. The use of public services to primarily control migrant workers rather than improve their welfare will worsen economic inequality and create new political opportunities around which outsiders can organize and protest down the road. This raises the question of why migrants might eventually protest instead of continuing to solve their own problems by organizing as a community, but authorities have not left these resourceful interventions alone and have actively thwarted some of these efforts. Cracking down on community-based solutions such as private schools, health clinics, and legal aid centers, for example, may backfire by weakening and undermining the same alternatives to formal institutions that meet migrants' needs and therefore mollify them for now.

The theory advanced in this book exhibits a broader pattern of individualization underway in Chinese politics. Individuation undermines collective action and provides a narrow avenue for people to redress grievances and make demands while disincentivizing organizing on a larger scale.[9] It builds in flexibility for different bureaus and levels of government to adapt policies for local political economies, but it is not without costs. Dealing with people one by one takes resources, including time and money, and may only provide a stopgap for the state if the problem is structural or cannot be solved by a single locality. The implications of politically atomizing migrant workers in China are wide-ranging, including deepening inequality, affecting future economic prospects, failing to improve migrant welfare and citizenship, and adding to the authoritarian state's social control toolbox.

This book focused on conceptual development of the theory of political atomization as a larger phenomenon and set aside causes of variation for future research. Researchers who aim to center the pattern of variation may build on the empirical findings detailed in Chapters 3 through 6 to identify causes of variation. Patterns of regulation, such as those around public schools and private substitutes in Chapter 4, offer breadcrumbs for generating work on which level and unit of analysis could be most fruitful. Are the key differences between, for example, regional and municipal policies, industry sectors and formal versus informal work, levels of administration within the state, interprovincial and intra-provincial migrants, or something else? Within China, does political atomization work for controlling other segments of society besides migrants? In a cross-national analysis, is China more similar to other developing countries or to other authoritarian regimes? How does political atomization transcend levels of economic development and regime type as a tool in the state toolbox regardless of these categories?

Downstream economic effects are inevitable because migrant workers make up about a third of the Chinese labor force. Economic development in China requires restructuring in ways that depend on a healthy labor force and flexibility to move forward. Migrants will need to be part of any successful efforts to industrially upgrade and restructure the national economy, and those who are underserved will have a hard time adjusting to an economy less reliant on low-end manufacturing exports. Without support, it will be difficult to transform from a producer on the factory line to a middle-class consumer and to go from making refrigerators to buying them for their new homes. Educational inequality makes migrant workers more likely to save more for precautionary reasons and therefore lowers their consumption (Yan 2017). Restrictions on mobility, no matter how subtle, affect the labor market and impose friction for current and future generations of registered rural residents venturing into cities.

Creating policies and maintaining practices to bring migrants into the state's bureaucratic fold take time and money. For local governments struggling with inadequate financial transfers to incorporate more people into their urban welfare entitlement schemes, deflecting and demobilizing take more total work and resources than outright denying migrant demands. Making new configurations of public service provision in their part of the national hodgepodge is expensive without an eventual overhaul of the entire system. And while Xi Jinping declared victory in early 2021 in lifting almost 100 million impoverished people and thereby eradicating extreme poverty, wide income inequalities continue to exist. Individualization aids in solving some political problems but contributes to other larger economic complications.

Persistent political atomization is not only bad for economic growth but also harmful to migrants' well-being. If their welfare is not the main driver behind social policy toward them and no centralized public service provision takes their specific mobile needs into account, then they are likely to suffer the main consequences. Problems associated with lack of consistent access to high quality social services tend to compound over time. Students who cannot enter a certified primary school are unlikely to fare well in higher levels of education, earn high enough scores on the college entrance exam to enter university, or find stable, well-paying jobs that can help them accelerate their savings, gain wealth, and move into another socioeconomic class. Sick workers can easily deplete their family savings or lose their jobs in the city if a visit to a private clinic is insufficient and they must go to a more advanced urban public hospital, and those with chronic illnesses or serious injuries may never recover their health. Housing insecurity and apartment demolitions force workers to relocate to another part of the city or return to their home village empty-handed without any other social safety net. As part of an aging population across the country, retirees without pensions may have poor quality of life and be unable to support other vulnerable family members. Social policy in service of other government goals is detrimental to this already marginalized group of people.

The hopes of many migrants become truncated over time as experiences of political atomization trickle through their circles. A construction worker from Guizhou Province in southwest China whom I met had spiky, bleached blonde hair and stood out among his older coworkers, whose weathered hands showed how much longer they had been working in the industry than him. At the construction site where he lived and worked outside the Sixth Ring Road in Beijing, our conversation unfolded as we discussed his access to public services. To him, that question was connected to workers' dreams and hopes for life after spending a few years making money in the construction industry. He suddenly seemed confused, so I repeated and rephrased what we had just discussed in case things were unclear, whereupon he clarified that he understood. Educational opportunities and vocational training were not available to help him move up through the layers of subcontracting, and it was improbable he would be promoted within the company. Relying on his physical health while in his early twenties, he knew that too was limited because physical therapy, long-term workplace injury compensation, or anything similar would be unlikely if he got hurt on the job. He paused with a puzzled look on his face and said, "I do not think much about education and health care policy or about anything in general that might improve my life ... I do not have any dreams."[10] Political atomization dampens his and others' expectations about their future opportunities in a country where institutions appear designed to hinder their progress, not help it.

Migrant citizenship in the city is contingent and comprised of new gradations of second-class status. Differential access to urban public goods drives wedges between rural migrants that are separate from those that divide registered rural residents and urban registrants. Provisional citizenship may appear at first glance to be a step forward in gradual urban inclusion, but it is distinct and may not necessarily or automatically lead to full integration. Because their standing in the eyes of the state can change with each new eligibility rule or obstacle to usage introduced, citizenship remains pliable enough for social control (Chan 2024). Localized treatment of migrant workers makes it harder to carry out a national overhaul down the line if the central government opts to unify the provincial, municipal, and district points of policy implementation and service delivery. The same applies for efforts to make benefits transferrable or to redistribute funding for local governments to be able to provide adequate services to those living and working within their jurisdictions.

Decentralization and local adaptation, contrary to expectation, do not automatically improve migrant welfare. Local governments have information to better tailor benefits than the central government, suggesting that devolution of responsibility and funding should empower them to build and enhance schemes that serve those in their municipality.[11] That same knowledge, however, also informs how they can best channel and contain migrant demands while preserving an important pool of labor. Mobile populations need an integrated, centrally coordinated, and transferrable system of benefits because movement is a defining characteristic of the group. Leaving decisions and implementation to local authorities means that different bureaus and provincial, municipal, and district governments can play hot potato with who holds ultimate accountability for a range of reasons, from an unfunded mandate from above to depoliticization of claims in practice.

Political atomization fragments a marginalized group by treating members as discrete individuals and requiring them to navigate an overly complicated system. Where decentralization could have made room for tailoring public goods for their needs, it instead has given local officials the flexibility to incorporate a few people while making it harder for the rest to make claims on their rights. This built-in selectivity is not obvious at first because the criteria for residence, eligibility, access, and use are convoluted. The fieldwork for this book involved speaking with officials and seeking documentary sources from a variety of government bureaus, including those involved in development and reform, education, human resources and social security, health and family planning, labor, public security, and more. Some would explain that only one small aspect of migrant services is within their purview and then send me to others for the complementary part of a policy. Provincial level officials would refer me to municipal or district counterparts whom they claimed to be directly responsible for a particular regulation in formulation and implementation, and the inverse happened when I followed through with their suggestions. The upshot is that while a few make their way through the byzantine scheme, most never do because they do not have the appropriate paperwork, do not qualify based on points systems or other rules, cannot afford additional so-called voluntary donations and fees, cannot access benefits at the point of delivery, or simply give up out of frustration with obstacle after obstacle.

Local authorities are also able to avoid much of the blame for deficient migrant incorporation. If an authority excludes someone by fiat, it is clear why that person could not attain services. When that same authority denies a person because of insufficient paperwork to prove eligibility or calls upon a dormant policy, the responsibility falls either to the migrant to make their case or to bureaucrats and frontline service providers who, according to them, are only enforcing rules and doing their job. Local authorities can divert blame to others, such as when a district official faults city or provincial policy or vice versa when the district is alleged to be giving migrant workers the runaround. This strategy has inherent tensions, and the central government can conveniently divert responsibility when policy formulation and implementation are left to lower-level officials.

Authorities have in effect updated and repurposed institutions of population management in China. Mobile groups of people challenge and push the state in how they can manage them while preserving their labor and relative acquiescence. Social stability is a government priority that steps outside the conventional bounds of the coercive arm of the state. Policies supporting social stability and economic development may overlap at times and counteract each other in some ways or at least redirect attention to other issues such as containing and channeling migrant demands. Most migrants are vulnerable and powerless, but they are able to subvert elements of the process, even as the cumulative effects of individualization are still corrosive. The array of central, provincial, and municipal-level guidelines, procedures, and practices suggest that there needs to be a much broader focus than *hukou* reform to substantially improve the lives of those who move around in China and treat them as full citizens regardless of where they live and work.

POLITICAL ATOMIZATION IN THE WORLD

China is not alone in politically atomizing marginalized people or using public service provision as a tool of social control. From a comparative perspective, other countries face similar challenges of fostering urbanization, dealing with internal migration, reforming the welfare state, facilitating development, and managing the labor force. While presenting and sharing my research along the way for this book, I was struck by how often people commented that they had seen political atomization at work in a variety of other contexts and that there was no existing concept or theory that adequately captured the phenomenon. Those conversations encouraged me to consider how and why this operates in not only other authoritarian regimes or developing countries but also in industrialized democracies. Softer forms of social control through seemingly mundane decisions are substantial and clear in the aggregate.

Countries such as Brazil and India contend with development challenges comparable to those of China. Electoral incentives have a role in shaping these policies in democracies,[12] but they are not the only factor at play. Redistributive policies can be divisive and exclusionary depending on whom the programs target and what criteria authorities choose in designing schemes. Conditional cash transfer programs in Latin America may selectively distribute benefits, and officials can tinker with how they specify conditions to divide and conquer among those served (or not) by the program. Bolsa Família has enhanced democracy in Brazil (Pereira 2015), but there are paperwork requirements that may be difficult for the poor to complete, segmented medical service delivery, and uneven quality in schooling (Sánchez-Ancochea and Mattei 2011).[13] Irregular provision of health care and education leaves open spaces for political individualization to work through social assistance programs like Bolsa Família. Future research could expand on how political atomization works in these democratic regimes, in what areas of social policy they run, and which segments of the population they target.

Authorities in industrialized democracies such as the United States can also resort to political atomization. Parallels between the treatment of internal migrants in China and immigrants in Western countries are evident in the selective policies that make it easier for certain people to become citizens and harder for others, depending on whom the government perceives to be desirable and deems deserving of social citizenship.[14] Rhetoric around the work and worthiness of American immigrants mirrors policy and neighborhood park conversations about the role and status of migrant workers in China. Individuals from both groups technically have a path to full citizenship (whether it is social citizenship or national citizenship), but the number of people who can jump through all of the bureaucratic hoops is limited. Recipients of welfare aid, regardless of national citizenship status, may also be deflected or demobilized as they try to access better urban public schools or low-income housing for which they are supposedly eligible.

Countries with different regime types and levels of development share commonalities in their treatment of the poor. Governments "create incentives and services to smooth the path to preferred behaviors ... [and] ... work continually to manage low-income populations and transform them into cooperative subjects of the market and polity" (Soss et al. 2011: 1–2).[15] Diversion has been common in U.S. state local welfare policies since at least the mid 1990s. To divert clients away from public assistance, some states implemented eligibility rules that steered applicants away with work search requirements and short-term cash payments in lieu of enrollment in the system (Blank 2002). Formal and informal diversion in welfare may also restrict people's access to and eligibility for Medicaid (Maloy et al. 1999). Tactics of diversion are a subset of deflecting through phantom services and entail a mark of atomization in practice.

Political atomization works under different regime types and in countries with developing as well as developed economies. The utility and seeming ubiquity of the phenomenon suggest that wealth and resources, be they economic or political, are insufficient for explaining certain patterns of public service provision and inclusion by the state. Other policy goals such as social control may become part of the sets of rules and practices that determine on the ground whether someone can receive adequate health insurance coverage or other benefits that are owed to them. In cases where officials consider other de facto aims alongside supporting recipients' well-being, policies may fall short of helping those they are said to support. Containing and channeling demands is a pragmatic way to deal with populations whose presence cannot be ignored and is often necessary for the local economy to function and grow. The process of providing public goods is itself a political arena and worth studying as part of authoritarian leaders' toolboxes. More research on how atomized social service provision connects to and advances our understanding of authoritarian resilience and the exchange of benefits for loyalty would show why the perceived exchange of diffuse promised benefits, as opposed to actual targeted perks, can induce support and acquiescence.

The relationship between force-based social control and methods beyond coercion merits more study. Violence is a key component of the Weberian state, but it does not explain all citizen compliance nor fully capture the myriad of methods the state uses in political control. Softer forms may achieve the same goals over a large swath of the population without resorting to sending in the police or military. Points systems and new ways of determining eligibility for urban benefits contain migrant requests before they coalesce into a collective demand that spills into the streets. Or hard and soft forms may complement each other in paired or sequential practices, wherein approaches such as political atomization presage physical coercion. Those migrant workers who leave after warnings of private school shutdowns to come obey the softer procedures, while the few holdouts who wait until demolition face forceful eviction and removal. Other situations may involve authorities using different tools concurrently, such as during campaigns to crack down on and regulate illegal health clinics. The mix of approaches employed by different states may vary by social group, level of marginalization, perceived collective political threat, local economic need, availability of state resources, and other trade-offs.

EMBEDDED INEQUALITY AND THE STATE

Inequality sometimes serves the state in spite of its numerous negative consequences. Many advocates and government officials themselves acknowledge how social, economic, and political disparities harm people and outcomes of interest to the state. But in other ways, maintaining, deepening, and changing the contours of inequality enable the state to undermine collective class consciousness and govern over marginalized groups in the population. Contingent citizenship tends to favor the governments, who dictate the boundaries and conditions. Through them, officials can effectively modify who counts as a full citizen and what concrete entitlements they receive in accordance with that. Individuation brings into the fold a few who meet the eligibility requirements, have the paperwork in hand, and can navigate administrative hurdles while leaving most behind with phantom services and less recourse to organize group-wide resistance to the policies that buttress inequality. This particular form of powerlessness combined with liminal hope of meaningful incorporation places blame on the individual for failing to qualify or gain access instead of the broader system for neglecting to meet their needs.

The institutional structures behind inequality are deeply embedded in social policy. These systemic constraints include formal public service provision policies, implementation of them in practice, and informal substitutes that collectively act as barriers to equitable distribution, better health and education, and upward socioeconomic mobility. Though they are not the only sources or areas of concern, education, health care, housing, and other public goods support the livelihoods and welfare of migrant workers in their everyday lives. Insofar as the provision of benefits itself is distributed inequitably and generates disparity through this differentiated allocation, it engenders some of the same problems it seeks to solve. It is no wonder that migrants in China have turned to seeking replacement institutions and muddling through when they cannot depend on this patchy, unpredictable coverage. Private schools and illegal clinics are band-aid solutions, but they do not address the underlying problem of institutional deflection. Indeed, they may push national overhauls and reforms further down the line when they function well enough for the time being.

Chinese authorities and other leaders who use political atomization seek a desired zone of control in which some level and kind of inequality exist but not too much. Excessive inequality would be harmful and invite dissent, which could potentially be politically and socially destabilizing. This desired zone of control generates a number of questions for future research. How can scholars conceptualize and measure this zone of control in order to systematically assess what kinds or levels of inequality would serve the state? In what policy areas besides public goods provision could political atomization work? What are the bounds of this zone, and why are some governments able to stay within these limits to capitalize on inequality while others exceed the upper or lower boundaries and therefore cannot exploit disparities to support their rule? Under what political, economic, and social conditions does the desired zone of control narrow or widen?

Migrants and others who experience political atomization face structural inequalities that individuals alone cannot permanently dismantle by themselves. People problem solving one by one can address immediate needs for health care and education but cannot overcome systemic barriers to reliable, meaningful, and long-term access to public services. Full inclusion and social citizenship in the city appear to potentially be in sight, which has not always been the case, but remain out of reach for most who move to the city for higher wages and job opportunities. Parents sending their children to a private migrant school this year have no guarantees of being able to enroll them in urban public schools next year, and there is no mechanism to ensure that participants in informal insurance groups on one job site will be able to eventually have formal social insurance that they can use regardless of where they are currently living and working and that will reimburse them at sufficient rates for trips to urban hospitals. Meeting their needs now, no matter how resourceful or desperate they are, is not a well-defined stepping stone to incorporation in the future. They endure a Sisyphean task in vying with systemic sources of inequality to access benefits owed to them.

Chinese migrant workers are marginalized members of society who bear the additional burden of having to overcome being deflected and demobilized. The channeling and containing itself, such as chasing down labor contracts never offered to them or shuffling paperwork between government bureaus and schools, costs them time and money. People with precarious jobs who work long hours as construction workers, nannies, security guards, and other positions cannot afford to waste either of those resources. Keeping them busy with, for example, proving eligibility for benefits, amassing points to change their residency status, or seeking a school that will accept migrant students for enrollment conveniently displaces their free time, disposable income, and willingness to make group-wide demands on the state for incorporation.

Person by person solutions to increase equity can unintentionally help cement structural sources of inequality. Rural-to-urban migrants in China must meet their needs somehow for pragmatic reasons in addition to their well-being, so their improvised modes of survival are unavoidable. Unfortunately, their turning to informal substitutes or otherwise making do inadvertently eases the burden on the state to redress structural issues. Each migrant student that stays in the village under the care of their grandparents is one less place district or municipal officials have to find or create in an urban public school, and each patient who opts to visit a private health clinic is one less person struggling to pay out-of-pocket costs for treatment in a public hospital in the city. Central and local officials are then under less pressure to rectify the broader policies that deflect and demobilize migrant recipients, and the practices of political atomization can remain intact.

Political atomization is insidious because it implicitly indicates that Chinese migrant workers and others who experience it must and can earn inclusion. It appears they may do so by being better citizens, working harder or longer in the city, entering into formal housing arrangements, or performing other indicators that qualify them as worthy of urban citizenship. Structures of inequality are rooted in the convergence of central directives, local policies, and frontline practices. The effect of shifting the blame to individual migrants and obscuring who is responsible for the patchwork further makes it difficult to organize collectively. Individual-level schemes and solutions are no match for systemic depoliticization and demobilization.

Notes

1 INEQUALITY AND THE AUTOCRAT'S TOOLBOX

1. This book focuses on one component of local citizenship, namely migrants' social citizenship. According to one influential, widely used typology, there are three types of citizenship: civil, political, and social (Marshall 1950). Social citizenship entails a right to some level of economic welfare and security and the right to social services available to everyone, such as education.
2. A transcript of the March 2014 press conference on the new urbanization plan is available at http://china.org.cn/china/2014-03/19/content_31836248_2.htm.
3. Ibid.
4. See Wallace (2014) on urban bias in China.
5. On patronage and clientelism in democracies, see Kitschelt and Wilkinson (2007).
6. A transcript and video of the speech are available online at https://news.cgtn.com/news/30516a4d32597a6333566d54/share_p.html.
7. On public perceptions of inequality in China, see Whyte (2010a).
8. See Unger and Siu (2019) for more on shifts in migrant worker trends.
9. On weak state capacity and ineffective bureaucratic control in pollution enforcement in China, see van der Kamp (2023).

2 A THEORY OF POLITICAL ATOMIZATION

1. Interviews with migrant workers, Beijing, September 2010.
2. See Pun and Lu (2010a) for more on the labor subcontracting system in construction in China.
3. In the development and formation of "political atomization" as a concept, I sought to follow Gerring's (1999) eight criteria (familiarity, resonance, parsimony, coherence, differentiation, depth, theoretical utility, and field utility) for good concepts and adopted a similar approach of balancing trade-offs over adhering to specific rules.

4. See State Council of the People's Republic of China (2014).
5. Interview with a factory–government liaison, Dongguan, December 2010.
6. Interviews with a factory–government liaison, Dongguan, December 2010 and an economics scholar, Guangzhou, January 2011.
7. The number is calculated from China Labour Bulletin's Strike Map: https://maps.clb.org.hk/su/T8YpqfO6.
8. Ibid.
9. See Guangzhou White Paper on Labor Dispute Litigation (广州劳动争议诉讼情况白皮书, *Guangzhou laodong zhengyi susong qingkuang baipishu*), www.gzcourt.gov.cn/upfile/File/201705/12/101657100.pdf.
10. Interviews with migrant workers, Beijing, December 2010 and an NGO staff member, Chengdu, July 2012.
11. Interviews with migrant workers, Beijing, December 2010 and Chengdu, July 2012.
12. See Jaros (2019) on why provincial policies tend to favor the largest and most economically developed cities.
13. Interview with a migrant worker, Beijing, July 2017.
14. Paired comparisons were conducted where available and appropriate. The Bo Xilai scandal erupted while I traveled to Chongqing and the surrounding area. Beijing is uniquely situated as the capital city of China.
15. See the United Nations Development Programme for more on HDI: http://hdr.undp.org/en/content/human-development-index-hdi. The three dimensions are health (measured by life expectancy at birth), education (measured by mean years of schooling for adults aged twenty-five and older and expected years of schooling for children of school entering age), and standard of living (measured by gross national income per capita).
16. Interviewees were mainly recruited through snowball sampling with a goal of maximizing different nodes. All interview notes were coded to help identify patterns. An iterative approach to research design provided space for "ground-level up theorizing" (O'Brien 2006: 36–37). I was fortunate that I conducted the initial bulk of the fieldwork for this project at a time when field access was greater than it is now. From 2010 to 2012, I spent a year and a half in China conducting interviews and gathering ethnographic observations. The scope and depth of this project in revealing the lived experience of migrant workers, service providers, and street-level bureaucrats are less available. Follow-up fieldwork during trips in the summer of 2017 and winter of 2019 have shown that the structures and experiences remain largely consistent.
17. See Hwang (2022) on how integration with the global economy affects social insurance coverage.
18. See Svolik (2012) on another form of cooptation through authoritarian parties.
19. See, for example, the International Organization of Migration World Migration Report 2020 at www.iom.int/wmr/.
20. See Yan (2010) on the individualization of Chinese society.
21. Interviews with a scholar, Shanghai, April 2012 and a high-skilled migrant, Beijing, July 2012.

22. Interviews with a migrant employer, Chengdu, January 2011; doctors, Hangzhou, April 2012; and a government official, Chengdu, May 2012.
23. Interviews with a migrant NGO staff member Guangzhou, December 2010; principal, Beijing, June 2012; and a migrant worker, Beijing, July 2017.
24. Interviews with a migrant worker, Beijing, December 2011; a migrant activist, Beijing, January 2012; government official, Beijing, March 2012; and a migrant worker, Beijing, July 2017.
25. Interviews with teachers, Beijing, March 2012.
26. Interviews with doctors, Hangzhou, April 2012; Beijing, June 2012; and Shanghai, July 2012.
27. Interviews with migrant workers, Shanghai, July 2017 and Chengdu, July 2017.
28. Interviews with migrant workers, Beijing, December 2011 and Beijing, July 2017.
29. Interviews with migrant workers, Beijing, December 2010; Hangzhou, April 2012; and Guangzhou, July 2017.
30. Interviews with a migrant NGO staff member, Guangzhou, December 2010 and migrant workers, Beijing, July 2017 and Guangzhou, July 2017.
31. Similarly, local governments incentivized state-owned enterprise workers to pursue narrow identities and particularistic claims that tended to divide and demoralize them (Chen 2019).
32. Interview with a migrant NGO staff member, Guangzhou, December 2010.
33. Interviews with a scholar-activist, Chengdu, May 2012; a government official, Chengdu, July 2012; and migrant workers, Chengdu, July 2012.
34. On different provinces' approaches to social policy, see Ratigan (2022). On the role of affiliated associations in education, see Gao and Tyson (2023).
35. Interviews with a migrant NGO staff member, Beijing, October 2010; a government official, Beijing, March 2012; a migrant NGO staff member, Chengdu, May 2012; a migrant NGO staff member, Shanghai, May 2012; and a scholar-activist, Chengdu, July 2017.
36. See Harvey (2005) for a history of the doctrine of neoliberalism.

3 DEFLECTING MIGRANT WORKERS

1. The author thanks *The China Journal* for permission to reuse the article on which much of this chapter is based: Chan, Alexsia T. and Kevin J. O'Brien. 2019. "Phantom Services: Deflecting Migrant Workers in China." *The China Journal* 81: 103–122.
2. Enrollment in social insurance programs increased nationwide in the 2000s and into the 2010s. For more on social insurance and, in particular, health insurance policies, see Zhang (2012) and Huang (2014).
3. On public schools in Shanghai accepting migrant children but also instituting other forms of discrimination, see Lan (2014).
4. On different kinds of low-cost housing, see Wu (2002) and Huang (2012).
5. Privately run schools, known as "people-run schools" (*minban xuexiao*), provide education to migrant children who cannot attend public schools. See Kwong (2004), Chan and Wang (2009), and Teets (2012). Similarly,

with regard to medical benefits, migrants often use illegal "black clinics" (*hei zhensuo*) for health care instead of participating in insurance programs or going to public hospitals. On other obstacles that block access to health services, see Li and Wu (2010).

6. For more on how the *hukou* system perpetuates the rural–urban divide in China, see Cheng and Selden (1994), Chan (1994a), Chan (1994b), Solinger (1999), Chan and Zhang (1999), Fan (2002), Wang (2005), Chan and Buckingham (2008), Chan (2009), Whyte (2010), Wu (2010), and Chan et al. (2018). On how China uses the *hukou* system to manage urbanization, see Wallace (2014).
7. On migrant eligibility for the "Minimum Livelihood Guarantee" (*zuidi shenghuo baozhang*) program, see Solinger (2013) and Leung and Xiao (2015).
8. See Chan and Buckingham (2008) on how *hukou* reform since the late 1990s has become increasingly localized. Many cities and towns now have discretion over the yearly quota and criteria for who can become a registered permanent resident.
9. See Cheng and Selden (1994), Chan (1994a), Chan and Zhang (1999), Solinger (1999), Fan (2002), Wang (2005), Chan and Buckingham (2008), Chan (2009), Whyte (2010), Wu (2010), and Chan et al. (2018).
10. See Chan and Buckingham (2008), Chan (2009), and Chan et al. (2018).
11. This is part of a general decline in the working-age population in China.
12. Seventy percent of them first move with their spouse and later bring their children along to their destination.
13. Basic medical insurance coverage across the country increased from less than 50 percent in 2005 to 87 percent in 2008 to 95 percent in 2011 (State Council of the People's Republic of China 2012, Yu 2015).
14. In 2011, only 21 percent of migrants participated in a plan.
15. Total spending is expected to reach 1 trillion USD by 2020 (Gardner 2017).
16. Interview with a doctor, Guangzhou, July 2017. These initiatives (and studies of them) remain largely at the level of proposed institutional reforms and new policies yet to be seen in practice. For example, on the integration of pension and health schemes, see Müller (2017).
17. These initiatives include ones that touch on urbanization, *hukou* reform, fiscal transfers, and land policy. See Gao et al. (2019) and Howell and Duckett (2019) on reforms of social policy during the Hu–Wen Era.
18. Interview with a social welfare scholar, Beijing, March 2012; Interview with a former education official, Chengdu, May 2012; also interview with a migrant education NGO staff member, Shanghai, July 2017.
19. Interview with an informal worker, Beijing, September 2010; Interviews with construction workers, Beijing, December 2010; Interview with a migrant NGO leader, Guangzhou, December 2010; also interview with a migrant worker, Guangzhou, July 2017.
20. Significant gaps exist between migrants who can apply for a *hukou* transfer and those who are successful at acquiring one in Beijing because of eligibility requirements (Liu and Shi 2020).
21. Many of these policies were intended to induce migrants to settle in small and medium-sized cities instead of the overcrowded provincial capital. Some

cities within Guangdong Province, such as Shenzhen and Zhongshan, have set up their own points systems as well. See Guo and Liang (2017).

22. Application materials include: (1) degree certificates or certificates of professional qualification, (2) a valid form of identification, (3) proof of residence in Guangdong Province, (4) a marital status certificate, (5) a health certificate, and (6) an already signed employment contract (Guangdong Province Public Security 2009a).
23. The system is similar to points systems used by some countries for immigrants (Interview with a Shanghai public administration scholar, Hong Kong, March 2012).
24. Shenzhen municipality opened up 10,000 permanent residency spots in 2017, but these are reserved for applicants with the most points and will only benefit a tiny fraction of the city's millions of migrant workers (He 2017). See Guo and Liang (2017).
25. There are three main differences between migrants holding Shanghai residence permits and residents with Shanghai *hukou*. For example, residence permit holders cannot get permanent residence for their parents, apply for the city's minimum livelihood (welfare) program, or apply for government-subsidized affordable housing (Shanghai Municipal Information Office 2013).
26. Points systems are not the only way that some migrants are favored over others. Many highly educated, better-off migrants can apply for an urban *hukou* during their years at university or obtain health insurance through their employers, and many can pay for their children to attend local schools. As an official said in Chengdu, "High-skilled senior personnel are encouraged to come and have no problem accessing services" (Interview with a municipal development cadre, May 2012).
27. Interviews with a scholar in Chengdu, July 2012 and July 2017.
28. For example, although some Foxconn workers were told that they would receive benefits as soon as they started working and insurance could be purchased on a monthly basis, they reported that they were classified as temporary workers and would only became eligible to purchase insurance after four to six months (Interview with an informal worker, Chengdu, July 2012; Interview with an NGO leader, Chengdu, July 2012). For more on Foxconn workers, see Pun and Chan (2012).
29. Interview with a migrant legal aid center director, Guangzhou, December 2010.
30. Interviews with school principals, Beijing, March 2012; also interview with a migrant education NGO staff member, Shanghai, July 2017.
31. On placing the onus on workers to figure out how to access services, see Shanghai Daily (2013). At this press conference, Mao Dali, deputy director of the Shanghai Human Resources and Social Security Bureau, said that nonlocals "can calculate the points themselves and know [in] which area they need to work hard to fill the gap."
32. Interviews with informal workers, Beijing, December 2011; Interviews with informal workers and construction workers, Chengdu, July 2012; also interview with a migrant worker, Beijing, July 2017.
33. Interview with a scholar, Chengdu, May 2012.
34. Interviews with a migrant activist, Beijing, November 2010 and January 2012.

35. Elsewhere, land seizures have turned violent, especially when residents have faced off with hired thugs (Wines and Ansfield 2010, Ong 2018).
36. Interviews with migrant workers, Hangzhou, April 2012; Guangzhou, July 2017; and Chengdu, July 2017; and with a doctor, Guangzhou, July 2017.
37. The more specific people's attribution of blame, the more likely it is that they protest (Javeline 2003).
38. Based on data from the National Bureau of Statistics of China (2017a). The numbers had been about the same five years earlier (Zhang and Li 2016). For a study of education spending in Shanghai, see Zhou and Wang (2016).
39. Interviews with a social welfare scholar in Beijing, March 2012; a political scientist in Shanghai, April 2012; and a public policy scholar in Beijing, July 2017.
40. For example, Beijing municipality's 13th Five-Year Plan (2016–2020) calls for reducing the population of six central districts by 15 percent and limiting Beijing's total population to 23 million.
41. Interview with a scholar in Chengdu, July 2017.
42. On "legal-bureaucratic absorption" and being forced to bargain with bureaucrats in their offices rather than taking to the streets to protest, see Lee and Zhang (2013) and Chuang (2014).
43. In 2011, county welfare officials in Sichuan province introduced new rules for low-income social insurance (*zuidi shenghuo baozhang*, or *dibao*) that, for instance, disqualified anyone living with employable adult children, which made many elderly evictees ineligible for this welfare assistance.

4 DEMOBILIZING MIGRANT WORKERS

1. "People-run" schools began as popular, voluntary village institutions during the Yan'an Period in the mid-1940s (Robinson 1986). Throughout the Maoist Era, they served as vehicles for inculcating political and educational values (Wang 2002). This form of education became hyperpoliticized during the Great Leap Forward in 1958 and the Cultural Revolution from 1966 to 1976. In contemporary China, the term "people-run" schools usually refers to private migrant schools set up to provide education for migrant children living in cities where they are barred from enrolling in public school.
2. See the chapter by Chan, Mok, and Tang (2004) in Wong, White, and Gui (2004) for a case study of education reform in Shanghai. See Yu and Crowley (2020) for a list of national and Beijing municipal policies and regulations.
3. Interview with a migrant worker activist, Beijing, January 2012.
4. Interviews with teachers, Beijing, June 2012.
5. Interview with a teacher, Beijing, March 2012.
6. For comparison, China's national GDP per capita was US$4,486.60 in 2010 (United Nations 2020).
7. The Economist (2012).
8. This was according to a 2012 report by the National Population and Family Planning Commission and is likely a conservative number (Chen 2012).
9. For example, one frequently cited news article began, "Shanghai will this year become the first Chinese city to provide free education to all school-age

children of migrant workers, through more government investment in facilities and teachers" (Zhi 2010).

10. Interviews with a migrant NGO staff member, Beijing, October 2010; a migrant NGO staff member, Shanghai, April 2012; a migrant NGO staff member, Shanghai, May 2012; and a migrant NGO staff member, Shanghai, July 2017.
11. Interview with a migrant employer, Chengdu, January 2011.
12. Interviews with a scholar–activist, Chengdu, May 2012 and a principal, Chengdu, May 2012.
13. Chengdu's comparatively better service provision for migrant workers extends beyond the substantive policy area of education. According to the 2010 *Population Research* report on the "Current Living Situation of Migrant Population in China" by the Department of Floating Population Service and Management of National Population and Family Planning Commission of China, 57.3 percent of migrants in Beijing and 49.3 percent of migrants in Shanghai participated in health insurance. In contrast, the participation rate in Chengdu was much higher at 83.7 percent (Department of Floating Population Service and Management of the National Population and Family Planning Commission of China 2010).
14. These are prevailing patterns. Some variation and district discretion exists within cities.
15. Interview with a migrant NGO staff member, Beijing, October 2010 and a migrant NGO staff member, Shanghai, May 2012.
16. Interview with a migrant NGO staff member, Beijing, October 2010.
17. Interview with a migrant NGO staff member, Beijing, October 2010.
18. Interview with a migrant NGO staff member, Beijing, October 2010.
19. Interview with a migrant NGO staff member, Beijing, October 2010 and Canaves and Feng (2010).
20. Interviews with an NGO staff member, Beijing, December 2011 and a teacher, Beijing, March 2012.
21. Interview with a government official, Beijing, March 2012.
22. Interviews with a migrant worker, Beijing, September 2010 and a migrant worker, December 2011.
23. Interview with a migrant activist, Beijing, December 2010 and a teacher, Beijing, March 2012.
24. The 2006 policy of abolishing school fees significantly increased citizens' (especially rural residents') demands for greater government responsibility for financing compulsory education (Lü 2014).
25. Interview with a migrant worker activist, Beijing, November 2010 and a migrant worker, Beijing, December 2011.
26. Interview with a migrant NGO staff member, Beijing, October 2010.
27. Interview with a migrant NGO staff member, Shanghai, April 2012.
28. Interview with a government official, Beijing, March 2012.
29. See Li and Xiong (2019) on gratitude education of migrant children in Beijing.
30. Interview with a government official, Beijing, March 2012.
31. Interview with a principal, Beijing, June 2012.
32. Interview with a migrant worker, Beijing, December 2011.

33. Interview with a migrant worker, Beijing, September 2010 and a teacher, Beijing, March 2012.
34. Interview with a public policy scholar, Beijing, July 2017.
35. Interview with a migrant worker, Beijing, July 2017.
36. Interviews with a migrant worker, Beijing, December 2010 and a government official, Beijing, December 2010.
37. Interviews with principals and teachers, Beijing, March 2012.
38. Interview with a principal, Beijing, June 2012.
39. Interview with a migrant worker, Beijing, July 2017.
40. Interview with a migrant NGO staff member, Shanghai, July 2017.
41. Interview with a political science scholar, Shanghai, April 2012.
42. Interview with an NGO staff member, Shanghai, May 2012.
43. Interview with an NGO staff member, Shanghai, May 2012.
44. Interview with an NGO staff member, Shanghai, April 2012.
45. Interview with an NGO staff member, Shanghai, May 2012.
46. Interviews with a political science scholar, Shanghai, April 2012 and an NGO staff member, Shanghai, April 2012.
47. Interview with a migration scholar, Shanghai, April 2012.
48. Interview with a migrant NGO staff member, Shanghai, July 2017.
49. Interviews with an NGO staff member, Shanghai, April 2012 and an NGO staff member, Shanghai, May 2012.
50. Interviews with migrant workers, Shanghai, July 2017.
51. Interview with a migrant worker, Shanghai, July 2017.
52. Interview with a migrant NGO staff member, Shanghai, April 2012.
53. Interview with an NGO staff member, Beijing, October 2010.
54. Interview with a teacher, Beijing, March 2012.
55. Interviews with an NGO staff member, Beijing, October 2010; teachers, Beijing, March 2012; and an NGO staff member, Shanghai, April 2012.
56. Interview with an NGO staff member, Shanghai, April 2012.
57. Interview with a migrant NGO staff member, Shanghai, July 2017.
58. Interview with a social welfare scholar, Beijing, March 2012.
59. Interview with a principal, Chengdu, May 2012.
60. Interviews with a scholar–activist, Chengdu, May 2012 and follow-up, Chengdu July 2017.
61. Interviews with a principal, Chengdu, May 2012 and a government official, Chengdu, May 2012.
62. Interview with a scholar–activist, Chengdu, May 2012.
63. Interview with a scholar–activist, Chengdu, July 2017.
64. Interviews with migrant workers, Chengdu, July 2017.
65. Interviews with migration scholar, Chengdu, January 2011; a government official, Chengdu, May 2012; and an NGO staff member, Chengdu, July 2012.
66. Interview with a government official, Chengdu, May 2012.
67. Interview with a scholar–activist, Chengdu, May 2012.
68. Interview with a migrant worker, Chengdu, July 2012.
69. Interview with a government official, Chengdu, May 2012.
70. Interview with an NGO staff member, Chengdu, July 2012.
71. Interview with a migrant worker, Chengdu, July 2012.

72. Interview with a migrant education NGO, Shanghai, July 2017.
73. Interview with a government official, Chengdu, May 2012.
74. Interview with a migrant worker, Guangzhou, July 2017.
75. Interview with a migrant worker, Guangzhou, July 2017.
76. Interviews with an NGO staff member, Guangzhou, December 2010 and a migrant worker, Guangzhou, July 2017.
77. Interview with a government official, Chengdu, May 2012.
78. Interview with an NGO staff member, Shanghai, April 2012.
79. Interview with a government official, Chengdu, May 2012.
80. Interviews with an NGO staff member, Shanghai, April 2012 and a government official, Chengdu, May 2012.
81. Interview with an NGO staff member, Shanghai, April 2012.
82. A string of uncoordinated knife attacks in Chinese schools from 2010 to 2012 also put the issue of school safety at the forefront of government officials' agendas.
83. Interview with a scholar–activist, Chengdu, May 2012.

5 PLAYING WITH INSTITUTIONAL LEEWAY

1. Interview with a migrant worker, Chengdu, July 2012.
2. On Chinese police officers as frontline bureaucrats, see Scoggins (2021).
3. When reform of the health care system began, the Chinese government reduced funding for public hospitals while still maintaining a foothold in its pricing structure. Before 1985, Chinese hospitals enjoyed full funding from the government. The early phases of reform in the 1980s and 1990s were marked by less reliance on state funding, decentralization of public health services, more autonomy for health facilities, increased freedom of movement for health workers, and decreased political control (Bloom and Gu 1997). The Central Pricing Commission set the general guidelines for pricing policy for providers for political reasons; they kept prices for most health services low and based on historical fees set in the 1950s instead of on economic considerations such as cost (Hsiao 1995). These policies were aimed at promoting social equality and affordability and, consequently, hospitals provided these services at cost or a net loss.
4. Interview with a migrant worker, Shanghai, July 2017.
5. Interview with migrant workers, Shanghai, July 2017.
6. On network structure between labor subcontractors and migrant workers in labor protests, see Wei and Chan (2022).
7. In the U.S., some public service bureaucrats incorporated immigrants and provided greater substantive responsiveness to their needs than local politicians (Marrow 2009).
8. Interview with a doctor, Beijing, June 2012.
9. Interview with a doctor, Shanghai, August 2012.
10. Interviews with a migrant worker, Beijing, December 2010; a factory manager, Dongguan, December 2010; and a doctor, Shanghai, July 2012.
11. Interviews with teachers, Beijing, March 2012.

12. Interviews with migrant NGO staff, Beijing, October 2010; teachers, Beijing, March 2012; and a migration scholar, Shanghai, April 2012.
13. Interviews with migrant NGO staff, Beijing, December 2011 and teachers, Beijing, March 2012.
14. Interview with migrant NGO staff, Shanghai, July 2017.
15. Interview with GONGO staff, Chengdu, July 2012.
16. Interview with a doctor, Beijing, June 2012.
17. Interview with a doctor, Shanghai, July 2012.
18. Interviews with a doctor and migrant workers, Hangzhou, April 2012. The doctor was referring the patient for surgery, so she would not directly benefit financially from encouraging the migrant worker to be admitted for surgery in her hospital that day.
19. Interview with a doctor, Guangzhou, July 2017.
20. Interview with a teacher, Beijing, March 2012.
21. Interview with a teacher, Beijing, March 2012.
22. This was part of an opportunity to interview and observe dozens of frontline service providers as part of an organized multi-site visit with officials, principals, school administrators, teachers, and a local scholar.
23. Interview with a teacher, Beijing, March 2012.
24. Cited in Chen (2018). These numbers are according to the Chinese Society of Education, which is affiliated with the Ministry of Education.
25. Interview with a teacher, Beijing, March 2012.
26. Interview with GONGO staff, Chengdu, July 2012.
27. Interview with a scholar, Beijing, December 2010. On how Shanghai, like Chengdu, was historically a place full of rural migrants, see Honig (1992).
28. Interviews with a scholar–activist, Chengdu, May 2012 and July 2017.
29. Interview with a scholar, Hong Kong, March 2012.
30. Interview with a migrant worker, Beijing, July 2017.
31. There is an extensive literature on informal institutions in comparative politics. See Helmke and Levitsky (2004) on a typology of formal–informal institution interaction and Tsai (2006) on adaptive informal institutions in China.
32. Interview with a migrant activist, Beijing, November 2010. He and his fellow activists also preferred the term "new worker" (*xin gongren*, 新工人) to "migrant worker."
33. As of the 1990s, government subsidies accounted for a mere 10 percent of public health facilities' total revenue, forcing hospitals to generate 90 percent of their budget from other revenue-generating activities (Yip and Hsiao 2009). Due to market-oriented reforms, Chinese hospitals relied on fees for medical services, especially high technology tests, and profits from pharmaceutical drug sales. In 1992, the Ministry of Health granted financial autonomy to hospitals to charge fees, keep income, and sell drugs for profit. At the same time, the government also set prices for new, high-tech diagnostic services above cost and allowed a 15 percent profit margin on pharmaceutical drugs, which hospital administrators took advantage of to increase revenues.
34. Doctors often earn 30 percent in kickbacks for prescribing certain companies' medicines (Li et al. 2012), and they earn bonuses according to how much revenue they generate for the hospital. By 2008, drug revenue

accounted for an average of 40 percent of the gross income of hospitals, much higher than the 15 to 25 percent common in most OECD countries (The World Bank 2010). Moreover, the combination of profit-driven hospitals and fee-for-service schemes led to the overuse of various diagnostic tests and procedures. In 2009, Chinese hospitals administered an average of eight intravenous drips per person, more than twice the world average rate at 2.5 to 3.3 annually (The World Bank 2010). The focus on generating revenue is necessary but sometimes distorts incentives away from socially desirable outcomes for public goods provision.

35. Interview with a doctor, Beijing, June 2012.
36. Interviews with doctors, Hangzhou, April 2012.
37. New sources of revenue included enterprises, NGOs, and schools themselves (Tsang 1996). Public schools are to rely more on a local tax base. It is common in cities for district governments to administer and fund primary education while municipal governments administer and fund secondary schools. Despite initiatives to hire more teachers, teacher salaries remain low. Moreover, schools collect additional fees from parents to offset rising costs. With education reform, there is a bigger market for consumer spending in education and additional pressure on school administrators and teachers to increase their school's rankings.
38. Household categories are grouped by permanent residence according to the report.
39. Interviews with teachers, Beijing, March 2012.
40. Interview with migrant NGO staff, Shanghai, July 2017.
41. Interview with a migrant activist, Beijing, November 2010.
42. Interview with migrant NGO staff, Beijing, October 2010.
43. Interview with a principal Chengdu, May 2012.
44. Interviews with a principal, Beijing, March 2012 and a scholar–activist, Chengdu, July 2017.
45. Interview with a migrant activist, Beijing, November 2010.
46. Interviews with teachers, Beijing, June 2012.
47. Interview with a migrant activist, Beijing, January 2012.
48. Interview with a doctor, Beijing, June 2012.
49. Interview with migrant NGO staff, Chengdu, July 2012.
50. Interview with migrant NGO staff, Guangzhou, December 2010.
51. Interview with a doctor, Beijing, June 2012.
52. Interview with a doctor, Beijing, June 2012.
53. Interview with migrant NGO staff, Guangzhou, December 2010.
54. Interview with a teacher, Beijing, March 2012.
55. Interview with a teacher, Beijing, March 2012.
56. Interview with a teacher, Beijing, March 2012.
57. Interview with a teacher, Beijing, March 2012.
58. Interview with a teacher, Beijing, March 2012.
59. Interview with a scholar–activist, Chengdu, July 2017.
60. Interview with a principal, Beijing, March 2012.
61. Interview with a teacher, Beijing, March 2012.
62. Interviews with teachers, Beijing, March 2012.

63. Interview with political science scholar, Shanghai, April 2012.
64. Interview with a migrant worker, Guangzhou, July 2017.

6 MAKING DO AND MUDDLING THROUGH

1. Interviews with a doctor and migrant worker, Beijing, June 2012.
2. Interview with a doctor, Guangzhou, July 2017.
3. The use of the term "self-reliance" here is not intended to evoke the Maoist concept.
4. Interview with a migrant employer, Guangzhou, July 2017.
5. Interview with a migrant worker, Guangzhou, July 2017.
6. Interview with a migrant worker, Beijing, July 2017.
7. See Li et al. (2020) on the challenges of primary health care in China.
8. See Huang (2020) on the expansion of social health insurance in China more broadly.
9. Interview with a migrant worker, Beijing, July 2017.
10. According to the National Bureau of Statistics, 94.8 percent of villages had clinics in 2019 (National Bureau of Statistics of China 2020). See Müller (2019) on township health centers in China.
11. Interview with a migrant worker, Chengdu, July 2012.
12. Interview with a migrant worker, Chengdu, July 2012.
13. Interviews with migrant workers, Chengdu, July 2012.
14. Interviews with migrant workers, Chengdu, July 2012.
15. See Li (2014) on illegal private clinics in a migrant village in Beijing.
16. Interview with a doctor, Shanghai, August 2012.
17. Cited in Li and Blanchard (2013).
18. Interview with a health care scholar, Chengdu, May 2012.
19. See Sun (2020) on campaign-style policy implementation in another area of public benefits, affordable housing provision.
20. Interviews with doctors, Beijing, June 2012 and a doctor, Shanghai, August 2012.
21. Interview with a migrant worker, Beijing, July 2017.
22. Interview with a migrant worker, Beijing, December 2010.
23. Interview with a migrant worker, Beijing, July 2017.
24. Interview with a migrant activist, Beijing, November 2010.
25. Interview with legal aid center staff, Guangzhou, December 2010.
26. Interview with a company manager, Chengdu, January 2011.
27. Interview with an urban planning scholar, Beijing, 2010.
28. Interview with a teacher, Beijing, March 2012.
29. Interview with NGO staff, Chengdu, July 2012.
30. On the "left-behind" children of migrants in rural China, see Murphy (2020).
31. Interview with migrant legal aid clinic staff, Guangzhou, December 2010.
32. Interview with NGO staff, Shanghai, July 2017.
33. See National Bureau of Statistics of China (2014, 2015a) for the breakdown of insurance coverage by insurance types.
34. Interview with a migrant worker, Chengdu, July 2012.

35. Interview with a migrant worker, Chengdu, July 2012.
36. Interview with a migrant worker, Chengdu, July 2012.
37. Interviews with migrant workers, Chengdu, July 2012.
38. Interview with a migrant worker, Chengdu, July 2012.
39. Interviews with migrant workers, Chengdu, July 2012.
40. Interview with a public policy scholar, Beijing, July 2017. See Chuang (2020) on rural people losing their rights to village land.
41. Interview with a government–factory liaison, Dongguan, December 2010.
42. Interview with a government official, Chengdu, July 2012.
43. Interview with a migrant worker, Beijing, September 2010.
44. Interview with a migrant worker, Beijing, September 2010.
45. Interview with a construction company manager, Chengdu, January 2011. He added that this multi-layered system of subcontractors sometimes led to problems when a sub-contractor absconded with wages instead of paying their workers.
46. See Pun and Lu (2010) for an account of how the labor subcontracting system generates a culture of violence and frequent wage arrears.
47. Interview with a migrant worker, Chengdu, July 2012.
48. Interview with a doctor, Shanghai, July 2012.
49. Interviews with migrant workers, Beijing, December 2010.
50. Interview with a migrant activist, Beijing, November 2010.
51. Interview with a health care scholar, Chengdu, May 2012.
52. Interview with a health care scholar, Chengdu, May 2012.
53. Interview with a doctor, Beijing, June 2012.
54. Interview with a scholar-activist, Chengdu, May 2012.
55. Interview with a migrant worker, Beijing, July 2012.
56. Interview with a migrant worker, Guangzhou, July 2017.
57. Interview with a migrant worker, Beijing, September 2010.
58. Interview with a migrant worker, Beijing, December 2011.
59. Interview with a government official, Chengdu, May 2012.
60. Interview with an education scholar, Beijing, June 2012.
61. Interview with a principal, Beijing, June 2012.
62. Interview with a migrant worker, Beijing, July 2017.

7 CONCLUSION

1. Interview with a government official, Chengdu, May 2012.
2. Interview with a public policy scholar, Beijing, July 2017.
3. Interview with a social welfare scholar, Beijing, July 2017. See Pan (2020) on how *dibao* distribution is used to preempt threats to political order.
4. See Scott (2009) on people keeping the state at a distance and state evasion and state prevention in Southeast Asia.
5. See Chan (2023) on the authoritarian crisis response to COVID-19 in China, another governance issue with unintended consequences. Sources of control that enable the state to mobilize resources and people hamper the flexibility and nimbleness needed to adapt amid uncertainty.

6. Interview with a migrant worker, Beijing, December 2011.
7. Interview with a scholar-activist, Chengdu, May 2012.
8. Interview with a migrant activist, Beijing, January 2012.
9. For an example of the importance of political community cohesiveness for welfare, see Singh (2015) on subnationalism and social development in India.
10. Interview with a migrant worker, Beijing, December 2010.
11. See, for example, Ho (2019) on the provision of drinking water to urban residents in Shenzhen and Beijing.
12. For example, see Hunter and Power (2007) on social policy, including Bolsa Família, and the 2006 Brazilian elections and Auerbach (2020) on party workers and public goods provision in urban India.
13. See Teichman (2008) on conditional cash transfer programs in Chile and Mexico.
14. See Bloemraad et al. (2019) on social citizenship, deservingness, and redistribution in Western societies.
15. Paternalistic welfare programs, especially in the United States, operate under a philosophy of the social contract and make recipients satisfy behavioral requirements, such as working or staying in school (Mead 1998).

References

1 INEQUALITY AND THE AUTOCRAT'S TOOLBOX

Ang, Yuen Yuen. 2016. *How China Escaped the Poverty Trap*. Ithaca: Cornell University Press.
Albertus, Michael, Sofia Fenner, and Dan Slater. 2018. *Coercive Distribution*. New York: Cambridge University Press.
Bratton, Michael and Nicholas van de Walle. 1997. *Democratic Experiments in Africa: Regime Transitions in Comparative Perspective*. New York: Cambridge University Press.
Brownlee, Jason. 2007. *Authoritarianism in an Age of Democratization*. Cambridge: Cambridge University Press.
Bueno de Mesquita, Bruce and Alastair Smith. 2010. "Leader Survival, Revolutions, and the Nature of Government Finance." *American Journal of Political Science* 54(4): 936–950.
Bueno de Mesquita, Bruce, Alastair Smith, Randolph M. Siverson, and James D. Morrow. 2003. *The Logic of Political Survival*. Cambridge, MA: MIT Press.
Chan, Alexsia T. 2024. "Pliable Citizenship: Migrant Inequality in the Xi Jinping Era." In Esarey, Ashley and Rongbin Han (eds.), *The Xi Jinping Effect*. Seattle: University of Washington Press.
Chan, Kam Wing. 1994. *Cities with Invisible Walls: Reinterpreting Urbanization in Post-1949 China*. New York: Oxford University Press.
Chan, Kam Wing. 2009. "The Chinese Hukou System at 50." *Eurasian Geography and Economics* 50(2): 197–221.
Chan, Kam Wing and Will Buckingham. 2008. "Is China Abolishing the Hukou System?" *The China Quarterly* 195: 582–606.
Chan, Kam Wing, Fang Cai, Guanghua Wan, and Man Wang. 2018. *Urbanization with Chinese Characteristics: The Hukou System and Migration*. New York: Routledge.
Chan, Kam Wing and Li Zhang. 1999. "The Hukou System and Rural-Urban Migration in China: Processes and Changes." *The China Quarterly* 160: 818–855.

Cheng, Tiejun and Mark Selden. 1994. "The Origins and Social Consequences of China's Hukou System." *The China Quarterly* 139: 644–668.

Davenport, Christian. 2007. "State Repression and Political Order." *Annual Review of Political Science* 10(1): 1–23.

Diamond, Larry. 2015. "Facing up to the Democratic Recession." *Journal of Democracy* 26(1): 141–155.

Fan, C. Cindy. 2002. "The Elite, the Natives, and the Outsiders: Migration and Labor Market Segmentation in Urban China." *Annals of the Association of American Geographers* 92(1): 103–124.

Frantz, Erica and Andrea Kendall-Taylor. 2014. "A Dictator's Toolkit: Understanding How Co-Optation Affects Repression in Autocracies." *Journal of Peace Research* 51(3): 332–346.

Freedom House. 2017. "Populists and Autocrats: The Dual Threat to Global Democracy." Freedom in the World 2017 Report.

Gallagher, Mary E. 2017. *Authoritarian Legality in China: Law, Workers, and the State*. New York: Cambridge University Press.

Gallagher, Mary E. and Jonathan K. Hanson. 2009. "Coalitions, Carrots, and Sticks: Economic Inequality and Authoritarian States." *PS: Political Science & Politics* 42(4): 667–672.

Gallagher, Mary E. and Jonathan K. Hanson. 2015. "Power Tool or Dull Blade? Selectorate Theory for Autocracies." *Annual Review of Political Science* 18: 367–385.

Gandhi, Jennifer. 2008. *Political Institutions under Dictatorship*. Cambridge: Cambridge University Press.

Gandhi, Jennifer and Adam Przeworski. 2006. "Cooperation, Cooptation, and Rebellion Under Dictatorships." *Economics & Politics* 18(1): 1–26.

Gandhi, Jennifer and Adam Przeworski. 2007. "Authoritarian Institutions and the Survival of Autocrats." *Comparative Political Studies* 40(11): 1279–1301.

Garay, Candelaria. 2016. *Social Policy Expansion in Latin America*. New York: Cambridge University Press.

Gershenson, Dmitriy and Herschel I. Grossman. 2001. "Cooption and Repression in the Soviet Union." *Economics and Politics* 13(1): 31–47.

Göbel, Christian. 2011. "Authoritarian Consolidation." *European Political Science* 10: 176–190.

Guo, Zhonghua and Tuo Liang. 2017. "Differentiating Citizenship in Urban China: A Case Study of Dongguan City." *Citizenship Studies* 21(7): 773–791.

Hawkins, Kirk A. and David R. Hansen. 2006. "Dependent Civil Society: The Círculos Bolivarianos in Venezuela." *Latin American Research Review* 41(1): 102–132.

Holland, Alisha C. 2017. *Forbearance as Redistribution: The Politics of Informal Welfare in Latin America*. New York: Cambridge University Press.

Huang, Xian. 2020. *Social Protection under Authoritarianism: Health Politics and Policy in China*. New York: Oxford University Press.

Jamil, Rehan Rafay. 2021. "Understanding Expansion of Latin America's New Social Welfare Regimes." *Comparative Politics* 53(3): 549–566.

Kitschelt, Herbert and Steven I. Wilkinson (eds.). 2007. *Patrons, Clients, and Policies: Patterns of Democratic Accountability and Political Competition*. Cambridge: Cambridge University Press.

Knutsen, Carl Henrik and Magnus Rasmussen. 2017. "The Autocratic Welfare State: Old-Age Pensions, Credible Commitments, and Regime Survival." *Comparative Political Studies* 51(5): 659–695.
Lipsky, Michael. 1980. *Street-Level Bureaucracy: Dilemmas of the Individual in Public Services*. New York: Russell Sage Foundation.
Magaloni, Beatriz. 2008. "Credible Power-Sharing and the Longevity of Authoritarian Rule." *Comparative Political Studies* 41(4–5): 715–741.
Mares, Isabela and Matthew E. Carnes. 2009 "Social Policy in Developing Countries." *Annual Review of Political Science* 12: 93–113.
Marshall, T. H. 1950. "Citizenship and Social Class." In *The Citizenship Debates: A Reader*, 93–112. London: Pluto Press.
Nathan, Andrew J. 2003. "Authoritarian Resilience." *Journal of Democracy* 14(1): 6–17.
National Bureau of Statistics. 2022. "2021 Migrant Workers Monitoring Survey Report." www.stats.gov.cn/tjsj/zxfb/202204/t20220429_1830126.html.
O'Donnell, Guillermo A. 1979. *Modernization and Bureaucratic-Authoritarianism: Studies in South American Politics*. Berkeley: Institute of International Studies.
Pan, Jennifer. 2020. *Welfare for Autocrats: How Social Assistance in China Cares for its Rulers*. New York: Oxford University Press.
Pepinsky, Thomas. 2007. "Autocracy, Elections, and Fiscal Policy: Evidence from Malaysia." *Studies Comparative International Development* 42(1–2): 136–163.
Piven, Frances Fox and Richard A. Cloward. 1971. *Regulating the Poor: The Functions of Public Welfare*. New York: Vintage Books.
Pizzi, Elise and Yue Hu. 2022. "Does Governmental Policy Shape Migration Decisions? The Case of China's Hukou System." *Modern China* 48(5): 1050–1079.
Reuters. 2013. "China Urbanization Cost Could Top $106 Billion a Year: Think-Thank." July 30. https://reut.rs/4685Nub.
Scott, James C. 1985. *Weapons of the Weak: Everyday Forms of Peasant Resistance*. New Haven: Yale University Press.
Scott, James C. 1998. *Seeing Like a State: How Certain Schemes to Improve the Human Condition Have Failed*. New Haven: Yale University Press.
Slater, Dan. 2010. *Ordering Power: Contentious Politics and Authoritarian Leviathans in Southeast Asia*. Cambridge: Cambridge University Press.
Solinger, Dorothy J. 1995. "China's Urban Transients in the Transition from Socialism and the Collapse of the Communist 'Urban Public Goods Regime.'" *Comparative Politics* 27(2): 127–146.
Solinger, Dorothy J. 1999. *Contesting Citizenship in Urban China: Peasant Migrants, the State, and the Logic of the Market*. Berkeley: University of California Press.
State Council of the People's Republic of China. 2014. "*Guojia xinxing chengzhen hua guihua* (National New-Type Urbanization Plan) (2014–2020)." www.gov.cn/zhengce/2014-03/16/content_2640075.htm.
Svolik, Milan W. 2012. *The Politics of Authoritarian Rule*. New York: Cambridge University Press.
Swider, Sarah. 2015. *Building China: The Rise of Informal Work and the New Precariat*. Ithaca: Cornell University Press.

The World Bank and Development Research Center of the State Council, The People's Republic of China. 2014. "Urban China: Toward Efficient, Inclusive, and Sustainable Urbanization." https://openknowledge.worldbank.org/handle/10986/18865.

Unger, Jonathan and Kaxton Siu. 2019. "Chinese Migrant Workers Across Four Decades: Shifts in Work Conditions, Urbanization, and Family Strategies." *Labor History* 60(6): 765–778.

van der Kamp, Denise Sienli. 2023. *Clean Air at What Cost? The Rise of Blunt Force Regulation in China*. New York: Cambridge University Press.

Wallace, Jeremy. 2014. *Cities and Stability: Urbanization, Redistribution, and Regime Survival*. New York: Oxford University Press.

Wang, Fei-ling. 2005. *Organizing through Division and Exclusion: China's Hukou System*. Stanford: Stanford University Press.

Wang, Zheng. 2014. "The Chinese Dream: Concept and Context." *Journal of Chinese Political Science* 19:1–13.

Wedeen, Lisa. 1999. *Ambiguities of Domination: Politics, Rhetoric, and Symbols in Contemporary Syria*. Chicago: University of Chicago Press.

Whyte, Martin King. 2010a. *Myth of the Social Volcano: Perceptions of Inequality and Distributive Injustice in Contemporary China*. Stanford: Stanford University Press.

Whyte, Martin King. 2010b. *One Country, Two Societies: Rural-Urban Inequality in Contemporary China*. Cambridge: Harvard University Press.

Wibbels, Erik and John S. Ahlquist. 2011. "Development, Trade, and Social Insurance." *International Studies Quarterly* 55(1): 125–149.

Wintrobe, Ronald. 1998. *The Political Economy of Dictatorship*. New York: Cambridge University Press.

Wu, Jieh-Min. 2010. "Rural Migrants Workers and China's Differential Citizenship: A Comparative Institutional Analysis." In Martin King Whyte (ed.), *One Country, Two Societies: Rural-Urban Inequality in Contemporary China*. Cambridge: Harvard University Press.

Xu, Xu. 2021. "To Repress or to Co-opt? Authoritarian Control in the Age of Digital Surveillance." *American Journal of Political Science* 65(2): 309–325.

2 A THEORY OF POLITICAL ATOMIZATION

Albertus, Michael, Sofia Fenner, and Dan Slater. 2018. *Coercive Distribution*. New York: Cambridge University Press.

Barnartt, Sharon N. 1996. "Disability Culture or Disability Consciousness?" *Journal of Disability Policy Studies* 7(2): 1–19.

Boehler, Patrick. 2013. "Pickle Index Measures Changing Tide of Chinese Migrant Workers." *South China Morning Post*. August 14. www.scmp.com/news/china-insider/article/1296315/pickle-index-measures-chinese-worker-migration.

Bueno de Mesquita, Bruce, Alastair Smith, Randolph M. Siverson, and James D. Morrow. 2003. *The Logic of Political Survival*. Cambridge: The MIT Press.

Chan, Alexsia T. 2024. "Pliable Citizenship: Migrant Inequality in the Xi Jinping Era." In Ashley Esarey and Rongbin Han (eds.), *The Xi Jinping Effect*. Seattle: University of Washington Press.

Chan, Alexsia T. and Kevin J. O'Brien. 2019. "Phantom Services: Deflecting Migrant Workers in China." *The China Journal* 81: 103–122.

Chan, Kam Wing and Will Buckingham. 2008. "Is China Abolishing the Hukou System?" *The China Quarterly* 195: 582–606.

Chan, Raymond K.H. and Ying Wang. 2009. "Controlled Decentralization: Minban Education Reform in China." *Journal of Comparative Social Welfare* 25(1): 27–36.

Chen, Feng and Xin Xu. 2012. "'Active Judiciary': Judicial Dismantling of Workers' Collective Action in China." *The China Journal* 67: 87–107.

Chen, Jiaxian and Dan Wang. 2021. "Class Consciousness of Rural Migrant Children in China." *The China Quarterly* 247: 814–834.

Chen, Xi. 2019. "The Logic of Fragmented Activism Among Chinese State-Owned Enterprise Workers." *The China Journal* 81: 58–80.

Chuang, Julia. 2014. "China's Rural Land Politics: Bureaucratic Absorption and the Muting of Rightful Resistance." *The China Quarterly* 219: 649–669.

Cui, Yuming, Jingjing Meng, and Changrong Lu. 2018. "Recent Developments in China's Labor Market: Labor Shortage, Rising Wages and Their Implications." *Review of Development Economics* 22: 1217–1238.

Diaz-Cayeros, Alberto, Federico Estevez, and Beatriz Magaloni. 2016. *The Political Logic of Poverty Relief: Electoral Strategies and Social Policy in Mexico*. New York: Cambridge University Press.

Duckett, Jane and Guohui Wang. 2017. "Why do Authoritarian Regimes Provide Public Goods? Policy Communities, External Shocks and Ideas in China's Rural Social Policy Making." *Europe-Asia Studies* 69(1): 92–109.

Edin, Maria. 2003. "State Capacity and Local Agent Control in China: CCP Cadre Management from a Township Perspective." *The China Quarterly* 173: 35–52.

Elfstrom, Manfred and Sarosh Kuruvilla. 2014. "The Changing Nature of Labor Unrest in China." *ILR Review* 67(2): 453–480.

Fu, Diana. 2017. *Mobilizing without the Masses: Control and Contention in China*. New York: Cambridge University Press.

Gallagher, Mary E. 2017. *Authoritarian Legality in China: Law, Workers, and the State*. New York: Cambridge University Press.

Gallagher, Mary and Jonathan K. Hanson. 2009. "Coalitions, Carrots, and Sticks: Economic Inequality and Authoritarian States." *PS: Political Science & Politics* 42(4): 667–672.

Gandhi, Jennifer and Adam Przeworski. 2006. "Cooperation, Cooptation, and Rebellion Under Dictatorships." *Economics & Politics* 18(1): 1–26.

Gandhi, Jennifer and Adam Przeworski. 2007. "Authoritarian Institutions and the Survival of Autocrats." *Comparative Political Studies* 40(11): 1279–1301.

Gao, Hong and Adam Tyson. 2023. "Affiliated Associations in China's Education Sector: Between Passive Autonomy, Discretion and Control." *The China Quarterly* 255: 697–715.

Garay, Candelaria. 2016. *Social Policy Expansion in Latin America*. New York: Cambridge University Press.

Gerring, John. 1999. "What Makes a Concept Good? A Critical Framework for Understanding Concept Formation in the Social Sciences." *Polity* 31(3): 357–393.

Harvey, David. 2005. *A Brief History of Neoliberalism*. New York: Oxford University Press.

Holland, Alisha C. 2017. *Forbearance as Redistribution: The Politics of Informal Welfare in Latin America*. New York: Cambridge University Press.

Hong, Ren-Jie, Yu-Chi Tseng, and Thung-Hong Lin. 2022. "Guarding a New Great Wall: The Politics of Household Registration Reforms and Public Provision in China." *The China Quarterly* 251: 776–797.

Huang, Xian. 2014. "Expansion of Chinese Social Health Insurance: Who Gets What, When and How?" *Journal of Contemporary China* 23(89): 923–951.

Huang, Youqin. 2012. "Low-Income Housing in Chinese Cities: Policies and Practices." *The China Quarterly* 212: 953.

Hwang, In Hyee. 2022. "Compensating for Instability? Economic Openness, Threat of Social Unrest, and Welfare Provision in China." *Studies in Comparative International Development* 57(2): 171–197.

Jaros, Kyle A. 2019. *China's Urban Champions: The Politics of Spatial Development*. Princeton: Princeton University Press.

Kipnis, Andrew. 2006. "*Suzhi*: A Keyword Approach." *The China Quarterly* 186: 295–313.

Klein, Ethel. 1987. "The Diffusion of Consciousness in the United States and Western Europe." In Mary Fainsod Katzenstein and Carol McClurg Mueller (eds.), *The Women's Movements of the United States and Western Europe*. Philadelphia: Temple University Press.

Knight, John and Ramani Gunatilaka. 2018. "Chapter 4: Rural-Urban Migration and Happiness in China." In John F. Helliwell, Richard Layard, and Jeffery D. Sachs (eds). *World Happiness Report 2018*. New York: Sustainable Development Solutions Network.

Lan, Pei-chia. 2014. "Segmented Incorporation: The Second Generation of Rural Migrants in Shanghai." *The China Quarterly* 217: 243–265.

Lee, Ching-Kwan and Yong Hong Zhang. 2013. "The Power of Instability: Unraveling the Microfoundations of Bargained Authoritarianism in China." *American Journal of Sociology* 118(6): 1–34.

Lee, James and Ya-Peng Zhu. 2006. "Urban Governance, Neoliberalism and Housing Reform in China." *The Pacific Review* 19(1): 39–61.

Leech, Beth L. 2002. "Asking Questions: Techniques for Semistructured Interviews." *PS: Political Science & Politics* 35(4): 665–668.

Li, Hongbin, Lei Li, Binzhen Wu, and Yanyan Xiong. 2012. "The End of Cheap Chinese Labor." *Journal of Economic Perspectives* 26(4): 57–74.

Lin, Yi. 2011. "Turning Rurality into Modernity: Suzhi Education in a Suburban Public School of Migrant Children in Xiamen." *The China Quarterly* 206: 313–330.

Marrow, Helen. 2009. "Immigrant Bureaucratic Incorporation: The Dual Roles of Professional Missions and Government Policies." *American Sociological Review* 74(October): 756–776.

Murphy, Rachel. 2004. "Turning Peasants into Modern Chinese Citizens: 'Population Quality' Discourse, Demographic Transition and Primary Education." *The China Quarterly* 177: 1–20.

O'Brien, Kevin J. 2006. "Discovery, Research Re(design) and Theory Building." In Maria Heimer and Stig Thogersen (eds.), *Doing Fieldwork in China*. Honolulu: University of Hawai'i Press.

O'Brien, Kevin J. and Lianjiang Li. 2006. *Rightful Resistance in Rural China*. New York: Cambridge University Press.

O'Brien, Kevin J. and Yanhua Deng. 2017. "Preventing Protest One Person at a Time: Psychological Coercion and Relational Repression in China." *China Review* 17(2): 179–201.

Offe, Claus. 1972. "Advanced Capitalism and the Welfare State." *Politics and Society* 2: 479–488.

People's Government of Beijing. 2018. "Report on the Work of the Government 2018 (part I)." March 27. www.ebeijing.gov.cn/Government/reports/t1513295.htm.

People's Republic of China Central People's Government. 2017. "Beijing City Master Plan (2016–2035) Released" (北京城市总体规划（2016年-2035年）》发布). September 30. www.gov.cn/xinwen/2017-09/30/content_5228705.htm.

Piven, Frances Fox and Richard A. Cloward. 1971. *Regulating the Poor: The Functions of Public Welfare*. New York: Vintage Books.

Pun, Ngai, and Huilin Lu. 2010a. "The Culture of Violence: The Labor Subcontracting System and Collective Action by Construction Workers in Post-Socialist China." *The China Journal* 64: 143–158.

Pun, Ngai, and Huilin Lu. 2010b. "Unfinished Proletarianization: Self, Anger, and Class Action among the Second Generation of Peasant-Workers in Present-Day China." *Modern China* 36(5): 493–519.

Qian, Zhenchao, Yuan Cheng, and Yue Qian. 2019. "Hukou, marriage, and access to wealth in Shanghai." *Journal of Ethnic and Migration Studies*: 1–17.

Ratigan, Kerry. 2022. *Local Politics and Social Policy in China: Let Some Get Healthy First*. New York: Cambridge University Press.

Ruhs, Martin. 2013. *The Price of Rights: Regulating International Labor Migration*. Princeton: Princeton University Press.

Schatz, Edward. 2009. "Ethnographic Immersion and the Study of Politics." In Edward Schatz (ed.), *Political Ethnography: What Immersion Contributes to the Study of Power*. Chicago: The University of Chicago Press.

Scott, James C. 1998. *Seeing Like A State: How Certain Schemes to Improve the Human Condition Have Failed*. New Haven: Yale University Press.

State Council of the People's Republic of China. 2014. "*Guojia xinxing chengzhen hua guihua* (National New-Type Urbanization Plan) (2014–2020)." www.gov.cn/zhengce/2014-03/16/content_2640075.htm.

Svolik, Milan W. 2012. *The Politics of Authoritarian Rule*. New York: Cambridge University Press.

Wong, Christine. 2009. "Rebuilding Government for the 21st Century: Can China Incrementally Reform the Public Sector?" *The China Quarterly* 200: 929–952.

Xinhua. 2019. "Beijing's Point-Based Hukou System to Open for Annual Application." May 17. www.xinhuanet.com/english/2019-05/17/c_138067093.htm.

Yan, Yunxiang. 2010. "The Chinese Path to Individualization." *The British Journal of Sociology* 61(3): 489–512.

Yang, Dali L. 2005. "China's Looming Labor Shortage." *Far Eastern Economic Review* 168(2): 19–24.

Zhang, Heather Xiaoquan. 2012. "Protecting Mobile Livelihoods: Actors' Responses to the Emerging Health Challenges in Beijing and Tianjin," *Modern China* 38(4): 446–478.

Zuo, Mandy. 2016. "Beijing Spells Out Strict Residency Rules for Migrants to the Capital." *South China Morning Post*. August 12. www.scmp.com/news/china/policies-politics/article/2002543/beijing-brings-strict-new-migration-policy-cut-citys.

3 DEFLECTING MIGRANT WORKERS

Becker, Jeffrey. 2012. "The Knowledge to Act: Chinese Migrant Labor Protests in Comparative Perspective." *Comparative Political Studies* 45(11): 1379–1404.

Cai, Yongshun. 2008. "Disruptive Collective Action in the Reform Era." In Kevin J. O'Brien (ed.), *Popular Protest in China*. Cambridge: Harvard University Press. 163–178.

Chan, Kam Wing. 1994a. *Cities with Invisible Walls: Reinterpreting Urbanization in Post-1949 China*. New York: Oxford University Press.

Chan, Kam Wing. 1994b. "Urbanization and Rural-Urban Migration in China since 1982: A New Baseline." *Modern China* 20(3): 243–281.

Chan, Kam Wing. 2009. "The Chinese Hukou System at 50." *Eurasian Geography and Economics* 50(2): 197–221.

Chan, Kam Wing, Fang Cai, Guanghua Wan, and Man Wang. 2018. *Urbanization with Chinese Characteristics: The Hukou System and Migration*. New York: Routledge.

Chan, Kam Wing and Li Zhang. 1999. "The Hukou System and Rural-Urban Migration in China: Processes and Changes." *The China Quarterly* 160: 818–855.

Chan, Kam Wing and Will Buckingham. 2008. "Is China Abolishing the Hukou System?" *The China Quarterly* 195: 582–606.

Chan, Raymond K. H. and Ying Wang. 2009. "Controlled Decentralization: Minban Education Reform in China." *Journal of Comparative Social Welfare* 25(1): 27–36.

Chen, Xi. 2009. "The Power of 'Troublemaking': Protest Tactics and Their Efficacy in China." *Comparative Politics* 41(4): 451–471.

Cheng, Tiejun and Mark Selden. 1994. "The Origins and Social Consequences of China's Hukou System." *The China Quarterly* 139: 644–668.

Chuang, Julia. 2014. "China's Rural Land Politics: Bureaucratic Absorption and the Muting of Rightful Resistance." *The China Quarterly* 219: 649–669.

Dong, Yiming and Charlotte Goodburn. 2020. "Residence Permits and Points Systems: New Forms of Educational and Social Stratification in Urban China." *Journal of Contemporary China* 29(125): 647–666.

Fan, C. Cindy. 2002. "The Elite, the Natives, and the Outsiders: Migration and Labor Market Segmentation in Urban China." *Annals of the Association of American Geographers* 92(1): 103–124.

Gao, Qin, Sui Yang, and Fuhua Zhai. 2019. "Social Policy and Income Inequality during the Hu-Wen Era: A Progressive Legacy?" *The China Quarterly* 237: 82–107.

Gardner, Bradley. 2017. *China's Great Migration: How the Poor Built a Prosperous Nation.* Oakland: Independent Institute.

Guangdong Province Public Security. 2009a. "Mingnian 1 yue 1 ri qi juzhu zheng qudai zanzhuzheng liudong renkou ban juzhu zheng xiangshou geng duo quanyi." www.gdga.gov.cn/ztbd/tjb/gddt/200912/t20091231_393075.html.

Guangdong Province Public Security. 2009b. "Guangdong sheng yinjin rencai shixing 'Guangdong sheng juzhu zheng' de zhanxing banfa." www.gdga.gov.cn/ztbd/tjb/qwfb/200912/t20091228_393063.html.

Guo, Zhonghua and Tuo Liang. 2017. "Differentiating Citizenship in Urban China: A Case Study of Dongguan City." *Citizenship Studies* 21(7): 773–791.

He, Huifeng. 2017. "China's Silicon Valley to Migrant Workers: No Degree? No Problem." *South China Morning Post.* July 19.

Howell, Jude and Jane Duckett. 2019. "Reassessing the Hu-Wen Era: A Golden Age or Lost Decade for Social Policy in China?" *The China Quarterly* 237: 1–14.

Hsing, You-tien. 2010a. *The Great Urban Transformation: Politics of Land and Property in China.* New York: Oxford University Press.

Hsing, You-tien. 2010b. "Urban Housing Mobilizations." In You-tien Hsing and Ching Kwan Lee (eds.), *Reclaiming Chinese Society: The New Social Activism.* New York: Routledge. 17–41.

Huang, Xian. 2014. "Expansion of Chinese Social Health Insurance: Who Gets What, When and How?" *Journal of Contemporary China* 23(89): 923–951.

Huang, Youqin. 2012. "Low-Income Housing in Chinese Cities: Policies and Practices." *The China Quarterly* 212: 953.

Immel, Philpp C. D. 2020. "High-Modernist Urban Planning in Beijing for Population Control." *Journal of Current Chinese Affairs* 49(3): 291–311.

Jacob, Rahul. 2011. "Residency Reforms Favour China's Wealthiest; Resentment Grows over Two-Tier System in Shenzhen and Guangzhou." *Financial Times.* September 12.

Javeline, Debra. 2003. "The Role of Blame in Collective Action: Evidence from Russia." *The American Political Science Review* 97(1): 107–121.

Kwong, Julia. 2004. "Educating Migrant Children: Negotiations between the State and Civil Society." *The China Quarterly* 180: 1073–1088.

Lan, Pei-chia. 2014. "Segmented Incorporation: The Second Generation of Rural Migrants in Shanghai." *The China Quarterly* 217: 243–265.

Lee, Ching-Kwan and Yong Hong Zhang. 2013. "The Power of Instability: Unraveling the Microfoundations of Bargained Authoritarianism in China." *American Journal of Sociology* 118(6): 1–34.

Leung, Joe C. B. and Meng Xiao. 2015. "The Institutionalization of Social Assistance." In Kinglun Ngok and Chak Kwan Chan (eds.), *China's Social Policy: Transformation and Challenges.* New York: Routledge. Ch. 3.

Li, Yan and Shufang Wu. 2010. "Migration and Health Constraints in China: A Social Strata Analysis." *Journal of Contemporary China* 19(64): 335–358.

Liu, Tao and Qiujie Shi. 2020. "Acquiring a Beijing hukou: Who Is Eligible and Who Is Successful?" *The China Quarterly.*

Ministry of Finance of the People's Republic of China. 2017. "2016 *nian caizheng shou zhi qingkuang* (Revenue and Expenditure Situation)." January 23. http://gks.mof.gov.cn/zhengfuxinxi/tongjishuju/201701/t20170123_2526014.html.

Morris, Carwyn. 2022. "Spatial Governance in Beijing: Informality, Illegality and the Displacement of the 'Low-end Population.'" *The China Quarterly* 251: 822–842.

Müller, Armin. 2017. "Functional Integration of China's Social Protection in Health and Pension Insurance." *Asian Survey* 57(6): 1110–1134.

National Bureau of Statistics of China. 2016a. "*2016 nian nongmin gong jiance diaocha baogao*." www.stats.gov.cn/tjsj/zxfb/201704/t20170428_1489334.html.

National Bureau of Statistics of China. 2016b. "2016 *Zhongguo tongji nianjian*." www.stats.gov.cn/tjsj/ndsj/2016/indexch.htm.

National Bureau of Statistics of China. 2017a. "2017 *Zhongguo tongji nianjian*." www.stats.gov.cn/tjsj/ndsj/2017/indexch.htm.

National Bureau of Statistics of China. 2017b. "2016: A Good Start for China's Economy during the 13th Five-Year Plan Period." www.stats.gov.cn/english/pressrelease/201701/t20170120_1455922.html.

National Bureau of Statistics. 2022. "2021 Migrant Workers Monitoring Survey Report." www.stats.gov.cn/tjsj/zxfb/202204/t20220429_1830126.html.

National Health and Family Planning Commission of China. 2014. "Summary of China's Migrant Population Report for 2013." http://en.nhc.gov.cn/2014-05/16/c_45960.htm.

National Health and Family Planning Commission of China. 2016. "*2016 nian 10 yue 19 ri zhuanti fabu hui cailiao: 'Zhongguo liudong renkou fazhan baogao 2016' neirong gaiyao*." www.nhfpc.gov.cn/xcs/s3574/201610/58881fa502e5481082eb9b34331e3eb2.shtml.

O'Brien, Kevin J. and Yanhua Deng. 2015. "Repression Backfires: Tactical Radicalization and Protest Spectacle in Rural China." *Journal of Contemporary China* 24(93): 457–470.

Ong, Lynette H. 2018. "Thugs and Outsourcing of State Repression in China." *The China Journal* 80: 94–110.

Peng, Chonghong and Julia Shu-Huah Wang. 2023. "Accommodating China's Floating Population: Local Variations and Determinants of Housing Policies for Rural Migrant Workers." *The China Quarterly*: 158–182.

Pun, Ngai and Jenny Chan. 2012. "Global Capital, the State, and Chinese Workers: The Foxconn Experience." *Modern China* 38(4): 383–410.

Reuters. 2013. "China Urbanization Cost Could top $106 Billion a Year: Think-tank." July 30.

Shanghai Daily. 2013. "Shanghai to Ease Residency Permits for Outsiders." June 20.

Shanghai Municipal Government. 2013. "Notice of Shanghai Municipal People's Government on Printing and Distributing the Trial Procedures for Management of Shanghai Residence Card Points." www.shanghai.gov.cn/shanghai/node27118/node27386/node27408/n31241/n31279/u26ai38733.html.

Shanghai Municipal Information Office. 2013. "Shanghai's New Regulations on Residence Permit Application and Management." http://en.shio.gov.cn/presscon/2013/06/28/1152383.html.

Solinger, Dorothy J. 1995. "China's Urban Transients in the Transition from Socialism and the Collapse of the Communist 'Urban Public Goods Regime.'" *Comparative Politics* 27(2): 127–146.
Solinger, Dorothy J. 1999. *Contesting Citizenship in Urban China: Peasant Migrants, the State, and the Logic of the Market*. Berkeley: University of California Press.
Solinger, Dorothy J. 2013. "Streets as Suspect: State Skepticism and the Current Losers in Urban China," *Critical Asian Studies* 45(1): 3–26.
State Council of the People's Republic of China. 2012. "Medical and Health Services in China," *White Paper*. http://english.gov.cn/archive/white_paper/2014/08/23/content_281474982986476.htm.
State Council of the People's Republic of China. 2017. "Health Care Reform Policies in First Half of 2017." http://english.gov.cn/policies/policy_watch/2017/08/12/content_281475785356366.htm.
Teets, Jessica C. 2012. "Reforming Service Delivery in China: The Emergence of a Social Innovation Model." *Journal of Chinese Political Science* 17(1): 15–32.
The Economist. 2014. "The Great Transition." March 22.
The Guardian. 2014. "China's Nail Houses: The Homeowners Who Refuse to Make Way." April 15.
The Wall Street Journal. 2013. "Easing Gaokao Restrictions: A New Year's Gift?" January.
Tse, Chun-wing. 2016. "Urban Residents' Prejudice and Integration of Rural Migrants into Urban China." *Journal of Contemporary China* 25(100): 579–595.
Wallace, Jeremy L. 2014. *Cities and Stability: Urbanization, Redistribution, and Regime Survival in China*. New York: Oxford University Press.
Wang, Fei-ling. 2005. *Organizing through Division and Exclusion: China's Hukou System*. Stanford: Stanford University Press.
Wang, Xiang. 2021. "Permits, Points, and Permanent Household Registration: Recalibrating Hukou Policy under 'Top-Level Design.'" *Journal of Current Chinese Affairs* 49(3): 269–290.
Wang, Yue and Haoyuan Huang. 2010. "'Hukou' Scoring System Quickens China's Pace Towards Urbanization." *Xinhua News*. November.
Whyte, Martin King. 2010. *One Country, Two Societies: Rural-Urban Inequality in Contemporary China*. Cambridge: Harvard University Press.
Wines, Michael and Jonathan Ansfield. 2010. "Trampled in a Land Rush, Chinese Resist." *The New York Times*. May 26.
Wu, Fulong. 2016. "State Dominance in Urban Redevelopment: Beyond Gentrification in Urban China." *Urban Affairs Review* 52(5): 631–658.
Wu, Jieh-Min. 2010. "Rural Migrants Workers and China's Differential Citizenship: A Comparative Institutional Analysis." In Martin King Whyte (ed.), *One Country, Two Societies: Rural-Urban Inequality in Contemporary China*. Cambridge: Harvard University Press. 55–84.
Wu, Weiping. 2002. "Migrant Housing in Urban China: Choices and Constraints." *Urban Affairs Review* 38(1): 90–119.
Xinhua. 2015. "Beijing Mulls Credit Points for Registration of Nonresidents." December 10.

Yu, Hao. 2015. “Universal Health Insurance Coverage for 1.3 Billion People: What Accounts for China’s Success?” *Health Policy* 119(9): 1145–1152.

Zhang, Heather Xiaoquan. 2012. “Protecting Mobile Livelihoods: Actors’ Responses to the Emerging Health Challenges in Beijing and Tianjin.” *Modern China* 38(4): 446–478.

Zhang, Li and Meng Li. 2016. “Local Fiscal Capability and Liberalization of Urban Hukou.” *Journal of Contemporary China* 25(102): 893–907.

Zhou, Yisu and Dan Wang. 2016. “Understanding the Constraints on the Supply of Public Education to the Migrant Population in China: Evidence from Shanghai.” *Journal of Contemporary China* 25(100): 563–578.

4 DEMOBILIZING MIGRANT WORKERS

Canaves, Sky and Sue Feng. 2010. “The Trials of Migrant Schools in Beijing.” *The Wall Street Journal*, March 5.

Cao, Xiaoqian. 2012. “上海人均GDP超北京全国最高.” *Dongfang Daily*, January 20. www.dfdaily.com/html/3/2012/1/20/733021.shtml.

Chan, David, Ka-ho Mok, and Anguo Tang. 2004. “Education.” In Linda Wong, Lynn T. White III, and Gui Shixun (eds.), *Social Policy Reform in Hong Kong and Shanghai: A Tale of Two Cities*, 85–126. M. E. Sharpe.

Chen, Xin. 2012. “Migrant Children Have Greater Chance of Missing Out on School.” *China Daily*, August 8. www.chinadaily.com.cn/cndy/2012-08/08/content_15651090.htm.

Chengdu Statistics Bureau. 2011. “Chengdu Statistical Yearbook 2011.”

China Labour Bulletin. 2020. “Migrant Workers and Their Children.” May 11. www.clb.org.hk/content/migrant-workers-and-their-children.

Choi, Chi-yuk. 2013. “The Shame of Sichuan’s Tofu Schools.” *South China Morning Post*, May 6. www.scmp.com/news/china/article/1230807/shame-sichuans-tofu-schools.

Department of Floating Population Service and Management of the National Population and Family Planning Commission of China. 2010. “Current Living Situation of Migrant Population in China.” *Population Research* (*Renkou Yanjiu*) 34(1): 6–18.

Friedman, Eli. 2022. *The Urbanization of People: The Politics of Development, Labor Markets, and Schooling in the Chinese City*. New York: Columbia University Press.

Froissart, Chloé. 2003. “The Hazards of the Right to an Education: A Study of the Schooling of Migrant Worker Children in Chengdu.” *China Perspectives* 48: 1–22.

Kwong, Julia. 2004. “Educating Migrant Children: Negotiations between the State and Civil Society.” *The China Quarterly* 180: 1073–1088.

Lai, Fang, Chengfang Liu, Renfu Luo, Linxiu Zhang, Xiaochen Ma, Yujie Bai, Brian Sharbono, and Scott Rozelle. 2014. “The Education of China’s Migrant Children: The Missing Link in China’s Education System.” *International Journal of Educational Development* 37: 68–77.

Lan, Pei-chia. 2014. “Segmented Incorporation: The Second Generation of Rural Migrants in Shanghai.” *The China Quarterly* 217: 243–265.

Levin, Dan. 2012. "A Chinese Education, for a Price." *The New York Times*.

Li, Jiayuan, Xing Ni, and Rui Wang. 2021. "Blame Avoidance in China's Cadre Responsibility System." *The China Quarterly* 247: 681–702.

Li, Miao and Yihan Xiong. 2019. "Producing the Morally Captive Guest: Discourse and Power in Gratitude Education of Migrant Children in Beijing." *The China Quarterly* 240: 1018–1038.

Liu, Chengfang. 2010. "Educating Beijing's Migrant Children: A Profile of the Weakest Link in China's Education System." http://iis-db.stanford.edu/docs/274/CFLIU_educating_Beijing_migrants_FF_Apr2010.pdf.

Lü, Xiaobo. 2014. "Social Policy and Regime Legitimacy: The Effects of Education Reform in China." *American Political Science Review* 108(2): 423–437.

Ministry of Education. 2019. "2018 National Education Statistical Bulletin" (2018年全国教育事业发展统计公报). www.moe.gov.cn/jyb_sjzl/sjzl_fztjgb/201907/t20190724_392041.html.

National Bureau of Statistics. 2020. "2019 Migrant Workers Monitoring Survey Report" (2019年农民工监测调查报告). www.stats.gov.cn/tjsj/zxfb/202004/t20200430_1742724.html.

National People's Congress. 1986. "Compulsory Education Law of the People's Republic of China." www.china.org.cn/government/laws/2007-04/17/content_1207402.htm.

National People's Congress. 2006. "Compulsory Education Law of the People's Republic of China." http://english.www.gov.cn/archive/laws_regulations/2014/08/23/content_281474983042154.htm.

Organization for Economic Co-Operation and Development. 2016. "Education in China: A Snapshot." www.oecd.org/china/Education-in-China-a-snapshot.pdf.

Robinson, Jean C. 1986. "Decentralization, Money, and Power: The Case of People-Run Schools in China." *Comparative Education Review* 30(1): 73–88.

The Economist. 2012. "Testing Times." *The Economist*, June 13. www.economist.com/blogs/analects/2012/06/university-entrance-exams.

United Nations. 2020. https://data.un.org/en/iso/cn.html.

Vortherms, Samantha A. 2019. "China's Missing Children: Political Barriers to Citizenship through the Household Registration System." *The China Quarterly* 238: 309–330.

Wan, Yi and Edward Vickers. 2022. "Towards Meritocratic Apartheid? Points Systems and Migrant Access to China's Urban Public Schools." *The China Quarterly* 249: 210–238.

Wang, Chengzhi. 2002. "Minban Education: The Planned Elimination of the 'People-Managed' Teachers in Reforming China." *International Journal of Educational Development* 22(2): 109–129.

Wang, Ou, Dongtao Qi, and Yangge Liu. 2023. "Administrative Burdens in Chinese Public Services: A Case of Selective Affinity." *The China Quarterly*.

Weaver, R. Kent. 1986. "The Politics of Blame Avoidance." *Journal of Public Policy* 6(4): 371–398.

Wong, Linda, Lynn T. White, and Shixun Gui. 2004. *Social Policy Reform in Hong Kong and Shanghai: A Tale of Two Cities*. M. E. Sharpe.

Yang, Juhua and Chengrong Duan. 2008. "A Comparative Analysis of Educational Opportunities for Migrant, Stay and Other Children in Rural China (*Nongcun*

Diqu Liudongertong, Liushou Ertong He Qita Ertong Jiaoyu Shehui Bijiao Yanjiu)." *Population Research* (*Renkou Yanjiu*) 32(1): 11–21.

Yu, Min and Christopher B. Crowley. 2020. "The Discursive Politics of Education Policy in China: Educating Migrant Children." *The China Quarterly* 241: 87–111.

Zhang, Junmian. 2012. "Top 10 Richest Provincial Regions in China 2011." http://china.org.cn/top10/2012-03/16/content_24912437_9.htm.

Zhi, Lin. 2010. "All Shanghai Migrant Workers' Children to Get Free Education This Year." *Xinhua News*, February 24. http://news.xinhuanet.com/english2010/china/2010-02/24/c_13186425.htm.

5 PLAYING WITH INSTITUTIONAL LEEWAY

Bloom, Gerald and Xingyuan Gu. 1997. "Health Sector Reform: Lessons from China." *Social Science and Medicine* 45(3): 351–360.

Blumenthal, David and William Hsiao. 2005. "Privatization and Its Discontents – The Evolving Chinese Health Care System." *The New England Journal of Medicine* 353(11): 1165–1170.

Chen, Laurie. 2018. "Chinese Parents Spend up to US$43,500 a Year on After-School Classes for Their Children." *South China Morning Post.* December 4. www.scmp.com/news/china/society/article/2176377/chinese-parents-spend-us43500-year-after-school-classes-their.

Goodburn, Charlotte. 2020. "Growing Up in (and Out of) Shenzhen: The Longer-Term Impacts of Rural-Urban Migration on Education and Labor Market Entry." *The China Journal* 83: 129–147.

Helmke, Gretchen and Steven Levitsky. 2004. "Informal Institutions and Comparative Politics: A Research Agenda." *Perspectives on Politics* 2(4): 725–740.

Honig, Emily. 1992. *Creating Chinese Ethnicity: Subei People in Shanghai, 1850–1980*. New Haven: Yale University Press.

Hsiao, William C. L. 1995. "The Chinese Health Care System: Lessons for Other Nations." *Social Science and Medicine* 41(8): 1047–1055. www.hsph.harvard.edu/health-care-financing/files/2012/09/hsiao_1995_-_the_chinese_health_care_system_-_lessons_for_other_nations.pdf.

Huang, Xian. 2021. "Peace in the Shadow of Unrest: *yinao* and the State Response in China." *The China Quarterly* 247: 724–748.

Li, Ling, Qiulin Chen, and Dillon Powers. 2012. "Chinese Healthcare Reform: A Shift toward Social Development." *Modern China* 38(6): 630–645.

Lipsky, Michael. 1980. *Street-Level Bureaucracy: Dilemmas of the Individual in Public Services*. New York: Russell Sage Foundation.

Liu, Xingzhu and Anne Mills. 2002. "Financing Reforms of Public Health Services in China: Lessons for Other Nations." *Social Science and Medicine* 54(11): 1691–1698.

Long, Qian, Ling Xu, Henk Bekedam, and Shenglan Tang. 2013. "Changes in Health Expenditures in China in 2000s: Has the Health System Reform Improved Affordability." *International Journal for Equity in Health* 12(40): 1–8.

Marrow, Helen B. 2009. "Immigrant Bureaucratic Incorporation: The Dual Roles of Professional Missions and Government Policies." *American Sociological Review* 74(October): 756–776.

Maynard-Moody, Steven Williams and Michael Craig Musheno. 2003. *Cops, Teachers, Counselors: Stories from the Front Lines of Public Service*. Ann Arbor: University of Michigan Press.

National Bureau of Statistics of China. 2020. "Households' Income and Consumption Expenditure in 2019." www.stats.gov.cn/english/PressRelease/202001/t20200119_1723719.html.

Scoggins, Suzanne E. 2021. *Policing China: Street-Level Cops in the Shadow of Protest*. Ithaca: Cornell University Press.

Sharma, Yojana. 2013. "Asia's Parents Suffering 'Education Fever.'" *BBC News*. October 22. www.bbc.co.uk/news/business-24537487.

Takada, Kazunori. 2013. "Bribery Serves as Life – Support for Chinese Hospitals." *Reuters*. July 23. www.reuters.com/article/2013/07/23/us-china-hospitals-bribery-idUSBRE96M12Y20130723.

The World Bank. 2010. "Fixing the Public Hospital System in China." http://siteresources.worldbank.org/HEALTHNUTRITIONANDPOPULATION/Resources/281627-1285186535266/FixingthePublicHospitalSystem.pdf.

Tsai, Kellee S. 2006. "Adaptive Informal Institutions and Endogenous Institutional Change in China." *World Politics* 59(1): 116–141.

Tsang, Mun C. 1996. "Financial Reform of Basic Education in China." *Economics of Education Review* 15(4): 423–444.

Wei, Haitao and Cheris Shun-ching Chan. 2022. "Working Without Wages: Network Structure and Migrant Construction Workers' Protests in China." *The China Quarterly* 252: 1140–1161.

Yip, Winnie and William Hsiao. 2009. "China's Health Care Reform: A Tentative Assessment." *China Economic Review* 20(4) (December): 613–619.

6 MAKING DO AND MUDDLING THROUGH

Bärnighausen, Till, Yuanli Liu, Xinping Zhang, and Rainer Sauerborn. 2007. "Willingness to Pay for Social Health Insurance among Informal Sector Workers in Wuhan, China: A Contingent Valuation Study." *BMC Health Services Research* 7(114): 1–16.

Chuang, Julia. 2020. *Beneath the China Boom: Labor, Citizenship, and the Making of a Rural Land Market*. Oakland: University of California Press.

Health Commission of Heilongjiang Province. 2015. 黑龙江省卫生计生舆情摘报 (2015年 第54期) (*Heilongjiang sheng weisheng jisheng yuqing zhai bao (2015 nian di 54 qi)*). June 19. http://wsjkw.hlj.gov.cn/pages/5f05817e896eb305f4de18f3.

Huang, Xian. 2020. *Social Protection under Authoritarianism: Health Politics and Policy in China*. New York: Oxford University Press.

Li, Hui and Ben Blanchard. 2013. "China's 'Black Clinics' Flourish as Government Debates Health Reform." *Reuters*. March 27.

Li, Xi, Harlan M. Krumholz, Winnie Yip, Kar Keung Cheng, Jan De Maeseneer, Qingyue Meng, Elias Mossialos, Chuang Li, Jiapeng Lu, Meng Su, Qiuli Zhang,

Dong Roman Xu, Liming Li, Sharon-Lise T. Normand, Richard Peo, Jing Li, Zengwu Wang, Hongbing Yan, Runlin Gao, Somsak Chunharas, Xin Gao, Raniero Guerra, Huijie Ji, Yang Ke, Zhigang Pan, Xianping Wu, Shuiyan Xiao, Xinying Xie, Yujuan Zhang, Jun Zhu, Shanzhu Zhu, and Shengshou Hu. 2020. "Quality of Primary Health Care in China: Challenges and Recommendations." *The Lancet* 395(10239): 1802–1812.

Li, Yan. 2014. "Illegal Private Clinics: Ideal Health Services Choices among Rural–Urban Migrants in China?" *Social Work in Public Health* 29: 473–480.

Morduch, Jonathan. 1999. "Between the State and the Market: Can Informal Insurance Patch the Safety Net?" *The World Bank Research Observer* 14(2): 187–207.

Müller, Armin. 2019. "Public Services and Informal Profits: Governing Township Health Centres in a Context of Misfit Regulatory Institutions." *The China Quarterly* 237: 108–130.

Murphy, Rachel. 2020. *The Children of China's Great Migration*. New York: Cambridge University Press.

National Bureau of Statistics of China. 2014. "2013 年全国农民工监测调查报告." www.stats.gov.cn/tjsj/zxfb/201405/t20140512_551585.html.

National Bureau of Statistics of China. 2015a. "2014年全国农民工监测调查报告." www.stats.gov.cn/tjsj/zxfb/201504/t20150429_797821.html.

National Bureau of Statistics of China. 2015b. "Statistical Communiqué of the People's Republic of China on the 2014 National Economic and Social Development." www.stats.gov.cn/english/PressRelease/201502/t20150228_687439.html.

National Bureau of Statistics of China. 2020. 中国统计年鉴(*Zhongguo tongji nianjian, China Statistical Yearbook*). www.stats.gov.cn/tjsj/ndsj/2020/indexch.htm.

National Health and Family Planning Commission of the People's Republic of China. 2013. 国家卫生计生委集中整顿基层医疗机构取缔黑诊所6626个 (*Guojia weisheng jisheng wei jizhong zhengdun jiceng yiliao jigou qudi hei zhensuo 6626 ge*). www.nhfpc.gov.cn/xcs/gzjb/201401/58fc6535ff68446dae9b865c23efaf49.shtml.

National Health Commission of the People's Republic of China. 2019. "Start of National Campaign to Build a Healthy China." http://en.nhc.gov.cn/2019-08/22/c_75590.htm.

People's Daily. 2015. "哈尔滨打击非法行医：'黑诊所'状况堪忧 患者称'图个方便.'" *People's Daily*, June 18. http://hlj.people.com.cn/n/2015/0618/c220024-25289882.html.

Pun, Ngai and Jenny Chan. 2012. "Global Capital, the State, and Chinese Workers: The Foxconn Experience." *Modern China* 38(4): 383–410.

Pun, Ngai and Huilin Lu. 2010. "The Culture of Violence: The Labor Subcontracting System and Collective Action by Construction Workers in Post-Socialist China." *The China Journal* 64: 143–158.

State Council. 2017. "Development of China's Public Health as an Essential Element of Human Rights" (*White Paper*). http://english.www.gov.cn/archive/white_paper/2017/09/29/content_281475894089810.htm.

Sun, Xin. 2020. "Campaign-Style Implementation and Affordable Housing Provision in China." *The China Journal* 84: 76–101.
Wu, Jieh-Min. 2010. "Rural Migrants Workers and China's Differential Citizenship: A Comparative Institutional Analysis." In Martin King Whyte (ed.), *One Country, Two Societies: Rural-Urban Inequality in Contemporary China*. Harvard University Press. 55–84.
Xinhua News. 2015. 根除'黑诊所'需要标本兼治 2015 (*Genchu 'hei zhensuo' xuyao biaoben jianzhi*). *Xinhua News*. April 19. http://news.xinhuanet.com/politics/2015-04/19/c_1115016520.htm.
Yang, Wei. 2020. "Understanding the Non-medical Costs of Healthcare: Evidence from Inpatient Care for Older People in China." *The China Quarterly* 242: 487–507.
Zhang, Xia. 2020. "'The People's Commune is Good': Precarious Labor, Migrant Masculinity and Post-Socialist Nostalgia in Contemporary China." *Critical Asian Studies* 52(4): 530–549.

7 CONCLUSION

Auerbach, Adam Michael. 2020. *Demanding Development: The Politics of Public Goods Provision in India's Urban Slums*. New York: Cambridge University Press.
Blank, Rebecca M. 2002. "Evaluating Welfare Reform in the United States." *Journal of Economic Literature* 40(4): 1105–1166.
Bloemraad, Irene, Will Kymlicka, Michèle Lamont, and Leanne S. Son Hing. 2019. "Membership without Social Citizenship? Deservingness and Redistribution as Grounds for Equality." *Daedalus* 148(3): 73–104.
Chan, Alexsia T. 2023. "Authoritarian Crisis Response to COVID-19 in China." In Alan W. Cafruny and Leila Talani (eds.), *The Political Economy of Global Responses to COVID-19*. Cham, Switzerland: Palgrave Macmillan.
Chan, Alexsia T. 2024. "Pliable Citizenship: Migrant Inequality in the Xi Jinping Era." In Ashley Esarey and Rongbin Han (eds.), *The Xi Jinping Effect*, Seattle: University of Washington Press. 129–150.
Ho, Selina. 2019. *Thirsty Cities: Social Contracts and Public Goods Provision in China and India*. New York: Cambridge University Press.
Hunter, Wendy and Timothy J. Power. 2007. "Rewarding Lula: Executive Power, Social Policy, and the Brazilian Elections of 2006." *Latin American Politics and Society* 49(1): 1–30.
Lipsky, Michael. 1980. *Street-Level Bureaucracy: Dilemmas of the Individual in Public Services*. New York: Russell Sage Foundation.
Maloy, Kathleen A., Ladonna A. Pavetti, Julie Darnell, and Peter Shin. 1999. "Diversion as a Work-Oriented Welfare Reform Strategy and Its Effect on Access to Medicaid: An Examination of the Experiences of Five Local Communities." Center for Health Policy Research.
Mead, Lawrence M. 1998. "Telling the Poor What to Do." *The Public Interest* 132: 97–112.
Pan, Jennifer. 2020. *Welfare for Autocrats: How Social Assistance in China Cares for Its Rulers*. New York: Oxford University Press.

Pereira, Anthony W. 2015. "*Bolsa Família* and Democracy in Brazil." *Third World Quarterly* 36(9): 1682–1699.

Sánchez-Ancochea, Diego and Lauro Mattei. 2011. "Bolsa Família, Poverty and Inequality: Political Economic Effects in the Short and Long Run." *Global Social Policy* 11(2–3): 299–318.

Scott, James C. 2009. *The Art of Not Being Governed: An Anarchist History of Upland Southeast Asia*. New Haven: Yale University Press.

Singh, Prerna. 2015. *How Solidarity Works for Welfare: Subnationalism and Social Development in India*. New York: Cambridge University Press.

Soss, Joe, Richard C. Fording, and Sanford F. Schram. 2011. *Disciplining the Poor: Neoliberal Paternalism and the Persistent Power of Race*. Chicago: University of Chicago Press.

Teichman, Judith. 2008. "Redistributive Conflict and Social Policy in Latin America." *World Development* 36(3): 446–460.

Thornton, Patricia M. 2017. "A New Urban Underclass? Making and Managing 'Vulnerable Groups' in Contemporary China." In Vivienne Shue and Patricia M. Thornton (eds.), *To Govern China: Evolving Practices of Power*. New York: Cambridge University Press. 257–281.

Wang, Feng. 2019. "China's Uphill Battle against Inequality." In Dorothy J. Solinger (ed.), *Polarized Cities: Portraits of Rich and Poor in Urban China*. New York: Rowman & Littlefield. 23–42.

Yan, Gu. 2017. "Compulsory Education for Children of Migrant Workers: Is *Hukou* the Biggest Obstacle?" In Karen Eggelston, Jean C. Oi, and Yiming Wang (eds.), *Challenges in the Process of China's Urbanization*. Stanford: Walter H. Shorenstein Asia-Pacific Research Center Books. 113–138.

Index

absorption, selective, 84, 85–86
activists, 72
Adidas, 27
Anhui Province, 15, 38, 132–133
authoritarian control, 7–9
authoritarian distribution, 9–11
autocrats, 1–3

Beijing
  Chaoyang District, 80
  Daxing District, 66, 80–81
  document-checking rules, 63
  Fengtai District, 65, 80
  GDP per capita, 78
  Haidian District, 80–81, 83
  household registration (*hukou*) system, 25, 69, 78
  migrant schools, 78, 80–81, 95, 96
  migrant workers, 101
  population cap, 12
  private schools, 65, 75, 91, 114
  public schools, 56, 64–65, 81–84, 141
  regulation and integration of migrants in, 18
  services for migrants, 25, 56, 63, 69
  Summer Olympics (2008), 94
  vocational schools, 60
  Xinjian Village, 66
Beijing Municipal Education Commission, 60
Beijing Municipal Health and Family Planning Commission, 129
Beijing Municipal Master Plan (2016–2035), 25
Beijing University, 115
Benxi, 69
black clinics (*hei zhensuo*), 123, 125, 129, 151
blame, avoiding, 93–96
boarding schools, 132–133
Bolivarian circles, 10
Brazil, 32, 157
  Bolsa Família, 157
building safety, 95
bureaucracy and bureaucrats, 51, 105
  co-migrant empathy, 107–108
  document-checking rules, 63
  inequality in service to the state, 49–50

cash flow, 137–138
catastrophic care, 133–134
CCP. *See* Chinese Communist Party (CCP)
"the center treats; local governments pay" (*zhongyang qingke, dangdi maidan*, 中央请客，当地买单), 44
certification
  fake papers, 139–140
  of private schools, 87–89, 93
charity, 110
Chengdu, Sichuan Province
  GDP per capita, 79
  household registration (*hukou*, 户口) system, 136
  migrant schools, 79, 88
  migrant workers, 101, 104–105, 108, 111, 135
  private schools, 78, 115
  public hospitals, 111

Chengdu, Sichuan Province (cont.)
public schools, 64, 69, 78, 79, 89–90, 95
regulation and integration of migrants in, 18, 96
school fees, 89
services for migrants, 15, 25, 56, 62, 65, 69, 79, 91
teacher wage, 89
child care, 132, 141–142
children
left-behind, 76, 132
of migrants. *See* migrant children
China
annual disposable income, 113
Compulsory Education Law, 75
Healthy China Action Plan (2019–2030), 127
household registration. *See* household registration (*hukou*, 户口) system
internal migration, 32
labor shortages, 26
labor unrest, 27–28
migrant workers in, 14, 30, 58–60. *See also* migrant workers (*nongmin gong*, 农民工)
National New-Type Urbanization Plan (*guojia xinxing chengzhen hua guihua*, 国家新型城镇化规划) (2014–2020), 4–5, 14, 24, 40
national policy, 58–60
political atomization, 23, 151–156
politics of inequality, 146–148
population management, 156
public expenditures, 68
public services, 11–13. *See also* public services
social services. *See* public services
State Council, 4–5
tax revenues, 68
urban population, 58
urbanization, 1, 39
Xi Jinping era, 5, 24, 48, 51, 72
Chinese Communist Party (CCP), 13, 46
Central Committee, 4–5
Chinese Dream, 40
Chinese labor force, 153. *See also* migrant workers (*nongmin gong*, 农民工)
high-skilled workers, 34
lower-skilled workers, 34, 36
Chongqing, 56, 60, 135
citizenship
gradations of, 13–17
pathways to, 51
pliable, 45, 49, 155
city(ies)
mega-cities, 24, 68–69
migrant deflection, 60–63, 67–69
migrant deflection away from, 64–67
class differences, 42
clientelism, 10
coercion, 2
college entrance exams (*gaokao*), 86, 107, 119, 142–143
co-migrant empathy, 107–112
common prosperity, 40
community problem solving, 125–127, 135–142
Compulsory Education Law, 75
construction workers
community-based solutions, 125
labor subcontracting, 137
lived experiences, 20–23, 101, 154
consumer spending, 114
cooperative labor groups, 135
corruption, 95
criticism, avoiding, 93–96
Culture and Art Museum of Migrant Workers, 101–102

Datong, 69
decentralization, 3, 45, 93, 113
deflecting migrant workers, 55–57, 71–72, 147
away from the city, 64–67
in the city, 60–63
rationale for, 67–69
demobilizing migrant workers, 73–74, 90–93, 96–97, 147
democracies, developing, 32–33
demographics, 28, 58
demolition, 116–120
deservingness, 37
developing countries, 10
developing democracies, 32–33
dibao (low-income assistance), 8, 71
dictators, 10
discrimination, 83, 116–120, 150
diversion, 158
doctors, 105–106, 108–110
differential treatment of patients, 116–118
earnings, 113

documentation, 63
  fake papers, 139–140
  five documents (*wuzheng*, 五证), 62–63, 82, 140
document-checking rules, 63
Dongguan, Guangdong Province, 25
  household registrations (*hukous*), 56
  segregated roads, 116
  Yue Yuen shoe factory complex, 27

earthquakes, 94–95
education, 150
  access to, 57, 60–63, 139–140, 141–142, 143, 150–151
  boarding schools, 132–133
  college entrance exams (*gaokao*), 86, 107, 142–143
  Compulsory Education Law, 12, 75
  consumer expenditure on, 114
  decentralization of, 113–115
  high school exams (*zhongkao*), 107
  migrant services, 18, 26–27, 96–97
  personalized services, 110–111
  private schools. *See* migrant schools
  public schools. *See* public schools
  for quality (*suzhi jiaoyu*, 素质教育), 26–27
  regular primary schools (*putong xiaoxue*, 普通小学), 59
  vocational school, 60
empathy for migrants
  co-migrant, 107–112
  conditional, 116–118
ethnographics, 30
evictions, 65–66
exclusion, 81–84, 93

fake papers, 139–140
family ties, 132
five documents (*wuzheng*, 五证), 62–63, 82, 140
floating population (*liudong renkou*, 流动人口), 34, 57
force, 2
Foxconn, 134
full inclusion, 87–88
funding, 44

gift giving, 109
GONGOs, 108
Guangdong Province
  labor shortages, 26
  Pearl River Delta, 26
  points system for residence permits, 60–61
  services for migrant workers, 41
Guangzhou
  household registrations (*hukous*), 25, 61
  public schools, 93

Hangzhou, 25
happiness, 30
Harbin, Heilongjiang Province, 129
HDI (Human Development Index), 29
health care
  access to, 50, 57, 59, 69, 127
  black clinics (*hei zhensuo*), 123, 125, 129, 151
  consumer expenditure on, 114
  costs, 66–67, 122–123, 128, 130–131
  decentralization of, 113
  differential treatment of patients, 116–118
  disturbance (*yinao*, 医闹), 113
  on-site medical clinics, 55
  private clinics, 19, 56, 128–130, 150
  providers, 108–110
  rural, 131–132
  service delivery, 105–106, 111, 113, 127
  traditional Chinese medicine, 129
health insurance
  catastrophic coverage, 133–134
  informal insurance groups, 138–139, 140
  making do without, 101, 128, 141–142
  migrant statistics, 59, 133
  rural, 38, 57, 66–67, 131–132
  sharing cards, 139–140
  workers' experiences with, 22
health savings accounts, 137
Healthy China Action Plan (2019–2030), 127
high school exams (*zhongkao*), 107
high-skilled migrants, 105, 108
high-skilled workers, 34
HMP (housing monetarization policy), 46
home ownership, 25
hongbao (red envelopes), 109
hospitals. *See* public hospitals
household registration (*hukou*, 户口) system, 5, 12, 24–25, 56, 57, 60–63, 69, 136
  reform, 24
housing, 103
  access to, 57
  low-income, 56
  for workers, 22

housing costs, 134
housing monetarization policy (HMP), 46
hukou system. *See* household registration (*hukou*, 户口) system
Human Development Index (HDI), 29

improvisation
  in communities, 125, 135–142
  by individuals, 125, 127–135
inclusion, 93
  contingent, 57–58
  full, 87–88, 89–90
  segregated, 84, 86–87
income inequality, 153
India, 32, 157
individual problem-solving, 125, 127–135
individualism, 42
individualization, 33, 41, 50. *See also* political atomization
industrialization, 14
inequality
  alternative explanations for, 2, 25–28
  embedded, 47–50, 159–162
  gradations of, 13–17
  income, 153
  politics of, 1–3, 7–17, 146–148
  reasons for, 2
  reinforcing, 69–70
  in service to the state, 49–50
  socioeconomic, 2
  structural, 13–17, 69–70
  wealth, 150
inequity, 2
informal institutions, 18, 112–115, 120
informal insurance groups, 138–139, 140
insurance. *See* health insurance; social insurance
integration, 93
  approaches to, 18, 96–97
  modes of, 77–79
internal migrants, 1, 43, 58–60
international migration, 32
interns, 134
intraregional migration, 132

judicial matters, 33

labor force. *See* Chinese labor force
labor NGOs, 48
labor shortages, 26
labor subcontracting, 137
labor unrest, 27–28

Latin America, 11, 33, 157
left-behind children, 76, 132
legal aid clinics, 115, 130–131
Li Keqiang, 24
local governments
  "the center treats; local governments pay" (*zhongyang qingke, dangdi maidan*, 中央请客，当地买单), 44
  co-migrant empathy, 111–112
  contingent inclusion of migrant workers, 57–58
  integration of migrants into urban public schools, 77–79
  political atomization, 68, 146–148
  regulation of private migrant schools, 77–79
local migration, 132
locals (*bendi*, 本地), 41
location of work, 131–133
lower-skilled workers, 34, 36
low-income assistance (*dibao*), 8, 71
low-income housing, 56
low-skilled migrants, 108

making do and muddling through, 122–124, 144–145
marginalization, 47–50, 161
marketization, 14
meal costs, 134
medical care. *See* health care
medical insurance. *See* health insurance
mega-cities, 24, 68–69
meritocracy, 42
methods, 29–30
migrant children
  discrimination against, 118–120
  education of, 18, 26–27, 74–77, 81–84, 103–104, 132–133
  private schools for, 18, 74–77
  in public schools, 86–87, 89–90
  in regular primary schools (*putong xiaoxue*, 普通小学), 59
  schools for, 84–86, 95
  separating, 86–87
  services for, 22
  statistics, 59, 76–77
migrant instructors, 110–111
migrant schools, 74–77. *See also* private schools
  facilities, 76
  safety of, 94–95
  self-managed, 112

subsidies for, 85–86
suppression of, 80–81, 95, 151
teachers, 75–76
migrant workers (*nongmin gong*, 农民工), 41
community problem-solving, 125, 135–142
contingent inclusion of, 57–58
deflecting, 55–57, 60–63, 64–69, 71–72, 147
demobilizing, 73–74, 96–97, 147
demographics, 58
differentiation of, 34–40, 49
discrimination against, 116–120
empathy for, 107–112, 116–118
exclusion of, 93
full inclusion of, 87–88
happiness of, 30
health care, 103–104
health insurance coverage, 59, 133
high-skilled, 34, 105, 108
inclusion of, 93
individual problem-solving, 125, 127–135
integration of, 77–79, 96–97
internal migrants, 1, 43, 58–60
interns, 134
left-behind children of, 76, 132
lived experiences, 20–23, 38, 92–93, 122
lower-skilled, 34
low-skilled, 108
making and using informal substitutes, 112–115
making do and muddling through, 18–19, 122–124, 142–145, 148
marginalization of, 46, 161
monthly income, 59
playing with institutional leeway, 101–103, 120–121
practical priorities, 18, 103–105, 148
public services for, 7–8, 10, 24, 33, 42, 57–58
regional distinctions, 41
resourcefulness, 18, 103–105, 135, 148
right to education, 12
scraping together needs, 124–127
second-class citizenship, 15
second-generation, 14, 28
self-identification of, 37
self-reliance, 124
statistics, 58–60
student workers, 134
wages, 134, 136–137
work location, 131–133
working within existing institutions, 105–112
migration
internal, 32
international, 32
intraregional, 132
local, 132
pull factors, 32
push factors, 32
modernization, 39

nail households (*dingzihu*, 钉子户), 66
National Development and Reform Commission (NDRC), 35
National New-Type Urbanization Plan (*guojia xinxing chengzhen hua guihua*, 国家新型城镇化规划) (2014–2020), 4–5, 14, 24, 40
national policy, 58–60
NDRC (National Development and Reform Commission), 35
neoliberalism, 46
neopatrimonialism, 10
new-type urbanization, 39
NGOs (nongovernmental organizations), 48
Nike, 27
nongovernmental organizations (NGOs), 48

outsiders (*waidi*, 外地), 41

paperwork, 63
document-checking rules, 63
fake papers, 139–140
five documents (*wuzheng*, 五证), 62–63, 82, 140
patronage, 10
Pearl River Delta, 26
pensions, 57, 103
people-centered (*yiren weiben*, 以人为本) urbanization, 5, 39
people-run schools (*minban xuexiao*). *See* private schools
phantom services, 55–57, 70, 71–72, 147
pickle index, 35
points systems, 60–63, 69, 91
policymaking, 44
political atomization, 2–3, 146–148
alternative explanations, 2, 25–28
concept of, 1–2, 8, 23–25, 30–34
demobilizing demand with, 90–93
identifying, 20–23

political atomization (cont.)
  implications for China, 151–156
  limits of, 148–151
  migrant improvising and, 142–144
  persistence or endurance, 41–47
  process of, 2, 23, 34–40
  pushing visible results and avoiding blame and criticism, 93–96
  resistance against, 151
  theory of, 50–51
  trade-offs and risks of, 47–48
  in the world, 157–159
politics
  of inequality, 1–3, 7–17, 146–148
  rural land, 33
popular action, 72
population caps, 12, 59
population management, 156
poverty, 16, 153
private health clinics, 19, 128–130, 150
private schools, 115, 150. *See also* migrant schools
  certification of, 50, 87–89, 93
  fees, 92, 114–115
  funding, 75
  legalizing, 88–89
  management of, 18, 69
  overview, 74–77
  regulation of, 18, 56, 73–74, 77–79, 93, 96–97
  selective absorption of, 85–86
  self-managed, 112
private tutoring, 110–111
privatization, 46
prosperity, common, 40
protest prevention, 33
protests, 151
public expenditures, 68
public hospitals
  co-migrant empathy in, 108–109, 111
  costs, 130
  decentralization of, 103–104
  differential treatment of patients in, 117–118
  funding of, 103–104
public institutions
  playing with institutional leeway, 101–103, 120–121, 148
  working within, 105–112
public schools
  classroom size restrictions, 64–65
  competition for rankings, 118–119
  decentralization of, 103–104
  discrimination against migrants in, 118–120
  eligibility requirements, 151
  full inclusion of migrant children in, 87–88
  funding of, 84, 86, 103–104, 114
  incorporating migrants into, 69, 89–90
  integration of migrants into, 56, 77–79, 93
  keeping migrants out of, 56, 81–84
  management of, 18
  required documents, 82
  required donations, 82–83
  separating migrants in, 86–87
  urban, 77–79
public security, 146
public services. *See also* public hospitals; public schools
  access to, 111
  decentralization of, 3, 45, 93, 113
  eligibility criteria, 42, 57, 60–63
  exclusion from, 141–142
  funding of, 44
  inequality of, 49–50
  informal substitutes, 18, 112–115, 120
  localization of, 57–58
  for migrants, 7–8, 10, 24, 33, 42, 57–58
  phantom services, 55–57, 70, 71–72, 147
  as social control, 13, 33
  without elections, 11–13
  workers' experiences of accessing and using, 20–23

quality
  education for (*suzhi jiaoyu*, 素质教育), 26–27
  of life, 28

regional development, 151
regional distinctions, 41, 49
regular primary schools (*putong xiaoxue*, 普通小学), 59
regulation
  approaches to, 18
  of private schools, 18, 56, 73–74, 77–79, 93, 96–97
residence permits, 60–63
resourcefulness, 103–105, 135, 148
rural health care, 131–132
rural health insurance, 66–67, 131–132, 140
rural land politics, 33

rural migrants. *See* migrant workers (*nongmin gong*, 农民工)
rural-urban divide, 57
straddling, 131–133

safety, school, 94–95
Saucony, 27
scarcity, 43
school administrators, 106–107
school safety, 95
school services, 106–107. *See also* education
scraping together needs, 124–127
secondary vocational schools, 60, 86
second-generation migrants, 28
segregated inclusion, 84, 86–87
segregated roads, 116
selective absorption, 84, 85–86
self-identity, 37
self-made substitutes, 112
self-managed (*ziban*, 自办) schools, 112
self-run insurance, 19
Shaanxi Province, 76
Shandong Province, 142–143
Shanghai
document-checking rules, 63
GDP per capita, 79
household registrations (*hukous*), 25, 56
migrant schools, 84–86
migrant students, 12
population cap, 12, 26
public schools, 56, 64, 84–87, 89, 91–92, 95, 114
regulation and integration of migrants in, 18, 96
residence permits, 60, 61–62
services for migrants, 25, 38, 56, 65, 67, 69, 78–79
vocational high schools, 86
World Expo (2010), 94
sharing insurance cards, 139–140
Sichuan Earthquake (2008), 94–95
Sichuan Province, 15, 26
social control
public services as, 13, 33
soft forms of, 2
time wasting, 96–97
social insurance
making do without, 19, 101, 128, 133–134
sharing cards, 139–140
social management (*shehui guanli*, 社会管理), 71
social policy, 49–50, 51
social protection policies, 10
social services. *See* public services
socioeconomic inequality, 2
Solinger, Dorothy, 14
Southeast Asia, 10
state, embedded inequality and, 159–162
statistics, 58–60
strikes, 27–28
structural inequality
gradations of, 13–17
reinforcing, 69–70
student workers, 134
Sub-Saharan Africa, 10
Summer Olympics (Beijing, 2008), 94
suzhi jiaoyu (素质教育, education for quality), 26–27

tax revenues, 68
teachers, 106–108
discrimination against migrant children, 119–120
personalized, 110–111
salaries, 115
time wasting, 96–97
tofu-dreg schoolhouses, 95
traditional Chinese medicine, 106, 129
Tsinghua University, 78, 115

United States
political atomization in, 157–158
welfare system, 33
urban public schools. *See also* public schools
integration of migrants into, 77–79
urban public services. *See also* public services
workers' experiences of accessing and using, 20–23
urban villages (*cheng zhongcun*, 城中村), 93
urbanization, 1, 39
National New-Type Urbanization Plan (*guojia xinxing chengzhen hua guihua*, 国家新型城镇化规划) (2014–2020), 4–5, 14, 24, 40
new-type, 39
people-centered (*yiren weiben*, 以人为本), 5, 39
wrangling, 4–7

Venezuela, 10
visible results, 93–96
vocational schools, 60, 86, 134

wages, 136–137
wealth, 25–26
wealth inequality, 150
welfare states, 150
welfare systems
  in developing democracies, 32–33
  funding of, 44
Western countries, 157–158
Western Europe, 33
Western medicine, 106
work location, 131–133
worker activism, 33
workers' compensation, 133–134
workers' compensation
    disputes, 117–118
work-related injury disputes, 117–118
work-related injury insurance, 133
World Expo (Shanghai, 2010), 94
worthiness, 37

Xi Jinping, 13, 17, 153
Xi Jinping era, 5, 24, 48, 51, 72
Xiamen, 56
Xinjian Village (Beijing), 66
Xu Xianping, 5

Yang Zhiming, 5
Yue Yuen shoe factory, 27

Zhejiang Province, 132–133

Studies of the Weatherhead East Asian Institute
Columbia University

Selected Titles
(Complete list at: weai.columbia.edu/content/publications)

In Search of Admiration and Respect: Chinese Cultural Diplomacy in the United States, 1875–1974, by Yanqiu Zheng. University of Michigan Press, 2024.

Perilous Wagers: Gambling, Dignity, and Day Laborers in Post-Fukushima Tokyo, by Klaus K. Y. Hammering. Cornell University Press, 2024.

The Chinese Computer: A Global History of the Information Age, by Thomas S. Mullaney. The MIT Press, 2024.

Beauty Matters: Modern Japanese Literature and the Question of Aesthetics, 1890–1930, by Anri Yasuda. Columbia University Press, 2024.

Revolutionary Becomings: Documentary Media in Twentieth-Century China, by Ying Qian. Columbia University Press, 2024.

Waiting for the Cool Moon: Anti-imperialist Struggles in the Heart of Japan's Empire, by Wendy Matsumura. Duke University Press, 2024.

Beauty Regimes: A History of Power and Modern Empire in the Philippines, 1898–1941, by Genevieve Clutario. Duke University Press, 2023.

Afterlives of Letters: The Transnational Origins of Modern Literature in China, Japan, and Korea, by Satoru Hashimoto. Columbia University Press, 2023.

Republican Vietnam, 1963–1975: War, Society, Diaspora, edited by Trinh M. Luu and Tuong Vu. University of Hawai'i Press, 2023.

Territorializing Manchuria: The Transnational Frontier and Literatures of East Asia, by Miya Xie. Harvard East Asian Monographs, 2023.

Takamure Itsue, Japanese Antiquity, and Matricultural Paradigms that Address the Crisis of Modernity: A Woman from the Land of Fire, by Yasuko Sato. Palgrave Macmillan, 2023.

Rejuvenating Communism: Youth Organizations and Elite Renewal in Post-Mao China, by Jérôme Doyon. University of Michigan Press, 2023.

From Japanese Empire to American Hegemony: Koreans and Okinawans in the Resettlement of Northeast Asia, by Matthew R. Augustine. University of Hawai'i Press, 2023.

For EU product safety concerns, contact us at Calle de José Abascal, 56–1°, 28003 Madrid, Spain or eugpsr@cambridge.org.

www.ingramcontent.com/pod-product-compliance
Lightning Source LLC
Chambersburg PA
CBHW071248180926
51613CB00002B/163
* 9 7 8 1 0 0 9 3 5 5 6 3 6 *